WORDS
FROM
WITHIN

JAY F. DOWNS

iUniverse, Inc.
Bloomington

WORDS FROM WITHIN

iUniverse books may be ordered through booksellers or by contacting:

iUniverse
1663 Liberty Drive
Bloomington, IN 47403
www.iuniverse.com
1-800-Authors (1-800-288-4677)

ISBN: 978-1-4759-3012-2 (sc)
ISBN: 978-1-4759-3019-1 (ebk)

Library of Congress Control Number: 2012909887

Printed in the United States of America

iUniverse rev. date: 07/18/2012

Illustrations by Jeanie Downs

Contents

THIS BOOK IS DEDICATED TO

JEANIE, JASON,

JORDAN & JILLIAN

WHO TAUGHT ME

THE MEANING OF

THESE WORDS

I WOULD ALSO LIKE TO

ACKNOWLEDGE

PASTOR ANDY LUNT,

WHOSE SERMONS

GAVE ME THE

INSPIRATION

FOR MANY OF

THESE POEMS

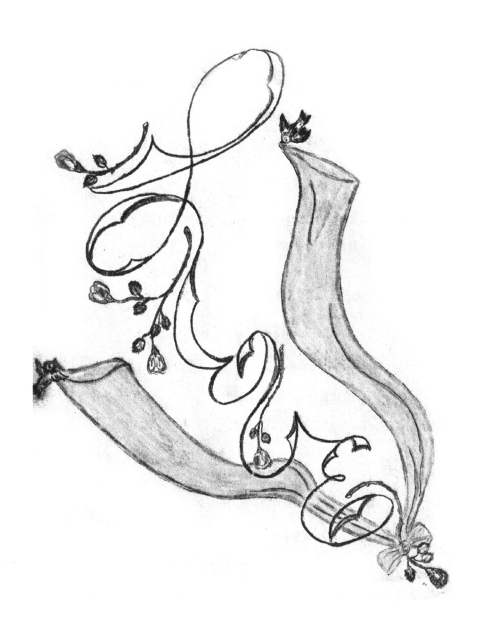

DREAM GIRL

TODAY I SAW A DREAM:

    EYES AS CLEAR AS A MOUNTAIN STREAM;

    HAIR LIKE A GENTLE WATERFALL;

    SKIN MADE OF THE PUREST, SOFT SILK;

    LIPS, UNTOUCHED, LIKE A NEWBORN ROSE;

    FEATURES CARVED BY A MASTER'S HANDS;

    DIMPLES, WHERE SHEER JOY SHOWS ITSELF;

    VOICE OF INTEREST, TALENT, AND LOVE.

THIS ANGEL WAS MY DREAM—AND I HOPE, MORE!

VISION

YOU ARE A VISION OF LOVELINESS

AS I SEE YOU WALK TOWARD ME;

YOUR BEAUTIFUL FACE, SO CALM, YOUR

EVEN MORE BEAUTIFUL, TRUSTING EYES

FILL ME WITH PEACE AND CONTENTMENT,

WHILE AT THE SAME TIME MAKE ME FEEL

ALL-POWERFUL, COMPLETELY LOVING,

AND MY HEART BURSTS WITHIN ME!

YOU ARE A VISION OF LOVELINESS,

BUT, FOR ME, ONLY A VISION!

THE MEETING

I MET HER TODAY:

    LIKE A FAWN SHE SEEMED,
    SLIGHTLY WILD AND YET TAME,

    BOUNCING AROUND WITH THE JOY OF BEING ALIVE,
    LEGS SLIM YET GRACEFUL AND STRONG,

    WITH A WISP OF A WAIST,
    SO THAT SHE SEEMED ALMOST FRAGILE;

    AND YET IN HER EYES, WHICH COMPLETELY ENGULF
    YOU IN THE WATERS OF A LIGHT GREEN POOL,

    WAS THE SPARK OF LIFE, A GREAT LOVE
    OF LIFE IN EVERY WAY POSSIBLE,

    SO THAT STRENGTH AND POWER
    SHONE FORTH LIKE THE SUN.

YES, I MET HER TODAY ------------------------- MY LOVE!

BY YOU

I AM THRILLED BY YOU,

AND FULFILLED BY YOU,

AND PLEASED BY YOU,

AND PRAISED BY YOU,

AND COMFORTED BY YOU,

AND EXCITED BY YOU,

AND HUMBLED BY YOU,

AND UPHELD BY YOU,

AND TICKLED BY YOU,

AND TENDED BY YOU,

AND INSPIRED BY YOU,

AND OVERJOYED BY YOU,

AND ENCOURAGED BY YOU,

AND TOUCHED BY YOU,

AND STRENGTHENED BY YOU,

AND SURROUNDED BY YOU,

AND WARMED BY YOU,

AND AWED BY YOU,

AND LOVED BY YOU;

AND I MUST BE . . . . BY YOU.

MY GIFT

TO YOU, MY LOVE, I GIVE ALL THAT I HAVE:

MY HANDS, QUICK AND STRONG TO HELP WHEN YOU'RE WEAK;
GENTLE AS A BREEZE WHEN CARESSING YOUR CHEEK;

MY EYES, SO THAT WITH THE TWINKLE YOU SEE THERE,
YOU'LL ALSO SEE A FLAME—HOW VERY MUCH I CARE;

MY MIND, AND WHAT ALL IT MAY POSSESS—
WIT, CHARM, AND DEEP THOUGHT FOR YOUR HAPPINESS;

MY VOICE, TO SHOW IN ALL THAT I SAY
I LOVE YOU MORE AND MORE EVERY DAY;

MY ARMS, TO LET YOU CRY AND CALM YOUR FRIGHT—
OR SIMPLY TO USE 'CAUSE YOU FIT JUST RIGHT;

MY FEET AND LEGS, SUPPORT FOR YOU NEAR,
ENABLING YOU TO WALK AHEAD WITHOUT FEAR;

MY HEART, WHERE YOUR LOVE OVERFLOWS THE BRIM,
MAKING SURE THE FLAME WILL NEVER DIM;

MYSELF AND ALL THAT I MAY BE,
THAT I CAN SOMEHOW HELP YOU TO LOVE ME;

ALL OF THIS I GIVE TO YOU, MY LOVE—
WHOEVER, WHEREVER, YOU ARE!

NEEDS

AS A ROSEBUD NEEDS SUN AND RAIN,

AS A NEWBORN BABE NEEDS TO GAIN,

AS A BLUEBIRD NEEDS WINGS TO FLY,

AS A FISH NEEDS WATER—OR DIE,

AS A SONG NEEDS SOMEONE TO SING,

AS A BELL NEEDS A CLAPPER TO RING,

AS WATER NEEDS SOMEWHERE TO RUN,

AS THOUGHTS NEED ACTION UNTIL DONE,

AS THE WIND NEEDS SOMEWHERE TO BLOW,

AS A ROAD NEEDS SOMEWHERE TO GO,

AS THE STARS NEED THE SKY ABOVE—

SO DO I NEED SOMEONE TO LOVE!

DECISION

I DON'T KNOW HOW TO LOVE YOU
SO YOU'LL ALWAYS KNOW I CARE;

I DON'T KNOW WHAT TO DO
TO FIX A SINK OR CHAIR;

I DON'T KNOW HOW TO RAISE A CHILD
OR PLAN FOR FUTURE DAYS;

I DON'T KNOW WHEN TO BE HARSH OR MILD
OR JUST WHAT ACTION PAYS;

I ONLY KNOW THAT I LOVE YOU
WITH EVERYTHING THAT'S IN ME;

I ONLY KNOW THAT I'LL BE TRUE—
THAT'S HOW IT'LL ALWAYS BE.

ONLY YOU KNOW HOW YOU FEEL, OR WHAT TO DO;
I CAN ONLY ASK, MY LOVE—IT'S UP TO YOU!

VALENTINE'S DAY

THIS IS ONE DAY OUT OF MANY,

AND SPECIAL YET, FOR SET ASIDE

TO LET US SHOW THE ONES WE LOVE

HOW EVERY DAY THIS LOVE ABIDES.

A GIFT WOULD SHOW TO YOU, PERHAPS,

JUST HOW I FEEL, AT LEAST IN PART;

BUT THE GREATEST GIFT YOU ALREADY HAVE—

HOPE IT WILL DO—IT IS MY HEART!

MA

THERE ARE TALL MAS AND SHORT MAS, FAT ONES
AND SKINNY, MAS WHO CAN DO JUST TONS
OF WORK, AND MAS THAT DON'T DO ANY;
MAS WITH NO TALENT, MAS WITH MANY;
THERE ARE GOOD MAS AND BAD MAS, PLEASANT
AND MEAN; CULTURED MAS WHO LIKE PHEASANT
AND OTHERS WHO LIKE BEANS; MAS WHO ARE
ATHLETES, MAS WHO GET TIRED IN A CAR;
HEALTHY MAS, KIND MAS, GENTLE AND BRAVE,
AND MAS WHO JUST LIKE TO RANT AND RAVE;
AMBITIOUS MAS, WHO PLAN ALL DAY LONG—
MAS WHO JUST SIT AND WONDER WHAT'S WRONG;
RELIGIOUS MAS—THEY'RE ALMOST A SAINT,
AND MAS WHO'D DO WELL TO MAKE A HAINT;
MAS FROM THE BOTTOM, MAS FROM THE TOP,
AND THEN THERE'S MINE—THE CREAM OF THE CROP!

THE COMING OF EASTER

EASTER—THE DAY OF LOVE FULFILLED!

THE LILY IS AN ANGEL WHO

SWEETLY SHOWS LOVE'S TRIUMPH TO US.

THIS IS PERFECTION—GOD'S TRUE LOVE.

BUT GOOD FRIDAY CAME JUST BEFORE.

THE DOGWOOD TELLS OF BETRAYAL,

HATE, LONELINESS, AND SUFFERING.

THIS IS THE TRIAL OF OUR LOVE.

GOOD FRIDAY WILL COME—THIS IS SURE;

EASTER MAY FOLLOW—OR MAY NOT.

I CANNOT SAY—I CAN ONLY

LOVE YOU COMPLETELY, FOREVER!

BEAUTY

YOU ARE TRULY BEAUTIFUL

IN THOUGHTS, ACTS, FACE, FORM, AND HAIR—

A SPECIAL, INNER BEAUTY;

I KNOW WHY—GOD PUT IT THERE!

HEALING

I FEEL! ONCE AGAIN I REALLY FEEL!

THINGS ARE NO LONGER TOO MUCH TROUBLE—
THEY COME WITH EASE—AND EVEN DELIGHT!

MY HEART IS WARM—WITH CARING YET!
AND DAYS ARE BRIGHT BOTH DAY AND NIGHT.

I SMILE AND LAUGH WITH JOY AGAIN,
AND LOVE ALL THINGS WITH ALL MY MIGHT!

I HOPE, AND DREAM, AND THEY'LL ALL COME TRUE!
AND MY SOUL SOARS TO A GREAT NEW HEIGHT!

HOW STRANGE! THE POWER OF TWO BEAUTIFUL
EYES, A SMILE, A WORD—AND ALL IS RIGHT!

I FEEL! ONCE AGAIN I REALLY FEEL!

HOME

WE KNOW OUR MOTHERS LOVE US

NO MATTER WHAT WE DO,

AND WE CAN ALWAYS GO HOME TO FEEL

SECURE AND PAMPERED ANEW;

BUT WE MAY HAVE NO PLACE TO CALL HOME,

SO FEEL UNLOVED, OF NO VALUE;

WE FEAR BEING REJECTED—AND ARE—

LOSING OUR JOB AND EVEN OUR SPOUSE TOO;

SO WHERE IS HOME WHEN IT'S

EITHER GONE OR MUCH TOO FAR AWAY?

IT'S WHERE GOD IS, AND HE MAKES

HIS HOME WITH US EACH DAY.

HE'S CALLING US HOME, WE'LL SEE,

IF WE'LL JUST LISTEN AND DARE,

BOTH NOW AND FOREVERMORE, IN

HIS FATHER'S HOUSE HE'S PREPARED.

FAMILY

WHAT IS THE THIN LINE
BETWEEN LOVE AND SMOTHERING,

POSSESSING A CHILD
AND GOOD MOTHERING?

THERE CAME A TIME WHEN
JESUS HAD TO DO

WHAT HE HAD BEEN CALLED
BY GOD TO SEE THROUGH,

NO MATTER WHAT HIS
FAMILY THOUGHT HE

SHOULD DO OR JUST HOW
TO ACT MOST SAFELY,

FOR FAMILIES CAN BE
THE SOURCE OF MUCH PAIN,

ABUSE, GUILT, VIOLENCE
AGAIN AND AGAIN;

BUT THE WATER OF
BAPTISM MAKE A NEW

KIND OF FAMILY—
THICKER THAN BLOOD TOO—

WHERE PEOPLE ARE HELD
IN SACRED WORTH STILL—

ACCEPTED, CARED FOR,
FREE TO DO GOD'S WILL;

THE CHURCH IS MORE THAN
LOVING FRIENDS EVEN—

IT'S THE FAMILY OF
GOD BOUND FOR HEAVEN!

WHAT IS LOVE?

WE TALK AND THINK AND SING LIKE A DOVE

ABOUT—INDEED, ARE IN LOVE WITH—LOVE.

LOVE IS A WARM, FUZZY, ECSTATIC FEELING,

AND CERTAINLY A MANY-SPLENDORED THING,

BUT THIS KIND OF LOVE IS FAR REMOVED

FROM SCRIPTURE, WHERE LOVE IS APPROVED

ONLY WHEN IT'S AN ACT OF THE WILL—

ACTING THAT WAY NO MATTER HOW YOU FEEL—

IT'S CARING FOR OTHERS IN SICKNESS AND HEALTH,

FOR BETTER OR WORSE, WITH NOTHING OR GREAT WEALTH,

FOR ACTIONS ARE HOW GOD SHOWS US THAT HE

LOVES US TOO, EVEN DYING FOR US WHEN WE

WERE UNLOVABLE, AND SO NOW WE MUST TAKE

THIS AS OUR GREAT COMMISSION—FOR LOVE'S SAKE!

IN MY FATHER'S EYES

I'M THE MOST IMPORTANT PERSON ON EARTH,
NOT JUST ONE OF THE OTHER GUYS,
BUT ONE OF INFINITE WORTH
IN MY FATHER'S EYES;

PLAYING GAMES, GOING FISHING, SHOOTING
BASKETS OR SHAGGING FLIES,
I'M SOMEONE FUN TO BE WITH
IN MY FATHER'S EYES;

I'M THE LAST-SECOND SPORTS HERO,
THE ONE WHO WINS THE PRIZE—
I'M THE "BESTEST OF THE BEST"
IN MY FATHER'S EYES;

AS I GROW UP—IT REALLY DOESN'T
MATTER WHAT MY SHAPE OR SIZE—
I KNOW I'M JUST ABOUT PERFECT
IN MY FATHER'S EYES;

ALL MY ACTIONS ARE GENTLEMANLY
AND MY DREAMS ALL REALIZED;
I'M ALL THAT I CAN EVER BE
IN MY FATHER'S EYES;

THERE ARE TWO FATHERS
WITH WHOM I HAVE FAMILY TIES—
TWO FATHERS TO WHOM I'M
THE APPLE OF THEIR EYES;

I WILL LIVE FOREVER WITH HIM—
ALL LOGIC THIS DEFIES—
BUT I'M A BELOVED CHILD
IN MY FATHER'S EYES!

PURE LOVE

YOU DON'T HAVE TO LOVE ME—
I WILL LOVE YOU STILL;
YOU DON'T HAVE TO LOVE ME—
I'LL FEEL HOW I FEEL.

MY LOVE DOESN'T DEPEND
ON WHAT YOU DO OR SAY;
MY LOVE COMES FROM WITHIN—
I'LL ALWAYS FEEL THIS WAY.

IT DOESN'T MATTER WHAT YOU'VE DONE—
I'LL ALWAYS FORGIVE AND FORGET;
IT DOESN'T MATTER WHAT IS PAST—
I KNOW THE BEST TO COME IS YET!

THIS IS HOW GOD LOVES EACH OF US—
IT'S NOT THE ORDINARY WAY—
THE QUESTION IS: DO EACH OF US
LOVE ONE ANOTHER THIS WAY?

THE ANSWER IS: OF COURSE, WE CAN'T
WITHOUT A CHANGE WITHIN US,
AND WE ARE FILLED WITH THE MIND AND
LOVE EXHIBITED BY JESUS!

PRODIGAL

IF WE'RE AWAY FROM GOD, WE'RE AWAY FROM HOME:

IF WE'RE AWAY FROM HOME, TOO FAR WE'VE ROAMED!

IF WE ARE IN A FAR COUNTRY, AN

      INHERITANCE CLAIMING OUR FATHER IS DEAD,

MAY WE COME TO OURSELVES AND KNOW,

      EVEN IF WE HAVE NO GIFT TO OFFER

FOR REPENTANCE, INSTEAD,

THE GIFT HAS ALREADY BEEN GIVEN BY HIM,

      AND WE WILL BE WELCOMED BACK HOME

BY A FATHER RUNNING TO US

      WITH OPEN ARMS AND UNDYING,

UNCONDITIONAL LOVE!

CUPPED HANDS

WE ARE WRITTEN IN THE PALM OF GOD'S HAND,
AND EVERYTHING ABOUT US TO HIM IS KNOWN;
BUT HE DOES NOT SIMPLY OPEN HIS HANDS
AND URGE US TO FLY OFF ON OUR OWN—

BUT HE CUPS HIS HANDS TO PROTECT US—
SO WE WON'T FALL DURING OUR ATTEMPTED FLIGHTS
AND HARM OURSELVES, BEFORE WE ARE READY
TO SPREAD OUR WINGS AND SOAR TO GREAT HEIGHTS.

HE CUPS HIS HANDS TO COMFORT US—
OUT OF HARSH WINDS THAT BLOW BELOW AND ABOVE—
SO THAT WE KNOW WE ARE ALWAYS PROTECTED
AND FEEL THE WARMTH OF HIS TRUE, PURE LOVE.

EACH OF US ARE HELD IN GOD'S CUPPED HANDS,
ALLOWED TO GROW UNDER HIS TENDER CARE
UNTIL WE BECOME THE ONE HE INTENDS
AND REACH THE ETERNAL HOME HE'S PREPARED.

A GIFT OF LOVE

MY GOD HAS GIVEN ME MANY THINGS:

HE GAVE ME A WONDERFUL WORLD
    TO BE BORN IN,

THE BEST HE COULD FIND
    FOR FAMILY AND FRIEND;

HE GAVE ME TRUE EYES TO SEE
    THE GOOD THINGS ALL ALONG—

THE BEAUTY, TRUTH, AND JOY
    IN ALL THINGS, RIGHT OR WRONG;

AND NOW, THE GREATEST GIFT OF ALL,
    UNBOUNDED LOVE AND GRACE TO SHOW:

A SHARING OF MIND, BODY, AND SOUL
    THAT NO ONE ELSE WILL EVER KNOW;

HE GAVE TO ME JUST WHAT I NEED,
    (I GUESS HE ALWAYS KNEW)

THE GREATEST GIFT OF ETERNITY—
    MY ANGEL, HE GAVE ME YOU!

GOD-LIKE

WHAT IS MORE LOVELY THAN A CHILD?

HE CRUMBLES THE HARDEST HEART!

THE FACE, THE VOICE, THE SIMPLE ACTS

OF LOVE WHICH HE IMPARTS

WILL MAKE US STOP AND REALIZE

GOD'S GREAT LOVE UNTO US—

IT'S AS IF OUR GOD HIMSELF

WERE THERE, SMILING UP AT US!

THE BEST

THERE MUST BE OTHER GOOD PARENTS
SOMEWHERE ON THIS BIG WIDE EARTH:

WHERE A CHILD HAS THE LOVE AND CARE
THAT I'VE HAD FROM MY DAY OF BIRTH;

WHERE HE'S TAUGHT TO WORK AND PLAY,
BUILDING CONFIDENCE IN ALL HE CAN DO;

WHERE, UNDER ALL THIS HE LEARNS
WHAT IT IS TO BE HONEST AND TRUE;

WHERE HE'S GIVEN THE LUXURY OF FREEDOM,
WITH THE TRUST THAT HE'LL ALWAYS CHOOSE RIGHT;

WHERE, IF HE SHOULD FAIL FOREVER,
THEIR LOVE WILL SHINE JUST AS BRIGHT;

WHERE CULTURE AND KNOWLEDGE ARE GOOD THINGS,
AND KIND THOUGHTS AS FREE AS THE AIR;

THERE MUST BE OTHER GOOD PARENTS,
BUT BETTER—I DON'T KNOW WHERE!

THANKS

THANK YOU, O LORD, FOR YOUR HELP FROM ABOVE;

THANK YOU FOR MY WIFE, WHO GAVE ME HER LOVE;

MAY I IN MY WEAKNESS FIND STRENGTH IN AND FROM YOU,

THAT I MAY BE ABLE TO GIVE HER ALL MY LOVE TOO.

WEDDING POEM

AT WEDDINGS MOST PEOPLE ARE HAPPY

AND SING ALOUD WITH A JOYFUL VOICE

FOR ONE OF THEIR OWN IS BEING WED—

THAT'S WHY TODAY THE ANGELS REJOICE!

A FATHER'S LOVE

A FATHER'S LOVE FOR HIS CHILD IS HIS STRONGEST ON EARTH:

IT STARTS WHEN HE SEES HIS FIRST CHILD GIVEN BIRTH;

FOR THIS BABE HE HOLDS IN HIS ARMS

HE COAXES HEAVEN TO PROTECT FROM ALL HARM;

HE GENTLY ROCKS WITH THE CHILD NESTLING IN HIS LAP,

THEN GAZES IN WONDER AT THE BEAUTY IN A NAP;

HE IS PROUD AS HIS CHILD GROWS BEFORE HIS EYES

BUT IS SAD TOO—HE'LL BE GONE BEFORE HE'LL REALIZE;

HE WANTS THE BEST FOR HIS CHILD IN EVERYTHING;

HE JOINS ALONG AS THE CHILD DANCES OR SINGS;

HE SIMPLY WATCHES IN AWE THE UNFOLDING SCENE

AND SNEAKS IN A KISS WITHOUT BEING SEEN.

HE LOVES TO ROMP AND PLAY WITH THIS CHILD

AND LAUGHS AS THE CHILD SUDDENLY GOES WILD;

HIS HEART LEAPS WHEN THE CHILD RUNS TOWARD HIM PELL
  MELL;

IT ACHES WHEN THE CHILD IS SICK—AND WANTS HIM WELL;

HE TRIES TO CAREFULLY CORRECT THE CHILD'S MISDEEDS,

AND CRIES TOO WHEN HE'S UNHAPPY OR DOESN'T HEED;

HE WONDERS IF THAT BASIC TRUST AND LOVE WILL SEE

THE CHILD THROUGH—AND AWAITS EACH RETURN EAGERLY.

A FATHER'S LOVE FOR HIS CHILD IS THE STRONGEST ON EARTH—

AREN'T WE GOD'S CHILDREN RIGHT HERE ON THE EARTH?

FIRST SON

FITTING IN YOUR ARMS, HIS FEET IN YOUR HAND,

YOU WONDER ABOUT THIS LITTLE MAN;

AS YOU LOOK DOWN INTO BIG EYES OF BLUE

YOU SUDDENLY FEEL HE'S WONDERING TOO;

HIS STARE GOES WITHIN AND STRIPS ALL AWAY,

ASKING, "HOW WILL YOU SHOW ME THE RIGHT WAY?"

YOU FEEL VERY WEAK AND POOR FOR THE TASK.

"HOW CAN I POSSIBLY TEACH HIM?" YOU ASK.

"WHAT CAN I DO OR POSSIBLY TELL . . ."

HE SMILES AND INSTANTLY BREAKS THE SPELL.

YOU'RE NOT ALONE, AND YOU KNOW IT NOW,

SO YOU WHISPER, "DON'T WORRY!" AND KISS HIS SOFT BROW.

HE SNUGGLES CLOSER, HIS EYES START TO CLOSE;

YOU THANK THE LORD THAT YOU'RE AMONG THOSE

ABLE TO BORROW A BIT OF THE LOVE

THAT COMES TO ALL FROM HEAVEN ABOVE.

MOTHERS SHARE THIS SPECIAL LOVE, THAT'S TRUE;

BUT, CUDDLING THEIR SON, FATHERS DO TOO!

ONE YEAR OLD

THROUGH MISTY EYES I SAW YOU

DRAW YOUR FIRST BREATH—

EYES WIDE OPEN TO THE WORLD,

A SMILE UPON YOUR FACE.

YOU JOINED US AT HOME, A TINY

BUMP IN A FILMY WHITE WORLD

WHERE YOU NURSED AND GREW MORE CUDDLY,

NOT WANTING TO GO TO SLEEP, IT SEEMED.

YOU BEGAN TO REACH FOR YOUR GYM SET

AND DEEPER INTO OUR HEARTS;

THEN YOU COULD ROLL OVER

AND HOLD YOURSELF UP.

BABY FOOD AND A CUP BROUGHT FORTH

A FLOOD OF EVENTS TO TREASURE:

> FEET REVOLVING AS YOU ATE
> GURGLING MILK DOWN YOUR FRONT
> PAT-Y-CAKE AND PEEK-A-BOO
> ALWAYS LYING STILL WHILE CHANGED
> BATHS TOGETHER, DA-DAS, STANDING

THAT HURT-FEELING LITTLE PUCKER
CRAWLING ALL OVER ME
OR UP—AND DOWN—THE STAIRS
ALWAYS SMILING FOR A PICTURE
YOUR SOFT, WISPY, ANGEL HAIR
THE DIAPERS THAT CAME AFTER A GRUNT
RIDING THAT PONY EVERYWHERE
THOSE EARLY MORNING VISITS IN BED
ROCKING YOU SQUEEKILY TO SLEEP
AN ARM DRAPED OVER MY SHOULDER
SCOOTING AROUND TO GET OFF THE BED
PUSHING YOUR WAGON ALL OVER
EATING WATERMELON IN THE POOL
WAVING BYE-BYE TO THREE PACIFIERS
CATCHING AND PITCHING YOUR BALL
RIDING IN THE WIND ON MY BICYCLE
POINTING AT ANY PLANE THAT PASSED
STROLLING TO THE GROCERY STORE
DANCING TO A LIVELY SONG
TURNING THE PAGES OF A BOOK
LIFTING EACH FOOT TO HELP UNDRESS
RIDING YOUR TYKE BIKE COMPLETE WITH MOTOR
THAT LAUGH WHEN YOU WERE TICKLED
SWINGING, OR DOING YOUR LAUNDRY
EATING ONE ORANGE SLICE AFTER ANOTHER
REACHING UP OR OUT FOR ME.
YOUR FIRST BIRTHDAY CAKE, ALL OVER YOU

THE CRYING AND FUSSING ARE FORGOTTEN

IN THE JOY AND DELIGHT OF THIS YEAR

THAT YOU'VE SHARED YOUR LIFE WITH US—

I HOPE YOU'VE BEEN AS HAPPY HERE!

BLESSED

HOW COULD ONE BE MORE BLESSED
THAN TO HAVE A GOLDEN BOY;

TO SEE HIM START TO WALK, THEN RUN,
AND JUMP AND JUMP FOR JOY,

TO HEAR HIM START TO TALK AND SAY
EVERYTHING FROM "DADDY" ON DOWN,

TO WATCH HIM PLAY WITH ANIMALS AND BALLS,
"BOMMY DOMMY HAT", CARS, AND CLOWN,

TO HAVE HIM TAKE YOUR HAND IN HIS,
AND SNUGGLE CLOSE AT NIGHT,

TO SEE HIS FACE WHEN A BIG GRIN COMES,
SAYING "PLEEZE" OR "CHRISTMAS TREE LIGHTS";

TO "HUG MY BOY" AND HAVE HIM KISS YOU
ONCE OR TWICE—THAT'S IT! IT'S TRUE!

THE ONLY WAY TO BE MORE BLESSED
IS HAVE NOT ONE—BUT TWO!

TWO LITTLE BOYS

ONE BOY OF ONE, THE OTHER PAST THREE
START OUR YEAR OFF JOYFULLY:

BEGINNING TO WALK AND TALK, YOU SEE,
BECOMING A BIG BOY, NATURALLY;

A POINTING FINGER TO "BEETLEBAUM" OR "DIG DUCK",
SAVED BY A SUPERHERO—GOOD LUCK;

CHEWING GUM AND RIDING A BIKE,
THE GYM SET AND TREE HOUSE YOU BOTH LIKE;

GOING TO THE GROCERY STORE OR GARAGE SALE,
ATTENDING THE PRE-SCHOOL, WITHOUT FAIL;

COLORING PICTURES TOO, "LOOK, MOMMY, DADDY"
A "COUNTING AND DRESSING AND WRITING HIS NAME" LADDIE;

A BIG-EARED BUNNY, TREAT SACK IN HAND,
TAKEN CARE OF ABLY BY—SPIDERMAN;

BRUSHING TEETH, NIGHTGOWN DRAGGING ALONG,
SAYING A PRAYER, SINGING A SONG;

WALKING HAND IN HAND, SLEEPING SIDE BY SIDE,
THE JOY YOU BRING TO ME I CANNOT HIDE;

A FACE STILL OF BEAUTY, A PUG NOSE FULL OF JOY—
I'LL THANK THE LORD FOREVER FOR YOU PRECIOUS LITTLE BOYS!

TO JILLIAN, 1977

AFTER TWO CHILDREN THAT WERE ONE IN A MILLION
WE WERE BLESSED WITH A THIRD—JILLIAN;

YOU CAME WITH SUCH EASE, AND HAVE BEEN THAT WAY SINCE,
WITH LITTLE FUSS OR CRYING, AND VERY FEW HINTS;

YOU WERE KISSED AND PULLED ON, RIGHT FROM THE BEGINNING,
BUT YOU TOOK IT CHARMINGLY AND CAME UP GRINNING;

YOU'D SURVEY THE SCENE WITH BIG EYES, AND GRIN,
THEN STRETCH OUT OR CURL UP AND SLEEP AGAIN;

YOUR KICKS AND GURGLES, YOU LAUGHING OUT LOUD
MAKES THE SUN SHINE THROUGH THE DARKEST CLOUD;

THERE'S NO SWEETER BABY, OF THAT THERE'S NO DOUBT
(EVEN IF YOUR EARS MIGHT A LITTLE STICK OUT);

YOU LOOK LIKE A PRINCESS IN OUTFITS OF PINK,
AND A MORE PRECIOUS ONE LIVES NOWHERE, I THINK

SO WE THANK THE LORD AND ANGELS ABOVE
FOR SENDING ANOTHER TO BRING US MORE LOVE.

THREE LITTLE FACES

LOOK AT THAT FACE—BRONZED,
    WITH HAIR TO MATCH;
ALREADY (LOOK OUT GIRLS) YOU'D
    BE QUITE A CATCH.
AND YOU'RE LEARNING TO READ AND
    WRITE NOW TOO,
AND THAT'S A <u>SIMPLE</u> WAY IN
    WHICH YOU GREW;
TRAVELING, YOU BECAME A BIG BOY—
    I KNOW,
AND IN <u>ALL</u> OF YOUR ACTIONS
    IT'S BEGINNING TO SHOW.
PLAYING CHESS OR TUMBLING FIGHTS—
    YOU'RE ON THE BALL;
MY LOVE FOR YOU IS LIKE THE HULK—
    JUST ABOUT TEN FEET TALL!

LOOK AT THAT FACE—BIG EYES, PUG
    NOSE, HAIR ALMOST WHITE,
IT'S A SHAME THE "TERRIBLE TWOS"
    GAVE YOU SUCH A FIGHT;
WITH POTTYING AND SHYNESS,
    NOT KNOWING HOW TO ACT,
YOU HAD A HARD TIME JUST
    STAYING ON TRACK;
BUT GROWING TOOK PLACE AMIDST
    SWEET LITTLE "HEAH"S
AND CARING AND SHARING CERTAINLY
    BROUGHT FORTH CHEERS;
A BRIGHT LITTLE BOY IS NOW
    SHINING THROUGH,
AND THROUGH IT ALL KNOW
    THAT DADDY LOVES YOU!

LOOK AT THAT FACE—A MIXTURE
    OF THE TWO—
PETITE BUT PERFECT, WITH LAUGHING
    EYES OF BLUE;
A CRAWL BECAME A WALK, THEN A
    RUN, EVEN A JUMP
AS YOU BEGAN TO EAT AND GROW
    (FINALLY OVER THE HUMP);
WHATEVER <u>THEY</u> DID, YOU WOULD DO,
    OR AT LEAST GIVE IT A TRY,
AND DISARM US WITH A GREAT BIG GRIN
    AND A SWEET LITTLE "HI";
A GIRL YOU ARE—A HORSEWOMAN YET—
    THAT NO ONE CAN DENY,
NOR THE FACT OF DADDY'S LOVE
    THAT REACHES TO THE SKY!

THREE LITTLE BODIES, 1979

THREE LITTLE BODIES, MADE PERFECTLY SO—
A JASON, A JORDAN, AND A JILLY-BO!

BUSY LITTLE HANDS, BUSY LITTLE MINDS,
DOING PROJECTS OF ALL SORTS OF KINDS:

READING AND WRITING AND COUNTING TOO
MIDST PEANUTS AND POPCORN—"'MELL POTTY" TOO;

TENNIS, FOOTBALL, AND BASEBALL—WHAT HITTERS—
OR JUST RIDING BIKES—YOU'RE NO QUITTERS;

BEACH BALLS AND SEA SHELLS AND GETTING WET—
THERE—OR IN OUR OWN BACKYARD GYM SET;

FUSSING AND TUSSLING—THAT'S PART OF IT TOO,
BUT BASIC TRAITS OF GOODNESS COME THROUGH;

YOU'RE GETTING BIGGER—AND THAT'S NOT HARD MATH—
FOR, ALL TOGETHER, WE CAN'T STILL TAKE A BATH;

SCHOOL BOYS AND BIG GIRL—GROWING UP, THAT'S TRUE,
SO, WHETHER DRAWING LOVE NOTES, DRESSING—OR TRYING TO—

PLAYING GAMES OR TUMBLING OR WATCHING TV,
TELLING A STORY OR CUDDLING—I LOVE YOU THREE!

TO J, J, J—1980

LOOK AT THAT BOY—PERFECT PHYSIQUE,
AND IN ALL WAYS CERTAINLY UNIQUE—
SERIOUS MINDED, HE CATCHES ON FAST
AND REMEMBERS THINGS LONG PAST;
DRACULA AND STAR WARS, BASEBALL AND CARDS,
READING, MATH, AND PUZZLES—HE TRIES HARD—
BEAUTIFUL ARTWORK AND HOME RUNS ARE A JOY
FOR HIM AND FOR ME—YOU'RE QUITE A BOY!

LOOK AT THAT BOY—LONG AND LEAN,
MISCHIEVOUS—YES, BUT CERTAINLY NOT MEAN;
SINGING HIS BEST SONG—AND NOT TOO BADLY—
STATING HIS OWN MIND—RIGHT, DADDY?
FINDING OUT HE CAN DO THINGS ALL ON HIS OWN,
LIKE TYING OR CATCHING OR SLIDING ALONE;
WHETHER SUPERMAN OR AN INDIAN, PLAYING WITH A TOY,
DOMINOES, OR WRITING—YOU'RE QUITE A BOY!

LOOK AT THAT GIRL—CUTE LITTLE FIGURE—
I'M NOT SURE ANYONE'S ANY BIGGER
IN DOING HER HOMEWORK OR TUMBLING JUST RIGHT
(ALTHOUGH SHE STILL CAN'T QUITE REACH THE LIGHT).
WITH DRY GING GIRL PANTS, "GINGLE BELLS" SHE SINGS,
SWEET DRESSES AND PURSES AND SPIDERHULK RINGS,
RUNNING TOWARD ME FOR A HUG OR A TWIRL,
HAIR BOUNCING WILDLY—YOU'RE QUITE A GIRL!

LOOK AT THOSE CHILDREN—A BEAUTIFUL THREE
(AND PEOPLE SAY THEY ALL LOOK JUST LIKE ME)—
HARD HEADED AND EXASPERATING AT TIMES, THAT'S TRUE,
BUT SUCH A JOY TO ME ALSO—I LOVE YOU!

LOVE, 1981

THE "DADDY'S HOME!" YELL, FEET FLYING FOR A HUG, THE
GAMES AND PIANO LESSONS, THE KISS WHEN LEAVING,
THE BEAR HUG AT NIGHT, THE LITTLE "I LOVE YOU"
NOTES—LOVE GIVEN.

IF EVER A FATHER LOVED CHILDREN THREE—IT'S ME!

THE HEALTHY, ACTIVE, COORDINATED INDIVIDUALLY
PERFECT BODIES, WITH BEAUTIFUL, EXPRESSIVE FACES
TO MATCH, THE LEARNING HOW TO READ, OR COUNT, OR
MULTIPLY, THE PERFECT TENNIS SWING, THE JOY UPON
WINNING A GAME—LOVE'S POTENTIAL.

IF EVER A FATHER CHERISHED THOSE SMILING FACES,
BEAUTIFUL BODIES, AND MINDS SO SLY—IT'S I!

THE PICTURES DRAWN, CANDY SHARED, SWEET SONGS
SUNG, WORK AT CHURCH, ONE HAND HOLDING ANOTHER'S,
HAPPY PLAY TOGETHER,

CLEANING UP, BOOKS READ, BIBLE VERSES LEARNED,
SPONTANEOUS,

BEAUTIFUL, MEANINGFUL PRAYERS—LOVE DISPLAYED.

IF EVER A FATHER HOPED FOR KIND ACTIONS, HELPFUL
DEEDS, PURE THOUGHTS, AND SOULS POINTED HEAVENLY—I
AM HE!

TO JASON, JORDAN, JILLIAN—1982

THIS YEAR'S GONE BY SO QUICKLY,
ALL THE EVENTS ARE A BLURRY HAZE;
AND YET YOU'VE BEEN SOMETHING SPECIAL
EACH OF ITS BUSTLE-Y DAYS:

A LITTLE GIRL—GROWING UP,
CUTE AND SPUNKY AND SWEET—
BUT NOT TOO BIG TO STILL RUN
FOR A HUG—WHAT A TREAT!

A KINDERGARTENER, FULL DRESSER NOW,
A SWIMMER TOO—SAKES ALIVE!
A BIG HELPER, AND THE SWEETEST GIRL
A DADDY COULD HAVE (FOR FIVE)!

A BIGGER BOY—FIRST GRADER NOW,
(MINUSES AND ALL),
A READER, RHYMER, PIANO PLAYER TOO,
BUT DON'T FORGET CARS AND BALL!

THE CUTEST, ROUNDEST, SWEETEST FACE
(REMINDS ME OF SOMEONE I KNOW),
PLAYFUL AND WITH THE KINDEST HEART
IS ENOUGH TO MAKE DADDY GLOW!

THE BIGGEST BOY—CAN IT BE
HE'S ALREADY IN THE FOURTH GRADE?
READER, WRITER, ARTIST, SPORTSMAN,
MUSICIAN (ALL SELF-MADE);

FACE AND BODY ARE GROWING UP,
THAT'S EVIDENT—YET CUDDLY STILL,
AND WHEN YOU SHOW HOW MUCH YOU CARE
YOU GIVE YOUR DAD A THRILL!

SO A BUSY YEAR HAS SWIFTLY GONE BY,
I'M SORRY FOR THE TIME I'VE MISSED WITH YOU,
BUT I HOPE YOU'VE STILL BEEN ABLE TO SEE
HOW TREMENDOUSLY MUCH I LOVE YOU!

TO JASON, JORDAN, JILLIAN—1983

YOU'RE NO LONGER LITTLE—IT'S CLEAR TO ME
AS I STILL LIFT YOU ACROBATICALLY,
OR YOU GIVE ME A HUG AND SIT ON MY KNEE,
IT'S NOW YOU WHO'S READING TO ME!

A BIG FIRST GRADER NOW—WELL, SORT OF—
DRESSING YOURSELF, A GI'L ON THE MOVE
WITH PIANO AND BALLET—YOU LOOK LIKE A DOVE—
DOLLS, BIKES, AND CLOTHES—ALL THINGS THAT YOU LOVE.

NO LITTLE GIRL COULD EVER BE
AS PRECIOUS AS YOU ARE TO ME!

YOU'RE NO LONGER LITTLE—IT'S PLAIN TO SEE;
JUST LOOK AT THE THINGS YOU DO TERRIFICALLY:
SWIM LIKE A FISH, SPELL LIKE A DICTIONARY,
PLAY THE PIANO AND DRAW CREATIVELY!

AND WHO COULD FORGET, ALL KIDDING ASIDE,
THE WAY YOU PLAYED FIRST, AND GAVE THE BALL A RIDE,
YOUR BASKETBALL, AND SCHOOL WORK—ALL DONE WITH PRIDE—
AND YOUR GROCERY LIST ITEM—A HORSE TO RIDE!

A CHIP OFF THE BLOCK, AN IMAGE OF ME—
YOU'RE AS PRECIOUS AS YOU CAN BE!

YOU'RE NO LONGER LITTLE—I MUST AGREE;
YOU'VE COME A LONG WAY DRAMATICALLY:
WHETHER CATCHING OR SECOND OR ON A HITTING SPREE,
TOOTLES I ENJOYED, BUT YOU'LL <u>ALWAYS</u> BE C. B.!

THERE'S STILL TIME FOR A HUG (BEFORE YOUR NEXT TRIP),
AND MUSICALLY SPEAKING, I'D SAY YOU WERE HIP
WITH PIANO, VIOLIN, AND CHOIR—NOW, NO LIP
OR I'LL ARM WRESTLE YOU WITH A NEW GRIP!

WHAT A BOY, GROWING BEAUTIFULLY—
YOU'RE AS PRECIOUS AS YOU CAN BE!

TO ALL THREE, AS I WATCH YOU GROW,
        I WANT TO SAY, "I LOVE YOU SO!"

TO JASON, JORDAN, JILLIAN—1984

THREE PEAS IN A POD, DEFINITELY THE SAME,
BUT EACH ONE OF YOU IS INTO YOUR OWN GAME;

ANYTHING THAT'S GOT A BIT OF ACTING IN IT
YOU'LL HOP AT IN HALF A MINUTE;

WHETHER PERFORMING MARYLAND'S HISTORY—WOW—
OR A SPECIAL SKIT, YOU'RE THE CAT'S MEOW!

ON A HORSE, CAR, OR LEGO, LOOK AT YOU GO;
WITH A BASEBALL, SCHOOLBOOK, OR PIANO.

YOUR DEDICATION AND TALENT'S RELEASED;
YOU'RE A WHIZ KID—CONSIDER 'FUR ELISE'!

WHAT A GIANT LEAP YOU'VE MADE
(FOR A SHORT THING), WITH SOME AID,

IN CONFIDENCE, ABILITY, AND DISNEY-FUN—
A SCHOOL-MARM IF I EVER SAW ONE!

IN SPELLING, OR PITCHING, OR DANCING, OR AI-YA,
YOU'RE CHAMPION "PARTNERS"—AND I SURE LOVE YA!

TO JASON, JORDAN, JILLIAN—1985

HOW GOD MUST SMILE WHEN HE LOOKS ON YOU,
THREE LITTLE CUTIES WITH YOUR EYES OF BLUE;

HOW, LIKE I, HE MUST THINK IT GRAND
THAT YOU STILL WANT TO HOLD YOUR DADDY'S HAND;

AND HE MUST GIVE A CHUCKLE—HE'S NO SAP—
WHEN YOU CURL UP (WELL, ALMOST) IN MY LAP;

AND HE HAS TO BE DEFINITELY PLEASED AS PUNCH
WHEN YOU DISPLAY TALENTS HE GAVE YOU—A BUNCH:

DAZZLING FINGERS ON THE KEYBOARD
(I ONLY WENT A LITTLE OVERBOARD),

WHIRLING AROUND A PARALLEL BAR
OR DRAWING A FANCY TRANSFORMER CAR,

DANCING OR SINGING—YOU'RE THE BEST YET—
OR DRIBBLING IN FOR A BASKET,

THREE LITTLE FISH, THREE TENNIS PROS;
WHEN HE GIVES TALENTS, THAT'S HOW IT GOES!

HE MUST BE PROUD THAT YOU'RE NO FOOL
AND DO YOUR BEST EVERY DAY IN SCHOOL;

AND HE MUST JUMP UP AND DOWN WITH JOY
TO SEE SUCH A LOVING GIRL AND BOYS;

THREE BEAUTIFUL CHILDREN—A WORK OF ART
FROM YOUR HEAD TO YOUR TOES—TO YOUR HEART.

I KNOW HOW HE FEELS—I FEEL THAT WAY TOO—
FOR ONLY GOD LOVES YOU MORE THAN I DO!

TO JASON, JORDAN, JILLIAN—1986

THREE LITTLE BIG ONES, BUT NO LONGER SMALL—
YOU'RE ALL CREEPING UPWARD, BUT NOT QUITE TALL;

IN ACTIONS YOU'RE PREDICTABLY UNPREDICTABLE;
"MESSY"'S NO PROBLEM—EXCEPT AT THE TABLE;

"CLEAN MY ROOM AND PRACTICE? WHY, THAT'S THAT MEAN?"
"SEE HOW SMART YOU ARE—THAT'S USING THE OLD BEAN!"

SINGING AND DANCING AND DRAWING—AND MATH;
BUT STILL HAVING TO SAY, "IT'S TIME FOR A BATH."

PLAY SOME, WATCH TV, RELAX FOR A WHILE—
KEEP WORKING HARD—YOU GOT REASON TO SMILE!

CARD SHARPS, POOL SHARKS, WITH PING PONG THROWN IN,
OR BASEBALL (SOFTBALL) AND TENNIS—YOU'RE SURE TO WIN!

A DATE? A BOY FRIEND? I'M NOT READY FOR THAT!
BUT IT'S COMING SO FAST I'D BETTER HOLD ON TO MY HAT!

YOU'RE ALL GOING PLACES—ONE CLASS OR ANOTHER—
YET STILL CAN ENJOY A SISTER OR BROTHER;

AND YOU ALL ARE STILL SO CUDDLY AND CUTE—
PLEASE STAY THAT WAY ALWAYS—AW, SHOOT,

WHY MESS AROUND? I'LL GO AHEAD AND SAY IT—
I LOVE YOU—MORE THAN A LITTLE BIT!

TO J, J, J—1987

THREE LOVELY FLOWERS
GROWING IN GOD'S LIGHT,
BLOSSOMING BEAUTIFULLY,
PLEASING TO THE SIGHT;

SECRETARY IS NOT ELEMENTARY,
MIDDLE SCHOOL IS NOT TRIVIAL,
AND THE FIRST YEAR IN HIGH SCHOOL
IS ALWAYS VERY SPECIAL;

BUT WHAT A YEAR IN NEW YORK
(AND BALTIMORE WASN'T BAD),
WITH THOSE NICE COMMERCIALS
AND MOVIES YOU'VE HAD;

FROM BASKETBALL STAR TO DANCING FIEND,
FROM STATE FAIR WINNER TO BALLERINA,
FROM BASEBALL CHAMP TO ARTIST SUPREME,
AND WE MUSN'T FORGET PAULINA!

A DRESSING ROOM ALL YOUR OWN—
THAT'S CERTAINLY QUITE A THRILL—
BUT THOSE LONG RIDES TO NEW YORK
CAN GET TO BE QUITE A PILL;

FROM SWIMMING UP TO FIFTY LAPS
TO ROLLER SKATES AND POGO BALL,
TENNIS AND POOL ARE CERTAINLY FINE,
BUT CAMPERS—YOU'RE NOT AT ALL!

YES, A LITTLE SKIN PROBLEM,
AND CURLY HAIR TO TOUCH,
BUT CLEANING AND COOKING
AND WASHING—NOT MUCH;

A LITTLE TEACHER, PRIM AND PROPER,
DRAWING CARTOONS BY THE HOUR,
MAGICAL SOUNDS FROM THE KEYBOARD,
SINGING ELVIS IN THE SHOWER;

A JUMPING, SCREECHING DRIVER,
A MOST ATTRACTIVE "BULLY",
A COMIC-READING MANIAC,
AN EXTRA MEETING WHOOPI;

A COMPUTER WHIZ ALL OUR OWN,
A SONG OR DANCE OR PLAY MAKER,
A POPCORN AND ORANGE JUICE TV WATCHER,
A CHOCOLATE CHIP COOKIE BAKER;

YOU'RE GROWING UP, THAT'S PLAIN TO SEE;
THE TELEPHONE NEVER STOPS RINGING,
AND NOTES APPEAR FROM FRIENDS SO DEAR
WITH INVITATIONS THEY'RE BRINGING;

BUT YOU'RE STILL JUST THE RIGHT SIZE
FOR ME TO HUG OR HOLD OR KISS,
FOR I'LL STILL LOVE YOU DEARLY
AS LONG AS THERE IS CHRISTMAS!

TO J, J, J,—1988

I'M NOT VERY CREATIVE
WHEN IT COMES TO MUSIC OR ART,
AND CAN'T EVEN SAY MUCH
WHEN SPEAKING FROM THE HEART;

BUT WHEN IT COMES TO CHILDREN,
I'M REALLY A SENSATION;
WITHOUT ANY DOUBT, Y'ALL
ARE MY BEST CREATION!

IF YOU ASK WHY, I'LL
SAY MORE THAN "BECAUSE";
I'LL BEGIN WITH A RAINBOW
FROM THE WIZARD OF OZ,

FROM SECRETARY TO MODERATOR,
THIS LADY'S ALWAYS TOPS;
AND EVEN AFTER SCHOOL,
THE TEACHING DOESN'T STOP;

GOODNESS AND SWEETNESS
MOST OF THE TIME—
YOUR HUGS HELP MY DAY
(AS WELL AS THIS RHYME);

WHETHER DRAWING OR BEING A
JUNGLE FIGHTER ALL YOUR OWN,
THIS STEEL-TOOTHED WISP HAS
DREAMS OF A SURGEON;

YOUR FINGERS FLY BEAUTIFULLY
OVER THE KEYBOARD STILL,
AND THE S.A.T. CHALLENGE
SPEAKS WELL OF YOUR SKILL;

THOUGH YOU'D STILL RATHER PLAY
AND IT BOTHERS ME SOME,
YOU'LL BE GROWN SOON ENOUGH—
RELAX, AND IT'LL COME;

A DRIVER IN OUR MIDST?
WHY, BLESS CLARA'S HEART!
IT'LL MAKE MOM'S HAIRSPRAY WILT
TO SEE YOU DIRECTING THE CART!

A WORLD PREMIERE, A HARDEE-HAR-HAR;
SHIELD ME FROM THOSE CHEESE RITZ BITS;
YOU'RE PREPARED FOR ANYTHING—
FROM TV SERIES TO SINGIN' THE HITS;

AND THOSE GIRLS STILL CALL YOU—
HOMECOMING'S HERE—WANT TO GO?
BUT NEW YORK ALSO BECKONS
AND YOU'RE PRETTY BUSY, SO . . .

IT'S BEEN A GOOD YEAR FOR ALL OF YOU—
YOU GRACIOUSLY GROW MORE AND MORE;
AND HOW MUCH DO I LOVE YOU NOW?
TRY HEAPS AND BUNCHES AND BUSHELS GALORE!

TO J, J, J—1989

THREE—CAN'T SAY LITTLE—CHILDREN
(AND GROWING BIGGER YET);
IT SEEMS YOU'VE GOTTEN THIS SIZE
FASTER THAN A JET;

BUT IT'S TIME FOR BRACES
AND DIFFERENT HAIR-DOS GALORE,
AND ONLY THE "RIGHT" CLOTHES
SO EVERYONE CAN ADORE;

THE TELEPHONE'S IN USE
FROM DUSK UNTIL LATE AT NIGHT,
AND INFO IS HANDY
ON ANY CAR IN SIGHT;

ONE CAR DIDN'T PASS
A CERTAIN BRAND NEW DRIVER,
AND FUNDS STARTED DWINDLING
AS CALL-BACKS DIDN'T DELIVER;

DEANNA, SHARON, BRIAN, AND—
TOO MANY TO MENTION;
ENOUGH CLEANING AND GOOD GRADES
KEPT YOU FROM LYNCHIN';

YOU HAD YOUR UPS
AND "DOWNS" TOO, OF COURSE—
8:00 ON SUNDAY MORN
LED YOU TO THE SOURCE;

THREE LOVELY CHILDREN,
EACH GREAT IN YOUR WAY;
I'M VERY PROUD OF YOU—
WHAT MORE CAN I SAY?

DON'T NEED TO CROW ABOUT IT,
NOR SING, DANCE, OR PLAY;
JUST KNOW THAT I LOVE YOU
EACH AND EVERY DAY!

TO J, J, J—1990

A LITTLE PRINCESS, THAT'S FOR SURE—
JUST LOOK IF YOU DON'T BELIEVE IT!
THOSE ON THE TELEPHONE RECOGNIZE THIS—
(HER ROOM IS WHERE YOU RETRIEVE IT)!

WONDERFUL CLASSES, DOING WELL,
ESPECIALLY IN MR. AB'S,
AND TOPS IN SELLING MAGAZINES
OR IN THE SCHOOL STORE, KEEPING TABS.

A DANCER YOU CONTINUE TO BE,
A SINGLES AND DOUBLES CHAMP THESE DAYS—
DEFINITELY A TEEN—AGER, LOOKING AHEAD,
AND, OF COURSE, DADDY'S GIRL, ALWAYS.

A VERY TALL PRINCE IS THIS ONE NOW,
AS HANDSOME AS CAN BE,
A THRIVING FRESHMAN COMING INTO
YOUR OWN, AS ALL CAN CLEARLY SEE.

FRESHMAN BOARD, ARTISTIC TOUCH,
I'M AFRAID IT'S LATIN TO ME—
HONORS HAVE ONLY BEGUN TO
COME TO YOU, LIKE GEOMETRY!

YOUR FINGERS STILL GRACE THE CLAVINOVA,
ANY CAR YOU KNOW BY FEATURES ALONE—
IF EVER YOUR BRACES ARE TAKEN OFF
THE GIRLS WON'T LET US TOUCH THE PHONE!

AS FOR THE PRINCE WHO BECAME A KING,
THE CALLS NEVER SEEM TO STOP;
FOR THE "HAIR-DO" ED VEEP OF THE SGA
AND MYF, WE NEEDED A COP!

PERHAPS IT WAS BOYS STATE (YEAH—RIGHT)
THAT GAVE YOU SUCH A GOOD START,
BUT YOU MADE THE MOST OF IT—
NATIONAL HONOREE, TALENT IN THE ARTS,

YOU GOT TO DANCE AND SING AND ACT
IN THE BEST EVER "WEST SIDE STORY",
AND WHO CAN FORGET YOU AS "THE DENTIST"
(AND MORE) IN THAT LITTLE SHOP SO GORY!

WE TRAVELED FAR—INTO THE SUNSET,
CAMPING AND SEEING ALL THE SIGHTS,
BUT ANYWHERE WE'RE ALL TOGETHER
SEEMS TO ME TO BE JUST RIGHT!

SO, FOR TWO PRINCES AND A PRINCESS,
IT'S BEEN A GOOD YEAR CLEAR THROUGH—
IT'S ALL RIGHT THAT YOU'RE GETTING BIGGER—
THERE'S JUST MORE TO LOVE OF YOU!

TO J, J, J—1991

THREE DIFFERENT NAMES YOU WERE CALLED
BY EACH OTHER—NOT—AS A THRILL;
YOU BECAME, IF YOU CAN IMAGINE,
A SCHLACE, A SNORD, AND A DILL.

THE YOUNGEST BECAME A FRESHMAN,
OR SHOULD I SAY "LADY", SO BUILT,
FOR EVEN WHEN A "MOST IMPROVED" VOLLEYBALL
PLAYER, YOU PLAYED IT TO THE HILT,

AND IT WAS NOTICED BY EVERYONE,
WHETHER YOU DANCED OR SANG,
YOU LOOKED LIKE A MODEL ON YOUR
VIDEO, AND THE TELEPHONE RANG AND RANG.

SCHOOL WAS GREAT, THEN HARD,
BUT SIZZLER HELPED NOW AND THEN;
AND HOMECOMING WITH YOUR BROTHERS
BROUGHT SPECIALS SMILES AGAIN.

THE TALL MAN GREW EVEN MORE,
AND YOUR TEETH BEGAN TO SHOW;
SCHOOL ACTIVITIES, LIKE TENNIS AND
A PLAY, AND YOUR REP BEGAN TO GROW;

YOUNG LIFE LED TO LAKE CHAMPION,
FOOS BALL AND LEARNING A LESSON,
AND HOW YOU GREW AND LOVED IT IN
JAMAICA ON A SPECIAL MISSION;

MATURITY BECKONED, AS DID
DRIVING A CAR BEFORE LONG,
AND YOU STEADILY PURSUED IT—
OF COURSE, WITH A BLARING SONG.

THE ACE ALSO BECAME A FROSH,
HEADING WEST FOR A "STARRY" LAND,
AFTER A WONDERFUL PERFORMANCE FOR
SENIORS, MAKING THEM YOUNG AGAIN;

AND THERE WAS NOTHING BETTER THAN "GOOD
OLD BILL", A PART JUST MADE FOR YOU—
THE BEST ACTOR, SINGER, AND DANCER WE KNOW,
AND YOU'VE MADE US PROUD OF YOU;

YOU'VE LONGED FOR INDEPENDENCE,
AND I BELIEVE HAVE FOUND IT;
NOW THE QUESTION IS TO USE
YOUR TALENT AS GOD SEES FIT.

FOR THIS IS WHAT WE WANT FOR YOU,
OUR DEAR CHILDREN, AS YOU'LL FIND—
TO CONTINUE TO GROW INTO THE ONES
WHOSE IMAGE GOD HAS IN MIND!

AND KNOW MY THOUGHTS AND PRAYERS
ARE WITH YOU WHEREVER YOU ARE,
AND MY LOVE WILL ALWAYS SURROUND YOU
FOR YOU ALL THREE, TO ME, ARE STARS!

TO J, J, J—1993

AT THE END OF THIS YEAR—
THE HARDEST OF MY LIFE—
I SEE A TIME THAT'S BEEN
FILLED WITH DISCORD AND STRIFE.

BUT I HOPE THAT WE'VE LEARNED
HOW VERY MUCH WE ALL CARE,
AND WHATEVER ONE NEEDS, WHEN,
WE'LL ALWAYS TRY TO BE THERE.

A PRINCESS WHO'S TURNED SIXTEEN—
AND INTO QUITE A BEAUTY—
ALSO FOUND A PIZZA JOB
AS YOUR FIRST "FOR PAY" DUTY;

A WONDERFUL WESTERN TRIP YOU DID TAKE,
BUT "PREFER TO DRIVE MYSELF NOW, THANK YOU"—
NUMBER ONE SINGLES TOOK YOU, ALBEIT MIXED,
ALL THE WAY TO THE STATE TOURNEY TOO!

IS THIS A SENIOR, OR A COLLEGE MAN?
SLEEPING IN LATE LETS ONE KNOW—
THE SPECIAL NOVELL COURSES THAT YOU'RE
TAKING PROMISE YOU SOME NEEDED DOUGH;

MUSIC'S NOT FORGOTTEN;
NOW IT'S JUST THE GUITAR,
BUT NOTHING TAKES PRECEDENCE
OVER A SHINY BLACK CAR!

IN YOUR WORLD TURNED UPSIDE DOWN,
YOU'VE KEPT YOUR FAITH AND COME THROUGH IT STRONG—
BLOCKBUSTER, CLEANING, COUNTRY DANCING HELPED
(AND SAMSON'S HAIR ONLY A MITE TOO LONG);

CONTINUING WELL IN COLLEGE AND
ENTERTAINING THE SENIORS MARVELOUSLY,
YOU'RE NOW PREPARED FOR THE WONDERFUL PLANS
GOD HAS IN STORE FOR YOU ESPECIALLY!

AND THIS IS MY PRAYER FOR ALL THREE OF YOU—
THAT HE MAY TAKE THE SPECIAL PERSON EACH OF YOU IS,
AND GUIDE YOU AND USE YOU AND MOLD YOU,
SO THAT <u>YOUR</u> WILL MAY BE <u>HIS</u>!

TO J, J, J—1994

THIS WAS A YEAR OF CHANGE
FOR THE BETTER, IT SEEMS—
MAY SAD MEMORIES OF THE PAST
BE LITTLE MORE THAN BAD DREAMS.

A PRINCESS STILL, BUT NOW
A COUNTY CHAMP TO BOOT—
WHAT A JOY YOUR TENNIS
WAS, AND FOR YOU TO ROOT!

BUT A GIANT STEP WAS EARLY MADE,
AS A COLLEGE STUDENT YOU BECAME,
AND OLAN MILLS HAD YET ANOTHER
TELEMARKETER—MARY BY NAME.

AND FRIEND SAM IS ANOTHER NAME
THAT POPS UP PRETTY PRONTO,
AS HE'S BECOME YOUR LONE RANGER'S
FAITHFUL COMPANION TONTO.

A SOPHOMORE, WHO KNOWS ALL
ABOUT EVERYTHING?
WELL, ASK HIM ANYTHING YOU LIKE
ABOUT A TENNIS SWING,

OR COMPUTERS, HOT CARS,
OR COMPUTER-AIDED DESIGN;
OR EVEN, FOR A PRICE, HE'LL
MAKE YOU A DANDY SIGN!

I HOPE YOU'LL DO WHATEVER YOU LIKE—
BUT BOSTON'S A LITTLE FAR—
I CERTAINLY WOULDN'T WANT TO MISS
THE STRAINS OF YOUR GUITAR!

FREE, AFTER ALL THE PROCEEDINGS
FINALLY WENT YOUR WAY,
TO FOLLOW THE PATH THAT GOD HAS
CHOSEN YOU TO WALK EACH DAY;

A CHANCE TO GROW, AND SEE,
AND UNDERSTAND ABOUT IT MORE
WAS GIVEN YOU, AS CALABAN
WAS LET LOOSE ON A NATIONAL TOUR!

AND, ON THE SIDE, YOU MADE
A TAPE OF SONGS WE LOVE TO HEAR,
AND SENIORS, TOO, ESPECIALLY,
AND SOON EVERYONE—DON'T FEAR.

SO AS YOU CHANGE INTO THE ONES
YOU'LL BE FOR ALL YOUR DAYS:
ACKNOWLEDGE HIM, FOLLOW HIM,
BE KIND, AND SMILE IS WHAT I PRAY.

TO J, J, J—1995

THREE LITTLE J-BIRDS, FLYING FROM THE NEST,
BUT GETTING SO BIG, WE KNOW THAT IT'S BEST:

A GRADUATE NOW, AND SOPHOMORE TOO—SMARTY—
CELEBRATED WITH A WONDERFUL, LOVELY TEA PARTY;

SCHOOL WORK, WHITE CAR (REPAIRED), AND CRAFTS GALORE,
FREEDOM AND CONFIDENCE GROWS—WONDER WHAT'S IN STORE?

A SOPHOMORE AGAIN, TOUGH COURSES FAR AWAY,
AND THE TASTE OF A JOB ALL DAY EVERY DAY

GIVES INSIGHT INTO YOUR FUTURE AND PLANS,
AS YOU TRAVEL AFAR AND BECOME A FINE MAN!

TRAVELING THE U.S. AND EUROPE, IT SEEMS,
COMES TO AN END AS YOU FOLLOW YOUR DREAMS—

A COLLEGE OPENS WIDE, A MUSIC TAPE COME OUT,
AND YOU ARE SO JOYFUL YOU JUST WANT TO SHOUT!

SO, AS EACH OF YOU TAKES ANOTHER GIANT STEP,
KNOW MY LOVE GOES WITH YOU—YEP, YEP, YEP!

TO J, J, J—1996

THREE COLLEGE STUDENTS PURSUING A COURSE
THAT WILL PROVIDE A SATISFYING, INCOME SOURCE;

MAKING GOOD PROGRESS TOWARD YOUR GOAL
AND ALSO, HOPEFULLY, BROADENING YOUR SOUL.

ALREADY AN "AA" DEGREE, AND NOT YET NINETEEN?
AND LET'S NOT FORGET "MARYLAND JUCO TENNIS QUEEN"!

A GARDENER, A "CRUISER"—AND DANCER ALL NIGHT—
A TOWSON DORM ROOM, AND DOING ALL RIGHT.

NOT GMI, NOT UMBC, AND NOT ROTC—
EVEN AFTER COMPLETING CAMP "OFFICER—TO-BE",

SO FORWARD AT TSU WHILE YOU DECIDE
WHAT ROAD TO TAKE FOR YOUR FUTURE RIDE!

ONE MORE STEP TO FULFILLING YOUR DREAM—
ACTING AND SINGING SEEM TO MAKE A NICE TEAM;

VERMONT AND NEW YORK ARE JUST THE BEGINNING
OF PLACES YOU'LL GO AS YOU ARE PERFORMING!

SO, AS EACH OF YOU TRAVELS THE WAY
THAT LIES BEFORE YOU, REMEMBER EACH DAY

THAT MY LOVE IS WITH YOU WHATEVER YOU DO,
AND BE ASSURED THAT GOD WILL ALWAYS GUIDE YOU!

TO J, J, J—1997

THE END OF YOUR TEENAGE YEARS, AND MORE—
AS EACH ONE PREPARED TO GO OUT OUR DOOR:

NOT TOO FAR, AND BACK REAL SOON,
A JOY YOU CONTINUE TO BE—
WITH A GORGEOUS APARTMENT YOU
WORKED ON EDUCATION ELEMENTARY;

A HARD WORKER TOO, NOT ONLY THERE,
BUT LANDSCAPING GROUNDS ALSO,
AND YOU STILL FOUND TIME TO ENJOY
A MORE AND MORE SERIOUS BEAU!

ANOTHER APARTMENT DWELLER LEFT
TO PURSUE COMPUTER INFO,
WHILE MUSIC ALSO DANCED IN YOUR HEAD
AS A USE, WITH ONE YEAR TO GO,

AND A NICE BREAK LIES AHEAD
IN LONDON, AND PARIS TOO—
IF BAGGY PANTS ARE IN, A
FASHION DESIGNER MAY BE YOU!

AND ONE IS A "GADUMATE" FINALLY,
WITH WONDERFUL HIGH PRAISE FROM ALL,
SO THAT THEY WANTED YOUR HELP
IN TEACHING CLASSES THIS FALL;

SO HOME AGAIN, EAT SPECIAL FOOD, OFF AGAIN—
WHO KNEW YOUR WHEREABOUTS WHEN?
BUT YOU HAVE YOUR FINGER IN LOTS OF
PIES, AND WHO KNOWS WHERE IT WILL END!

SO EACH OF YOU LOOKING UP—AND FORWARD,
BUT PLEASE KNOW WHATEVER MAY BE,
I AM WITH YOU EVERY STEP OF THE WAY
AND WILL LOVE YOU ETERNALLY!

TO J, J, J—1998

THREE LITTLE CHILDREN—UH, NOT ANY MORE!
THEY'RE ALL GROWN UP, ALMOST OUT THE DOOR:

STUDENT TEACHING—THAT DREADED PHRASE—
AND YOU HAVE YOUR HORROR STORIES TO TELL,
BUT YOU KEPT WITH IT, AND WORTHINGTON
MADE THINGS TURN OUT WONDERFULLY WELL!

THE STUDENTS ALL LOVED YOU
(DO I MENTION A YOUNG MAN ALSO?)
AND YOUR LONG, BEAUTIFUL HAIR—
BOTH HERE AND IN ARKANSAS!

DOING YOUR OWN THING—(IS THAT
ONE PAIR OF PANTS OR TWO?)
IN A GREAT NEW APARTMENT—
BETTER WITHOUT SCOOBIE-DOO!

YOU ALSO SEE THE END NEAR,
AND A GRADUATION DATE DUE.
IS IT POSSIBLE THE ATTENTION
OF A YOUNG LADY INSPIRES YOU?

YOU'VE LOVED IT ALL YOUR LIFE, AND
YOUR MUSIC HAS ALWAYS BEEN REAL,
BUT IT'S STILL A LONG WAY FROM
"CONRAD BIRDIE" TO A RECORD DEAL!

THE TRAINING AND TRIPS ARE REPAID,
(ON A BUS FROM THE TRAVEL PLAZA),
AS AN OFFER TO TEACH IS MADE
AND A SPECIAL TRIP TO AUSTRALIA!

SO, EACH OF YOU IS BEGINNING TO REACH
YOUR GOAL TO PERFORM, COMPUTE, OR TEACH,
AND, WHATEVER YOU DECIDE TO DO IN THE END,
KNOW THAT MY LOVE AND PRAYERS I SEND!

TO J, J, J—1999

THE END OF THE CENTURY—WHAT A THRILLING THING!
AND SOME EXCITING EVENTS THIS YEAR DID BRING:

WRITING BOTH SONGS AND PLAYS
FILLED IN NON-AUDITION DAYS,
BUT THIS SURELY DID YOU NO HARM
AS CONTRACTS FOLLOWED—TO PERFORM!

VOICE LESSONS PROVIDED MORE ELATION,
AS "ULUJAY" BECAME A CORPORATION;
AND YOUR NEW NAME—NOT LEGAL—
BECAME "WALKS WITH EAGLES"!

GRADUATION FINALLY, FINALLY CAME
AND FINDING A JOB BECAME YOUR AIM—
A GOOD ONE, THAT WILL EXPAND YOUR MIND
WAS ACHIEVED AND "YOU WERE A FIND"!

NEW FURNITURE—AND MUSICAL OPPORTUNITY
WAS THERE TO SEE WHAT YOU COULD BE,
AND WITHOUT THE SLIGHTEST QUIVER
YOU TRADED SLEEK BLACK FOR SILVER!

ALSO A GRADUATE, WITH NOTHING TO DO—
MODEL, TRAINER, AND A SCHOOLMARM TOO?
A TELEPHONE CALL, A CONVERSATION
AND IT SEEMED LIKE DIVINE INTERMENTION.

GT RESOURCE—YOUR VERY FIRST YEAR?
(NO ONE CAN BELIEVE IT—FAR OR NEAR.)
AUDITIONS AND RUNNING WAIT IN THE WINGS
WITH WRITING CHILDREN'S BOOKS AND OTHER THINGS.

A REWARDING YEAR IT CERTAINLY HAS BEEN
(WITHOUT MENTIONING CERTAIN GOOD FRIENDS),
SO WORK HARD, DO WELL, AND HAVE FUN—
AND REMEMBER—YOU'VE ONLY JUST BEGUN!

TO J, J, J—2000

A BRAND NEW YEAR—AND CENTURY TOO—
FINDS EXCITING EVENTS FOR EACH OF YOU:

ALTHOUGH WAITING IS STILL THE NAME OF THE GAME,
YOU'VE KEPT BUSY SINGING AND STAYING ALIVE
AND PREPARING YOURSELF IN ALL WAYS FOR FAME—
WHENEVER YOU GET THE "GO AHEAD" FROM JIVE!

WRITING, DIRECTING, AND ACTING IN PLAYS—
THEN, MAKING A "CD" IN THE STUDIO—
EVEN YOUR OWN APARTMENT IN NEW YORK PLACE
HINTS OF FUTURE SUCCESS FROM YOUR VIDEO!

A NEW JOB IN A BRAND NEW COMPANY
PROVIDES AN OPPORTUNITY FOR ADVANCEMENT—
WHILE YOU SUBMIT PROPOSALS SUCCESSFULLY,
YOU ALSO FIND IT TO BE VERY PLEASANT.

A NICE NEW QUIET APARTMENT YOU ALSO FIND,
WHERE YOU'RE NOT SO MUCH IN A TIZZY—
AS WELL AS A WONDERFUL COMPANION—
NO, I'M NOT TALKING ABOUT "GIZZY"!

COMPLETING AN ABSOLUTELY MARVELOUS YEAR
AS GT RESOURCE FOR PATAPSCO MIDDLE HIGH,
YOU TOPPED IT OFF WITH AN ENTIRE SUMMER
WITH "ANNE" AT THE "U OF PEI"!

WHAT TO DO NEXT? GOD WOULD INTERVENE,
AS YOU CONSIDERED ETHICS AND MORE SCHOOL;
WHILE BECOMING A TRUE RUNNING MACHINE,
AN ENGAGEMENT RING WAS ACCEPTED FROM MITCHEL!

OH, WHAT A YEAR—THE BEST YET MAY SAY SOME—
BUT JUST WAIT FOR THE MAGICAL YEAR TO COME!
AND KNOW THAT I'M PROUD OF ALL THAT YOU DO
IN YOUR DIFFERENT WAYS—AND I'LL ALWAYS LOVE YOU!

TO J, J, J,—2002

THIS WAS AN EVENTFUL YEAR, THERE'S NO DOUBT—
AND THE POSSIBILITIES FOR THE NEXT—WELL, WATCH OUT!

NEW YORK CITY, WITH ITS CONCRETE AND SMALL SPACE
GAVE WAY TO A COUNTRY HOME—IS THAT A SMILE ON YOUR FACE?

A SLOWDOWN IN MUSIC-MAKING LED TO NEW POSSIBILITIES,
AS ACTING AND FILMMAKING CAME FROM YOUR ABILITIES.

YOU MET THE ONE FOR YOU—ONE IN A MILLINIA—
AND SO YOU MARRIED THE SWEET AND LOVELY MISS PHILLIA!

ON THE JOB AND ON YOUR OWN, WEB DESIGNER ELITE, IT SEEMS—
ALSO MAKING ELECTRONIC MUSIC, AS YOU FOLLOW YOUR DREAMS.

HELPING IN EVERY WAY FOR GRADUATION AND THE BAR—SUCH
    STRESS—
WHILE BAKING DELICIOUS GOODIES AND SEARCHING FOR A NEW
    NEST

WHICH, MIRACULOUSLY, YOU FOUND AND MOVED—RIGHT AWAY
PREPARING IT FOR GUESTS AND YOUR FUTURE—OH, HAPPY DAY!

BIG STEPS TAKEN TOWARD YOUR DREAMS—
AND MAY THEY ALL COME TRUE—
KEEP DREAMING AND WORKING AND KNOW THAT
IN ALL YOU DO I LOVE YOU!

TO J, J, J,—2003

HERE ARE THE "QUITE A YEAR" TOP PICKS
FOR CHILDREN NOW DOUBLED TO SIX:

SWARMING AROUND YOU LIKE A BEEHIVE
ARE FILMS, PLAYS, AND A CD FOR JIVE,

AND WHAT'S A MORE PERFECT SETTING
THAN A NEW HOME FOR A WEDDING?

ANOTHER NEW HOME, RIGHT THERE BY THE MALL,
WITH TWO NEW CARS HAVE YOU BOTH WALKING TALL;

MUSIC AND WEBSITES AND GRAPHIC DESIGN
ARE THE PURSUITS YOU HAVE ON YOUR MIND.

AND YET ANOTHER GREAT HOME, BUILT ON TO MORE
(WITH MORE FAMILY COMING OUT YOUR BACK DOOR?)

A SUCCESSFUL YEAR "BED AND BREAKFAST"-ING
WHILE A YOUNG LAWYER SEEMS LIKE TYPE CASTING!

INDEED, A "MOVING" YEAR IT'S BEEN FOR YOU,
AND WE HOPE OUR LOVE HAS HELPED YOU THROUGH.

J'S, 2004

THIS YEAR BROUGHT MANY CHANGES TO US ALL,
AS WE BEGAN A COMPLETELY DIFFERENT LIFESTYLE TOO,
WORKING TO COMPLETE AND MOVE IN OUR HOME
AND THEN DECORATING AND RUNNING OUR BOOTHS:

A HONEYMOON BROUGHT IN THE NEW YEAR,
AS JIVE'S CHAPTER CAME TO AN END,
FREEING YOU TO WRITE AS YOU'D LIKE,
CONSIDER YOUR OPTIONS, AND AUDITION AGAIN.

YOUR OLD HOUSE SOLD, YOUR LARGE NEW HOME
BEGAN TO BE WHAT ALL YOU'D LIKE IT TO BE—
A COUNTRY SANCTUARY WITH MOUNTAIN VIEW
AND LOTS OF ROOM FOR A "COMING SOON" BABY!

MORE ON YOUR OWN, WITH AN EVER-GROWING
WEB DESIGN BUSINESS KEEPING YOU BUSY,
WHILE A NANNY DESIGNING CLOTHES AND
BAGS FOR A FASHION SHOW WASN'T EASY.

YOU ALSO WERE IN THE POSITION
OF DECIDING WHICH PATH TO TAKE,
AS FUTURE HEALTH AND HAPPINESS
DEPEND ON THE CHOICES YOU MAKE.

MORE B & B BUSINESS THAN EVER
BUT THAT WASN'T ENOUGH, IT SEEMS,
AS YOU FELT LED TO HELP THE TOWN,
BUILD EVEN MORE, AND FOLLOW YOUR DREAMS.

SO THE APPOMATTOX GALLERY WAS BORN—
A ROUSING SUCCESS FROM DAY ONE—
WITH EVEN MORE POTENTIAL LYING AHEAD,
AND FOR TWO RETIREES—JUST PLAIN FUN.

SO, AN EXCITING BUT TOUGH YEAR IT'S BEEN,
WITH FEELINGS NOT AS THEY SHOULD BE
AMONG THOSE WHO LOVE EACH OTHER AS DEARLY,
UNCONDITIONALLY, FOREVER—AS DO WE.

J'S, 2006

SIX LIVES, SEARCHING FOR THEIR WAY,
INDIVIDUALLY AND TOGETHER, EACH DAY:

STILL CLINGING HOPEFULLY TO THE DREAM
OF PERFORMING IN SOME WAY, SOMEDAY—
A MOVIE OPPORTUNITY, MORE SONGS COMING,
AND POTENTIAL VOICE-OVERS LEAD THE WAY.

PRODUCING A MOVIE, THEN DOING
OFFICE WORK AT HOME—WHAT A TRIP—
ESPECIALLY WHEN IT'S DONE WITH YOUR
MAIN INTEREST—A BABY ON YOUR HIP.

AN ACTUAL SELF-EMPLOYED WEB
DESIGNER ABLE TO MAKE IT WELL—
AND NOW EMPHASIS IS ALSO ON A
CD OF YOUR OWN MUSIC AS WELL.

ENTERING THE FASHION DESIGN WORLD
IS ALMOST CERTAINLY TO HAVE A GLITCH,
BUT YOU'VE WORKED AND LEARNED
AND "UNIFORMS" MAY JUST BE YOUR NICHE.

WITH THREE BUSINESSES ALREADY DOING WELL,
A COURTHOUSE THEATRE WAS ADDED THIS YEAR—
IT WAS STRESSFUL YET SATISFYING TO YOU—
FEMALE CITIZEN OF THE YEAR.

WILLING TO HELP IN EVERY POSSIBLE WAY,
CONTINUING TO GROW AND DO WELL
IN LAW, YOU EXPANDED EVEN MORE TO AN
ACTOR, SINGER, AND NARRATOR—DO TELL!

SO, ALL OF YOU ARE EXTREMELY BUSY—
IN EVER-CHANGING ACTIVITIES TOO—
BUT ONE THING THAT REMAINS CONSTANT
IS HOW VERY MUCH WE LOVE YOU!

2009

THIS WAS A YEAR WHERE ONE COULD POSSIBLY HAVE FELT
POOR,
AS ECONOMIC HARDSHIPS ABOUNDED LIKE NEVER BEFORE.

BUT, STILL RICH IN BLESSINGS, THING ARE MUCH BETTER,
SO I'D LIKE TO SUMMARIZE OUR YEAR IN THIS LETTER.

JASON AND SHARON DID WONDERFULLY WITH A DAUGHTER
AND SON,
AS DELIGHTFUL RIDLEY IS NOW FOUR AND SWEET GRIFFIN
TURNED ONE.

WORKING WHERE HE COULD, SHE SELLING TWO FILM
RIGHTS,
HE MADE A NEW CD, READY FOR NEW HEIGHTS.

JORDAN'S WEB-SITE BUSINESS STRUGGLED FOR A WHILE,
BUT, THROUGH EXCELLENCE AND WORK, HE'S PULLED
THROUGH IN STYLE

AND IS OUT-SOURCING JOBS, WITH ENOUGH BUT NOT YET
RICH,
AND PHILLIA HAS FOUND REAL ESTATE MAY NOW BE A
GREAT NICHE.

JILLIAN IS WRITING NEW BOOKS ON ALL SHE IS LEARNING—
A HOME STAGING COMPANY AND NEW IDEAS CHURNING;

RUNNING ANOTHER B & B HAS TAUGHT HER EVEN MORE,
AND SHE'S PLANNING AGAIN TO WELCOME GUESTS TO HER
    DOOR.

I'VE BEEN BUSY CREATING A COURSE AND GAMES GALORE,
AS I'VE COME UP WITH TWO—AND EIGHT EDITIONS OR
    MORE.

JEANIE STILL LOVES HER DOLLHOUSES AND HAS
    DECORATED SOME
TO WHERE A STORYBOOK ABOUT THEM IS READY TO COME.

WE'VE ALSO TRAVELED DOWN SOUTH TO FLORIDA THIS
    YEAR,
BUT OUR FAVORITE IS TO GO SEE GRANDCHILDREN, IT'S
    CLEAR.

SO WE'VE HAD A GOOD YEAR, IN THIS BEAUTIFUL PLACE
    HERE,
AND WE WISH YOU THE BEST AND A BLESSED, HAPPY NEW
    YEAR!

2010

MOM:

WHAT A YEAR IT'S BEEN. WHAT AN ACCOMPLISHMENT, DOWN TO A TEN!
A "MOTHER-OF-THE-BRIDE" DRESS IN PINK FITS JUST RIGHT,
ALL YOUR PETITE NEW CLOTHES NOT A BIT TOO TIGHT.
A NEW CAR FULL OF BOXES OF FAVORS AND CLOTHES,
SPECIAL DETAILS FOR OUR HEADS TO OUR TOES!

AN IDEA THAT HAD FESTERED FINALLY FLUTTERED TO LIFE,
A SWEET COLLABORATION BETWEEN HUSBAND AND WIFE.
A "DOLLHOUSE" BOOK NOW SOON ON THE WAY,
WITH PLENTY OF GIFT SHOPS ON SITE FOR DISPLAY.

YOUR OWN BRAND NEW HOME—OR "COTTONTALE COTTAGE"
WITH PLENTY OF PINK, DISHES, ROCKS, WATER, WATTAGE.
SPEAKING OF ROCKS . . . YOU'VE HAULED QUITE A FEW;
WHEN YOU PRAYED FOR ROCKS, HE GAVE YOU ONE OR TWO.
YOUR VERY OWN BARNSCRAPER, TWO FULL STORIES TALL,
WITH ENDLESS POSSIBILITIES—TOO MUCH TO RECALL!

DAD:

NOT ONLY "FATHER-OF-THE-BRIDE" BUT OFFICIANT TOO,
A SPECIAL POEM AND PRECIOUS MOMENT WITH YOU.
IN A NEW CAR YOU DROVE DOWN TO DISNEY AND BACK,
KEEPING YOUR MANY AMBITIONS ON TRACK:
"TRICKY TRIG" CAME AFTER 20 YEARS IN THE MAKING,
"STATE QUEST" IS READY FOR TOY FAIR AND THE TAKING,
"MAJOR WAGER" EDITIONS FOR THE AVID SPORTS LOVER—
THERE'S HARDLY A GAME THAT YOU HAVEN'T COVERED.

A CLEVER CHILDREN'S POEM, AMONG OTHER THINGS,
A COPYRIGHT AND TRADEMARK AND "FLUTTERFLY" HAS WINGS.
TEN REQUESTS WITH AUTOGRAPHS AND SOON MANY MORE,
AT LEAST A SALE TO COUPLES THAT COME THROUGH OUR DOOR.
MOVING ROCKS, STAINING BOARDS, RUNNING ELECTRICAL WIRE,
PAINTING ROOMS, MOVING IN; IT SEEMS YOU HARDLY TIRE.

NOW YOU'RE ALL MOVED IN A NEW HOME AND BARN SO COZY;
WE'RE JUST A HOP, SKIP, JUMP AWAY FOR WHEN YOU WANT TO MOSEY.
WHAT A BUSY YEAR IT'S BEEN! NO TIME FOR SITTING ON THE BENCH!
WE'VE DONE IT ALL—INCLUDING A THOUSAND AND ONE FOOT TRENCH.
BUT, AS YOU SAY, "WE'RE POISED AND READY FOR SUCCESS;
YOU CAN'T MAKE SOMETHING BEAUTIFUL WITHOUT A LITTLE MESS."

SAM AND ME:

THE BUSIEST YEAR YET—AND THAT'S SAYING A LOT;
ONE THING IS FOR SURE—WE GAVE IT ALL WE'VE GOT.
A FAIRYTALE WEDDING THAT NO ONE COULD TOP,
LAUNCHED EVEN GRANDER ADVENTURES, ONE AFTER ANOTHER, NON-STOP!
PINNACLE PLUMBING AND DESIGN REACHED ITS GOAL,
IN ALL THE CONSTRUCTION, NO HINT OF ITS TOLL.
PLUMBING, ELECTRICAL, GAS ARE A FEW
OF EXAMPLES OF ALL THE WONDERS YOU DO.
WATERLINE FROM THE WELL, ELECTRIC FROM THE HOUSE,
INTERNET FROM A SIGNAL RIGHT DOWN TO THE MOUSE.

I HAVE YET TO SEE WHAT YOU DON'T OVERCOME
THAT DOESN'T IMPRESS ME—AND MORE THAN JUST SOME.
I PAINTED AND PAINTED AND EVEN HELPED LAY THE FLOOR
AND "FLUTTERFLY" FOUND ME EVEN PAINTING SOME MORE.
A PICTURE A DAY, I TRIED TO PAINT WHAT YOU'D SEEN,
WITH A WEDDING AND B & B IN BETWEEN.

WONDERING WHAT ELSE WE COULD DO THAT TAKES WITS . . .
WE WALTZED RIGHT UP AND MOVED INTO THE RITZ!
THE FUN WE HAVE HAD, THE MOUNTAINS WE'VE CLIMBED,
THE MIRACLES WE'VE WITNESSED AND HOW EACH WERE TIMED.
THE INN AT WHITE OAK FINALLY OPENED ITS DOOR,
AND THE BLESSINGS OVERWHELMED US EACH DAY ALL THE MORE.

A GAYLORD AND DISNEY INSPIRATION UNFOLDS,
THE VILLAGE OF "WHITE OAK" WITH TREASURES UNTOLD,
A WHITE OAK COOKBOOK AND "WITHIN THE WALLS OF THE RITZ"—
AMONG OUR OTHER ENDEAVORS THAT SHOULD MAKE US SOME BITS.
EVERY MOMENT IS PRECIOUS, NOT A MOMENT TO WASTE,
A FULL LIFE OF LOVE AND EXPERIENCE AWAITS.
BUT IN 2010 EVERY DREAM DID COME TRUE;
WE SQUEEZED THE LIFE OUT OF EVERY MINUTE OR TWO.
AND NOW 2011 BECKONS US ALL WITH SO MUCH MORE—
ADVENTURES, SURPRISES, AND ALL THAT'S IN STORE!

Jillian Downs

TO JORDAN

IT'S HARD TO BE A MIDDLE CHILD
AT ANY TIME, THEY SAY—

AND BETWEEN A FLAMBOYANT ONE
AND A PRINCESS—NO WAY!

BUT YOU FIT IN PERFECTLY WITH
EITHER ONE—A BIG TEASE,

HOLDING YOUR OWN, DOING WHATEVER
THEY LIKED, IF YOU PLEASE.

YOU GREW INTO A TOWER OF
STRENGTH—AND NOT JUST TALL,

BUT INSIGHTFUL, CARING, CALMING,
UPLIFTING TO US ALL.

YOU'VE BLOSSOMED AND DEVELOPED A
KEEN WIT AND KEENER MIND,

WHILE STILL BEING A GOOD PERSON—
GENTLE, PATIENT, AND KIND.

AND NOW, AS YOU APPROACH THE NEXT
MAJOR STEP IN YOUR LIFE—

GOING AFTER YOUR DREAM IN SPITE
OF THE HARD WORK AND STRIFE—

REMEMBER THAT I'M PROUD OF YOU,
HAVE TRUST IN YOUR DECISIONS,

WILL MISS AND PRAY FOR YOU EACH DAY,
AND AM GLAD THAT YOU'RE MY SON!

TO JEANIE

IT'S TOO SOON FOR VALENTINE'S—
TOO EARLY FOR ANNIVERSARY,
BUT IT'S ALWAYS THE RIGHT TIME
TO TELL YOU WHAT YOU MEAN TO ME:

SPARKLING EYES THAT TWINKLED COQUETISHLY,

LOVELY HAIR FIXED HOWEVER DIFFERENTLY,

SMOOTH, SOFT SKIN THAT WAS TANNED NATURALLY,

A FULL FIGURE THAT CURVED APPROPRIATELY,

A SOFT VOICE THAT ALWAYS SPOKE SO KINDLY,

A MANNER THAT CHARMED SO GRACIOUSLY,

A SMILE THAT CAME FORTH GUSHINGLY

FROM LIPS SHAPED FOR KISSING SO PERFECTLY,

YOUR MIND SEEKING KNOWLEDGE SO JOYFULLY,

YOUR SOUL SEEKING GOD SO WORSHIPFULLY.

YES, IN EVERY WAY, YOU WERE BEAUTIFUL TO ME!

WE'RE OLDER NOW, AND A LITTLE LESS SVELTE,
BUT I WANTED YOU TO KNOW THAT I FELT
THE SAME ABOUT YOU NOW AS I DID THEN—
YOU'RE MY JOY, MY LOVER, AND MY FRIEND!

MY LOVE

WHO IS IT THAT JUST SENDS ME? MY LOVE.
WHO IS IT THAT BEFRIENDS ME? MY LOVE.

WHO IS IT THAT CARES FOR ME? MY LOVE.
WHO IS IT THAT SHARES WITH ME? MY LOVE

WHO IS IT THAT EASES MY PAIN? MY LOVE.
WHO IS IT THAT HELPS ME GAIN? MY LOVE.

WHO IS IT THAT TREATS ME SWEET? MY LOVE.
WHO FIXES ME WONDERFUL THINGS TO EAT? MY LOVE.

WHO IS IT THAT WALKS WITH ME? MY LOVE.
WHO IS IT THAT TALKS WITH ME? MY LOVE.

WHO IS IT THAT MAKES ME SMILE? MY LOVE.
WHO MAKES MY DAYS MORE WORTHWHILE? MY LOVE.

WHO ALWAYS TRIES TO MAKE THINGS RIGHT? MY LOVE.
WHO KEEPS ME WARM IN THE NIGHT? MY LOVE.

WHO OFFERS A PRAYER FOR ME? MY LOVE.
WHO IS ALWAYS THERE FOR ME? MY LOVE.
WHO IS IT THAT'S SOFT AND ROUND? MY LOVE.
WHO IS IT THAT I'M GLAD I FOUND? MY LOVE.

WHO IS IT THAT MAKES ME TINGLE? MY LOVE.
WHO KEPT ME FROM BEING SINGLE? MY LOVE.

WHO IS IT THAT'S MY SWEET LOVER? MY LOVE.
WHO TRIES NOT TO TAKE THE COVER? MY LOVE.

WHO IS IT THAT DRIVES ME WILD? MY LOVE.
WHO GAVE ME A WONDROUS CHILD? MY LOVE.

WHO IS IT THAT DECORATES MY LIFE?
YOU ARE THE LOVE OF MY LIFE—MY WIFE!

MAGNIFICENT MOM

I SEE HER AS A LITTLE GIRL
WITH HER DOLL, AS A MOTHER,
AND THUS BEGAN HER MISSION
MORE IMPORTANT THAN SISTER OR BROTHER.

AND WHEN IT WAS FULFILLED
THAT SHE BECAME A MOTHER OF THREE,
SHE PRAYED THAT SHE COULD BE ALIVE
TO BE THE BEST MOTHER SHE COULD BE.

SHE BUILT HER NEST WITH VERY LITTLE,
USING VERY ORDINARY THINGS,
BUT ALL THE WHILE EVERY DETAIL
WAS PLANNED TO MAKE THEIR HEARTS SING.

SHE ROCKED AND NURSED AND NURTURED
THEM SO THEY WOULD GROW UP STRONG;
SHE PLAYED WITH THEM ON THE FLOOR
AND TAUGHT THEM RIGHT FROM WRONG.

SHE COOKED AND BAKED DELICIOUS
MEALS, SO HEALTHY THEY WOULD GROW,
BUT ALONG WITH THEIR HEALTHY BODIES,
SHE FED THEIR MINDS AND SOULS ALSO.

SHE SEWED AND MADE THEM COSTUMES
AND EVEN A WEDDING TROUSSEAU;
SHE LISTENED TO ALL THEIR THOUGHTS
AND DREAMED WITH THEM WHERE THEY COULD GO.

SHE MADE HER HOME INTO A PLACE
WHERE THEY WOULD BE PROUD TO BE,
AND THE CHILDREN REVELED IN IT
AND BROUGHT AND SHOWED THEIR COMPANY.

BUT IT IS A PLACE, AND TOO SOON,
EACH WOULD FINALLY ROAM,
BUT THEY CAME TO REALIZE THAT
WHEREVER MOM WAS, IS HOME.

AS HARD TIMES CAME UPON THEM
AS, IT SEEMS, IT IS BOUND TO BE,
THROUGH TEARS SHE FELL UPON HER KNEES
AND PRAYED EVEN MORE FERVENTLY.

EVERY WAKING MOMENT IS STILL FILLED
WITH PRAYERS FOR THEM ALL—WHEN
HER PRAYERS INCREASED TO NOW INCLUDE
BEING HER BEST FOR GRANDCHILDREN.

DOWN ON THE FLOOR ONCE AGAIN
WITH GLUE OR PAINT OR CLAY,
INTERMINGLED WITH HUGS AND KISSES,
SHE MAKES EACH DAY A PARTY-DAY.

A LOVING FATHER KNEW WHAT HE WAS DOING
WHEN HE SAID TO HER, "COME,
I'VE GOT JUST THE THING FOR YOU—
YOU'LL BE ONE MAGNIFICENT MOM!"

TO MY WIFE ON MOTHER'S DAY

I'M SO GLAD YOU ARE THE MOTHER OF MY CHILDREN—

FROM THE WAY YOU TOOK CARE OF THEM EVEN
BEFORE THEY WERE BORN,

TO ALL THE NURTURING YOU GAVE EACH ONE
AS BABIES,

TO ALL THE SPECIAL THINGS YOU DID FOR THEM
AS THEY WERE GROWING UP,

TO KNOWING EXACTLY WHAT THEY NEEDED OR
WOULD BRING THEM JOY,

TO SUPPORTING THEM WHOLLY IN WHATEVER
THEY WERE DOING,

TO ALL THE LOVE YOU CONTINUE TO SHOW THEM
IN ALL YOU DO,

IN BEING THE BEST MOTHER ANY CHILD ANYWHERE
COULD EVER HAVE—

THANK YOU!

30 TH(OU)!

THIRTY THOUSAND DOLLARS SOUNDS LIKE A HIGH PRICE
WHEN TAKEN ALL AT ONCE INSTEAD OF EACH SLICE:

1000 A YEAR—IS THAT SO MUCH, REALLY,
FOR A BEST FRIEND AND LOVIN' GIVEN SO FREELY?

83.33 A MONTH IS NOT TOO MUCH TO PAY
FOR THE LAUGHTER AND JOY GIVEN ME EACH DAY;

19.23 A WEEK IS CERTAINLY WORTH THE PRICE
FOR A BEAUTIFUL HOME THAT HAS INCREASED TWICE;

2.74 A DAY IS HARDLY WORTH THE MENTION
FOR ALL THE GREAT MEALS AND SPECIAL ATTENTION;

11 CENTS AN HOUR IS JUST PIDDLING CHANGE—
TO THINK OF THE COMPANIONSHIP GAINED IN EXCHANGE;

.002 OF A CENT A MINUTE WE HARDLY CAN COUNT,
WHILE THE TREASURES I'M REAPING SEEM ONLY TO MOUNT;

.00003 OF A CENT FOR EACH SECOND WITH YOU
IS THE BARGAIN OF A LIFETIME—OKAY IF I CONTINUE?

YOU KNOW THAT I'M THRIFTY AND LIKE A GOOD DEAL—
BUT THE OVERWHELMING BLESSING THESE FIGURES REVEAL!

THESE 30 YEARS HAVE BEEN QUITE A TREAT FOR ME—
SO I WISH YOU MUCH LOVE AND "HAPPY ANNIVERSARY"!

33RD

MY FAVORITE NUMBER'S ALWAYS BEEN THIRTY-THREE,

BEGINNING 'WAY BACK WITH MY BASKETBALL JERSEY;

(BECAUSE THAT WAS JESUS' AGE

WHEN HE GAVE HIS LIFE MIDST ALL THE RAGE)

AND I ONLY RELISH IT EVEN MORE NOW,

SINCE YOU'VE HONORED ME THIS MANY YEARS, SOMEHOW,

BY BEING THE BEST WIFE AND MOTHER YOU COULD BE—

BY MAKING ME FEEL LOVED (AND NOT BE LONELY)—

BY CARING FOR EACH OF US SO COMPLETELY—

THANK YOU—HAPPY 33RD ANNIVERSARY!

Jay

TO JILLIAN AND SAM, ON YOUR WEDDING DAY

IT WAS HER SMILE IN 6TH GRADE,
YOU SAY, THAT CAUGHT YOUR EYE;
YOU TOLD YOUR MOM SHE WAS THE ONE
YOU'D BE WITH UNTIL YOU DIE.

A TRUE FRIEND YOU'VE ALWAYS BEEN,
STAYING FOCUSED ON ONLY ONE,
UNTIL YOUR PRAYERS WERE ANSWERED
AND MY DAUGHTER'S HEART YOU'D WON.

YOU ASKED ME FOR HER HAND;
I COULD SEE THE ANSWER ON HER FACE;
YOU'D REHEARSED, WAITED, AND PACED
FOR THIS VERY TIME AND PLACE.

AND WHERE ELSE TO NOW GET MARRIED
THAN THE PLACE "WHERE DREAMS COME TRUE"?
WITH THE LORD, YOU'VE PROVEN THAT
INDEED—IN FACT—THEY DO!

YOU'LL TRY TO MAKE HER HAPPY
WITH ALL YOU HAVE INSIDE,
AND YOU THANK GOD FOR THIS, HIS
CHOICE, TO BE YOUR SPECIAL BRIDE.

YOU ENVISION ALL HER BEAUTY,
HER SPIRIT, HER SOUL, HER HAIR—
YOU PROMISE YOURSELF TO MAKE
THIS A LIFETIME LOVE AFFAIR.

HER HAIR IS FIXED JUST RIGHT,
HER FACE GLOWS, HER WAIST'S SO SLENDER;
THE BLACK TUXEDOS ACCENTUATE
HER GOWN IN ALL ITS SPLENDER.

YOU REALIZE YOU ARE GETTING
MUCH MORE THAN SOME OTHERS KNOW,
FOR THERE ARE MORE TO HER
THAN WHAT HERE SIMPLY SHOWS:

THERE'S THE DELIGHTFUL LITTLE GIRL
YOU SAW ONCE UPON A TIME,
HER SMILE AND PLAYFUL WAYS
THAT MAKE YOU FEEL SUBLIME.

THERE'S THE LOVELY YOUNG LADY
SHE'LL REMAIN ALL OF YOUR DAYS—
THE ONE YOU FELL IN LOVE WITH—
ALL HER STRENGTH AND SPLENDID WAYS.

THERE'S THE BEAUTIFUL BRIDE-WIFE,
AND THOSE MOMENTS IN YOUR ARMS
THAT FILLS—NO, FULFILLS YOUR LIFE
AS SHE PRESENTS YOU ALL HER CHARMS.

THERE'S THE HOMEMAKER, BUSINESS
WOMAN, INNKEEPER, MOTHER-TO-BE?
THERE'S MORE TO THIS WOMAN
THAN IN A LIFETIME YOU'LL SEE.

YOU ARE A COMPLEMENTING PAIR,
TWO THAT LOVE WITH ALL YOUR MIGHT,
AND WHAT YOU CAN ACCOMPLISH
I HAVE MARVELED AT THE SIGHT.

FOR THIS IS YOUR WEDDING DAY, MUCH
GREATER THAT JUST SAYING, "I DO";
IT'S A HOPE YOU'VE CARRIED IN YOUR HEARTS,
A PRECIOUS DREAM COME TRUE!

A LOVE THAT'S WAITED SO LONG TO BURST
FORTH NOW COMES TO FULL BLOOM;
THE SHEER JOY ON BOTH YOUR FACES IS
EVIDENT TO ALL IN THE ROOM.

I WISH YOU GOD'S GOOD GRACE
THROUGHOUT YOUR TRULY BLESSED LIFE,
WITH ALL THE HAPPINESS AND LOVE
AWAITING YOU AS HUSBAND AND WIFE!

TO MR. THOMAS

FOR NINETEEN YEARS WE'VE RIDDEN TOGETHER—
MOST OF THE TIME, AT LEAST;
FOR NINETEEN YEARS I'VE OBSERVED SOME LITTLE
THINGS THAT HAVE NEVER CEASED:

AT 6:27 YOU'D ROUND THE CORNER
AND BACK INTO YOUR PLACE;
FORTY SECONDS LATER YOU'D EMERGE,
CHECK YOUR CAR LIKE A FLYING ACE,

WALK BEHIND MINE NO MATTER WHERE I PARKED,
THEN SLIP INTO YOUR SEAT,
AND WE WERE OFF ONCE AGAIN ON
AN ADVENTURE DOWN THE STEET;

TOPICS VARIED FROM DAY TO DAY—
OVER EVERY SUBJECT WE PROBABLY DID ROAM—
AND YOU KEPT ABREAST OF THEM ALL, UNLESS
I DECIDED TO SLEEP ALL THE WAY HOME;

NEITHER EARLY MORNING HOUR, NOR SLEET,
NOR SNOW, DID STOP US ON OUR WAY,
ALTHOUGH A COUPLE OF TIMES, I DO RECALL,
IN THE PARKING LOT WE SHOULD HAVE STAYED!

LEAVE A MINUTE EARLY? NOT ON YOUR LIFE!
YOU FULFILLED YOUR OBLIGATION
TO THE LETTER SO MUCH, THEY MADE YOU
TAKE A MUCH-DESERVED VACATION.

BUT, FINALLY, I COULD SEE YOU ANXIOUSLY
AWAITING THE TIME TO STOP—
YOU'D SAVED AND WORKED AND HAD EVERYTHING
PLANNED SO YOU'D COME OUT ON TOP.

NOW YOU'RE OFFICIALLY RETIRING AND
OUR CAR-POOLING MUST COME TO AN END—
THE CONSTANT THING YOU'VE BEEN TO ME IS
TRUSTWORTHY, HELPFUL, POLITE—AND FRIEND!

MISS STELLE

IT'S HARD TO IMAGINE ST. CHARLES
    WITHOUT THE IMAGE OF MISS STELLE;
IT'S LIKE A SUNDAY MORNING
    WITHOUT A RINGING CHURCH BELL.

THE MEMORIES COME FLOODING BACK
    OF DAYS SO LONG AGO,
YET THEY SEEM SO CLEAR
    THEY MUST BE STRONG ALSO:

ALL THE BASIC ENGLISH I LEARNED
    (AND LOVE OF POETRY TOO)
MADE ALL THE REST EASY AND FUN—
    LEARNED FROM YOU-KNOW-WHO;

THE FIRST CHRISTMAS PRESENT I EVER BOUGHT
    (I REMEMBER THE ROUGH, OILY FLOOR)
WAS AN OFFICIAL JUNIOR COMMANDO HAT
    FROM MISS STELLE'S GENERAL STORE;

EVERYONE IN TOWN, IT SEEMED,
    AT THE PICNIC, HAD A FEAST,
AND MISS BERTHA'S AND MISS STELLE'S TREATS
    WERE <u>NOT</u> AMONG THE LEAST;

THE BOOK CLUB—GOODNESS,
    WHAT WOULD IT EVER BE
WITHOUT THE ONE WHO
    INSPIRED IT, LITERALLY?

FOR EVERYONE WHO VISITED,
    DAFFODILS LINED THE WAY,
AND THE CHARM AND SUNNINESS
    INSIDE DIDN'T FADE AWAY.

TALKING WITH HER WAS AN EDUCATION,
    ALERT AND INTERESTING ALWAYS,
SHE REMAINED INTERESTED IN YOU
    AND YOUR THOUGHTS ALL HER DAYS.

FEELING BLESSED, A BLESSING TO ALL
    SHE REMAINED ALL THROUGH THE YEARS,
AND A GREAT JOY YOU HAVE TO FEEL
    EVEN THOUGH MIXED WITH TEARS.

OF ALL THE BOOKS SHE LOVED,
    SHE LOVED THE BIBLE BEST,
AND BELIEVING IN IT FAITHFULLY
    HAS BROUGHT HER ETERNAL REST.

THE WISDOM SHE BROUGHT TO ALL
    NO ONE CAN EVER TELL,
BUT I'M SURE GOD IS ENJOYING
    PERSONALLY—GRAND LADY MISS STELLE!

FULL OF LOVE

WELL, I MAY BE TOO LITTLE—
I'M NOT A TREE; I'M JUST A TWIG,
BUT WHEN IT COMES TO LOVING
I CAN LOVE REAL BIG!

      BECAUSE I'M FULL OF LOVE,
      JUST HUG ME UP REAL CLOSE,
      YOU'LL SEE, I'M FULL OF LOVE
      FROM MY HEAD DOWN TO MY TOES.

WELL, I MAY BE TOO TINY—
TOO YOUNG TO USE MOM'S ROUGE,
BUT WHEN IT COMES TO LOVING
I CAN LOVE REAL HUGE!

      BECAUSE I'M FULL OF LOVE,
      MY LOVE JUST OVERFLOWS;
      YOU SEE, I'M FRESH FROM GOD
      SO HIS LOVE JUST NATURALLY SHOWS.

WELL, I MAY BE TOO SMALL
TO DRIVE A BUS OR BARGE,
BUT WHEN IT COMES TO LOVING
I CAN LOVE REAL LARGE!

      BECAUSE I'M FULL OF LOVE—
      HEAVEN IS JUST LIKE ME;
      YOU SEE, I'M FULL OF LOVE;
      JUST LOOK AND YOU WILL SEE.

SO IF YOU THINK THAT YOU'RE TOO OLD
AND HAVE FORGOTTEN HOW TO LOVE,
JUST BECOME AS LITTLE CHILDREN
SENT STRAIGHT FROM GOD ABOVE!

      BECAUSE I'M FULL OF LOVE,
      YOU'D BETTER RUN FOR COVER
      IF YOU DON'T WANT TO BE LOVED,
      FOR I'M A LITTLE LOVER!

TWO DAYS OLD

AFTER MORE THAN 20 HOURS
YOU CAME INTO THIS WORLD.
AT 8, 14, AND 21,
A HEALTHY, PINK LITTLE GIRL.

IN YOUR TOBOGGAN HAT LIKE MINE
YOU EXUDED BABY CHARMS
AND WERE QUITE CONTENT, IT SEEMS,
ASLEEP INSIDE MY ARMS.

AS I HELD YOU SLEEPING
YOU WERE COMPLETELY UNAWARE
OF THE SURVEY TAKING PLACE,
STARTING WITH YOUR DARK, WAVY HAIR.

WITH A ROUND FACE AND HEART-SHAPED LIPS,
LONG FINGERS AND LITTLE PUG NOSE,
FOR YOU, EVERY TINY DETAIL
'PERFECT' SEEMS TO BE WHAT GOD CHOSE.

YOU LIKE TO HAVE YOUR HANDS FREE
AND MOVED YOUR HEAD THE OTHER WAY,
WHICH SHOWS AMAZING STRENGTH
FOR JUST YOUR 2ND DAY!

YOU'LL BE LOVED BY YOUR PARENTS
AND GRANDPARENTS TOO, YOU SEE,
SO WELCOME TO THE WORLD—
SWEET LITTLE LOVELY RIDLEY!

TWO DAYS OLD II

AS I HOLD YOU FOR THE FIRST TIME,
FITTING IN THE CROOK OF MY ARM,
I BEGIN TO SURVEY THIS BOY
LYING THERE ALL SNUGGLY AND WARM.

GOOD LIPS AND NOSE, DARK HAIR, ROUND CHEEKS,
AT "EIGHT, TEN" AND "TWENTY-ONE" LONG—
LIKE A "757" YOU CAME—
YOUR FACE LOOKS BOTH PEACEFUL AND STRONG.

RAISING YOUR HEAD FROM SIDE TO SIDE,
NICE EARS, A PERFECT LITTLE HEAD,
EXUBERANT KICKS OF YOUR LEGS,
AND A LUSTY CRY TO BE FED.

LONG FINGERS ON BLANKET-FREE HANDS,
BIG STEEL-BLUE EYES AND SOFT TAN SKIN—
I THINK YOU'LL BE, IN MANY WAYS,
A BEAUTIFUL MAN AMONG MEN.

YOU'LL BE HELPED BY MANY OTHERS
BEFORE YOU BECOME A MISTER,
GUIDED BY ALL THOSE WHO LOVE YOU—
ESPECIALLY A GREAT BIG SISTER.

A MIXTURE OF EAGLE AND LION,
KING OF THE AIR, KING OF THE EARTH—
OUR LITTLE GRIFFIN HAS ARRIVED—
TODAY WE CELEBRATE YOUR BIRTH!

SWEET WORDS

THE SOFTEST, GENTLEST, AND SWEETEST VOICE,

WHICH SPOKE ONLY TO ANGELS AT ONE TIME,

TOOK HIS TIME TO TALK ALOUD

ON EARTH WITH ITS GOOD AND GRIME.

BUT FINALLY CAME "MOMMY", "DADDY",

AND A NAME FOR BIG SISTER—"EE-AH",

AND ANYTHING ELSE HE HAD OBSERVED

OR THOUGHT OF AS AN IDEA.

BUT THE SWEETEST WORDS OF GRIFFIN

I KNOW—COMING OUT OF THE BLUE—

ACCOMPANIED BY A NATURAL HUG—

ARE THESE: "GRAND DADDY, I LOVE YOU."

A NEW VERSION OF "ROCK-A-BYE BABY"

(TO BE SUNG TO ITS TUNE)

ROCK-A-BYE BABY IN MOTHER'S ARMS

AS I BEHOLD YOUR MARVELOUS CHARMS:

SWEET LITTLE CHEEKS AND CUTE, TINY NOSE,

BEAUTIFUL EYES BEGINNING TO CLOSE.

ALL WRAPPED IN BLANKETS SNUG AS CAN BE,

ONE PERFECT HAND IS REACHING FOR ME;

THIS PRECIOUS MOMENT I'LL ALWAYS KEEP

AND CHERISH, WHILE ROCKING MY BABY TO SLEEP.

I PRAY TO HEAVEN AND GOD ABOVE

YOUR HEART WILL ALWAYS BE FILLED WITH LOVE

AND ANGELS WATCHING O'ER YOU WILL KEEP,

SO ROCK-A-BYE BABY—YOU'RE SOUND ASLEEP.

THE FORMATIVE YEARS

YOU AND THAT HOUSE ARE ONE AND THE SAME IN MY MIND.
ROOMS OF QUIET ACTION THAT, CALCULATED, EQUAL SOMETHING UNEQUAL.
YOU AND THAT HOUSE.
EVERY MORNING SO EARLY. CEREAL SOFTLY BEING CHEWED.
SACRED TO A CHILD LISTENING TO THE MYSTERIES OF A MAN.
THE CHAIR CREAKS ONLY SOME.
MUCH LESS, AT THIS HOUR, THAN IT WOULD LATER IN THE DAY,
SAY WHEN YOU RETURN TO A MAD HOUSE OF TEMPERS AND CHAOS.
BUT NOW IT'S JUST YOU AND THE HOUSE.
SILENT BEFORE THE SUN COMES UP.
IN YOUR CRINKLY PAJAMA SUIT.
HAIR CLEAN BUT SPLAYED EVERY WHICH WAY FROM SLEEPING ON IT.
NOW TINKERING IN THE BATHROOM
A SHAVE AND SOME AQUA VELVA.
ALWAYS ALBERTA VO5 FOR THAT UNTAMED BIT OF HAIR.
AS YOUR LIPS DISAPPEAR AND BROW FURROWS IN CONCENTRATION:
WILL IT LIE DOWN TODAY?
THE SMELLS LAY UPON ME IN MY BED.
THE SMELL OF EARLY MORNING. THE SMELL OF RISING.

AND WITH DISH IN SINK AND DAILY READING RETURNED TO ITS SPOT ON
TOP OF THE GRANNY CABINES AND WIFE KISSED AND WATCH ON AND RING
ON AND TIE TIED AND KEYS QUIET AND DOOR HUSHED OPEN AND CAREFULLY
CLOSED I LOVE YOU.
KNOWING YOUR CLOCKWORK
KNOWING YOU'LL BE BACK TO DO IT AGAIN EVERY DAY.
SLOWLY BUT SURELY I LOVE YOU SO MUCH I CAN SCARCE GO TO SLEEP.
I KNOW YOU SO WELL. YOU AND THAT HOUSE.
TAUGHT ME TO LOVE. SLOW BUT SURE.
SACRED LIKE THE SMELL OF CHANGE FROM YOUR POCKET TO THE CABINET.
I'D CLIMB ONTO THE SINK AND STICK MY FINGERS IN THE PENNIES AND DIMES.
YOU'RE A FACELESS LOVE. A BLANKET OF LOVE THAT COVERS MY NIGHT.
I SCARCELY CAN GO TO SLEEP KNOWING THE GIFT YOU'VE GIVEN ME.
MY LOVE FOR YOU IS A LONGING. A DEEP AND USELESS THING.

I USED TO HAVE A DREAM, FROM AN EARLY AGE, PROBABLY FIVE,
THAT YOU AND I WERE WALKING UP THE DRIVEWAY OF
THAT HOUSE, EACH OF US CARRYING A LOAD OF SOME KIND.
YOURS WAS RELATIVELY SMALL AND QUITE MANAGEABLE.
MINE, HOWEVER, WAS LARGE AND CUMBERSOME FOR MY SIZE.
I REMEMBER THE FEELING OF THAT LOAD TO THIS DAY.
I USED TO THINK I WAS MEANT FOR BIGGER THINGS THAN YOU
BUT NOW I THINK THE LOAD WAS YOU. WAS LOVE.
WAS LIVING UP TO YOU. TO WHAT YOU'D GIVEN ME.
THE SWEET TASTES OF MY LIFE.
THE DAYS OF UTTER JOY,
UNNOTICED THEN, SINCE I KNEW NOTHING ELSE,
ARE MEMORIES I RELISH AND AM SO GRATEFUL FOR:

THE CAREFULLY CRUSHED ICE IN YOUR WATER,
FUDGE BARS AFTER A BIKE RIDE,
THE SMELL OF OUR BASEBALL GLOVES AND TENNIS BALLS,
THE SUMMER, THE WATERMELON, THE CORN ON THE COB AND
SPARKLERS, THE COOL OF THE BASEMENT AFTER A SHOWER AND
POPCORN AND WET HAIR DRYING TO A GAME SHOW OR BALL GAME
OR CHESS OR DOMINOES OR CRAZY EIGHTS.
AND THE RECORD PLAYER.
YOU COULDN'T HELP BUT GRAB MOM AND DANCE
WHEN "'TIL I KISSED YOU" CAME ON AND SING ALONG.
"LISTEN TO THE DRUM PART ON THAT ONE!" BA DUM BA DUM.
IT ALL ADDS UP TO A LOVE THAT HURTS MY HEART.
THE SILLY VOICE YOU'D PUT ON WHILE TICKLING OUR BELLIES.
OR REPLACING TO WORDS TO THE CINDERELLS WORK SONG
WITH "MACARONI, MACARONI". GRAPE JELLY.
ENERGY FROM SOMEWHERE ONCE YOU CAME HOME TO US . . .
MY MEMORIES NEVER REST ON THE HARDENED FACE DURING MOMENTS OF
DISAPPOINTMENT. SITTING AT THE BREAKFAST TABLE OVER HOMEWORK
UNDONE. MY MIND DANCES PAST THOSE THINGS AND REMEMBERS
NOTHING NEGATIVE.

IT RESTS ON THE FEELING OF YOU AND THAT HOUSE.
US, IN THAT HOUSE. DOWN HOME.

SO, BEFORE I GO ON REPEATING MYSELF LET ME JUST SAY . . .

THANK YOU.

I LOVE YOU WITH ALL THAT I AM.
I AM YOUR SON.
THE CIRCLE IS COMPLETE.
AND NEVER UNDONE.

Jason Downs

THE INFORMATIVE YEARS

YOU AND THAT HOUSE ARE ONE AND THE SAME IN MY MIND.
YOU AND THAT HOUSE. ALWAYS AT ODDS WITH EACH OTHER.
YOU TRYING TO TAME IT. STRAIGHTEN IT. MAKE IT BETTER.
ALWAYS MOVING. FOR US. NEVER REALLY GETTING THERE.
BUT NOT REALLY NEEDING TO EITHER.
YOU'D ALREADY TAKEN US SO FAR.

YOU AND THAT HOUSE, LIKE YOUR FATHER AND HIS FARM.
CARVING OUT BEAUTY ON A LANDSCAPE LITTLE BITS AT A TIME.
WITH SWEAT. YOUR FACE TURNING BEET RED AND PERIODICALLY
BLOWING THE STRANDS OF HAIR AWAY UNSUCCESFULLY.
SCARCELY ABLE TO STAND THE HEAT.
FINDING REASON TO GO ON WHEN YOU'D STOP AND IMAGINE THE END.
THE FINAL PERFECT PICTURE.
OR IMAGINING THE FIRST TIME YOU'D EXPLAINED THAT VISION TO YOUR
HUSBAND OR TO ME OR TO ALL OF US AT THE DINNER TABLE.
THE LIGHT SPILLING FROM YOUR EYES LIKE A SECRET
YOU NEVER HAD ANY INTENTION OF KEEPING.
OPENING OUR MINDS TO A ROOM THAT HADN'T EXISTED ONLY MOMENTS
BEFORE. IMAGINING THE VIEW FROM THAT ROOM. FEELING THE BREEZE.

BUT IT'S SO HOT RIGHT NOW . . . YOU CAN'T SEEM TO GET COOL.
YOU ASK IF ANYONE ELSE IS HOT. YES. NO.
LIKE THE STICKY HOT OF A SUNDAY CHURCH PEW, NEXT TO YOU.
AND I'D STILL HOLD YOUR HAND AND YOU'D STILL LET ME.
BUT COULDN'T WAIT TO GET HOME TO RELIEF AROUND THE WAIST WHERE
BELTS OR ELASTIC SKIRT BANDS OR BRAS HAD COLLECTED HOT HUMID
     HEAT.
THE RELEASE ONCE HOME WAS DELICIOUS AND INTOXICATING.
SLIP INTO THE POOL. LIKE HEAVEN.
YOU PURSE YOUR LIPS AND CLOSE ONE EYE WITH PLEASURE.
FULLY CLOTHED TO STAY COOL LATER ON AS YOU WORK IN THE GARDEN.
A HAVEN. A HEAVEN. YOU AND THAT HOUSE.

A NEST OF LOVE AND PROTECTION AND YOUR STRUGGLE TO KEEP IT SO.
LIKE A BIRD, YOUR CONSTANT PRAYER.
AND YOU'D CONVERSE WITH THE TREES AND THE BIRDS
AND REMARK ON HOW WELL THEY'RE DOING.
BASK IN THE COLLECTIVE GOOD FORTUNE.

WALK ACROSS THE YARD SMILING AT SOMETHING YOU'VE SAID TO
    YOURSELF,
KNEES MUDDY, SWEAT DRIPPING, GLOVES ON, CLUMP OF WEEDS IN HAND,
TALKING TO ONE OF US . . . NO ONE AROUND AT THE MOMENT . . .
JUST ME WATCHING FROM THE BASEMENT WINDOW AND SMILING TOO.
AND LOVING YOU.
ASSERTING YOURSELF IN EACH CORNER OF OUR LIVES AND IN GOOD
    HANDS.
EVERYTHING GREW. EASILY AND BEAUTIFULLY, IN YOU AND THAT HOUSE.

LATER SITTING ON MY BED AND TALKING OF DREAMS WE WOULD WAX
PHILOSOPHICAL. TALK OF GOD AND LITTLE THINGS.
YOU'D REMIND ME THAT I COULD DO ANYTHING AND YOU'D STILL LOVE
    ME.
SUCH PRECIOUS LITTLE THINGS THAT GAVE ME WINGS TO GO AND BE AND
    SING.
SUCH SAD SONGS. I SO BADLY WANTED YOU TO SING BUT COULDN'T
    BEAR TO HEAR. "WHERE ARE YOU GOING, MY LITTLE ONE", "KISSES
    SWEETER THAN
WINE", "WHERE HAVE ALL THE FLOWERS GONE?" WHY THIS THEME, I
    WONDERED? NOW I KNOW THAT HAVING IS NOT HAVING.
NOTHING YOUR OWN.
TIME SO SHORT AND LOVE SO SWEET.
HANGING JUST OUT OF REACH LIKE THE LAST DAYS OF SUMMER

WHEN I'D COME TO YOU, HAVING BEEN CALLED FOR CARROTS, WITH
ITCHY LEGS AND SKINNED ARMS AND TANNED FACE AND COTTON MOUTH.
BUT THE FEELING FLEETING ONCE REFRESHED. FORGOTTON.
I DIDN'T NOTICE THEN YOUR ABSOLUTE AWARENESS.

IT WAS A WARM BATH BUT I COULDN'T TELL THE DIFFERENCE
BETWEEN WHAT WAS AND WHAT WAS WATER. IT WAS THE SAME.
WE WERE SO BUSY BEING COVERED IN CHOCOLATE CAKE MIX.
BATTER ON THE GRANNY CABINET. ON OUR LITTLE BODIES. IT DIDN'T
    MATTER.
OATMEAL COOKIES AND THE KITCHEN FLOOR.
WARM OVEN SMELLS AND COMPANY COMING ANY MINUTE.

"IS ANYONE ELSE BURNING UP IN HERE?"
JUST TO SHARE THE JOY WAS YOUR JOY.
YOUR AGILE LITTLE BODY ALWAYS MOVING TO THAT PURPOSE.
ALWAYS WATCHING FOR ONE THING OUT OF PLACE. IT WAS HOW YOU
    LOVED US. AS BIG AS THAT HOUSE. THE FINAL PERFECT PICTURE.
EVERY DETAIL CONSUMING YOU. EVERY DETAIL NOTICED.
AND JUST SO YOU KNOW . . . I NOTICED. SILLY FOR ME TO SAY THANK YOU.

I LOVE YOU WITH ALL THAT I AM.
I AM YOUR SON.
THE CIRCLE IS COMPLETE.
AND NEVER UNDONE.

Jason Downs

RICH MAN

VERY FEW DADS ARE DADS THAT WHO
POSSESS THE RICHES THAT MY DAD DOES DO . . .

A DAD FULL OF CHRIST WITH WISDOM SINCE YOUTH,
A DAD POSSESSING PEACE AND VERY MUCH COUTH;

A DAD FIRM IN FAITH WHO IS STABLE AND TRUE;
A RELIABLE DAD CAN'T BE FOUND MORE THAN YOU.

A DAD SO LOVING, SO GENTLE AND KIND;
A DAD LIKE YOU IS SUCH A RARE FIND.

A DAD WHO'S A FRIEND AND THERE BY MY SIDE,
A DAD WHO, WHEN I WAS SAD, HE TOO CRIED;

A DAD WHO HELPS AND LENDS A HAND;
A COURAGEOUS DAD THAT PERSEVERED SELLING LAND.

A DAD THAT LIVES THE LIFE HE HAD TAUGHT;
A LESSON THAT PRECIOUS COULD NEVER BE BOUGHT;

A GENEROUS DAD ALWAYS WILLING TO AID,
MIRACULOUSLY STRETCHING ALL THAT HE MADE;

A DAD THAT IS BRILLIANT IN MATH AND THE WORD,
POETRY, TRIG, CHILDREN'S BOOKS IS UNHEARD;

A DAD THAT SHOOTS HOOPS AND PLAYS TENNIS TOO;
I WON WOMEN'S SINGLES ALL BECAUSE OF YOU;

A DAD THERE FOR SOFTBALL, TENNIS, AND DANCE,
TOWSON, OPPORTUNITIES—ALL TO GIVE ME A CHANCE;

A DAD WHO IS SELFLESS AND WANTS ME TO SHINE;
THERE ISN'T A DAD WHO WAS EVER SO FINE;

A DAD WHO IS HEALTHY AND STRONG EVERY DAY;
A DAD WHO MOVES MOUNTAINS AND IN THE MORNING'S OKAY;

A DAD WHO GOD BLESSES IN EVERY WAY
TO REMIND YOU HOW PRECIOUS YOU ARE DAY-TO-DAY;

VERY FEW DADS POSSESS THE RICHES YOU DO,
AND NONE COULD EVER BE MORE LOVED THAN YOU.

Jillian Downs

PERPETUAL MOTHER'S DAY

YOU'RE THE TRUE MOTHER OF ALL—
AND ESPECIALLY OUR THREE—
SINCE YOU CAN HARDLY RESIST
EVEN PASSING BY A SWEET BABY.

YOU PRAYED FOR OUR CHILDREN
EVEN BEFORE THEY WERE BORN,
AND YOU CONTINUE TODAY,
EITHER FULL OF JOY OR FORLORN.

YOU MADE THEIR ROOMS SPECIAL,
ALL GREENERY AND WHITE,
AND WOULDN'T BE SATISFIED
UNTIL IT WAS JUST RIGHT.

YOU COOKED EACH THING CAREFULLY,
ASSURING IT WAS NUTRITIOUS AND GOOD;
THAT CARE EXTENDED TO ALL THEY DID
AND NOT JUST TO MARVELOUS FOOD.

YOU SUPPORTED EACH ONE'S DREAM
AND TOLD THEM WHAT TO DO:
TRUST IN GOD AND NEVER GIVE UP,
AND YOUR EVERY DREAM CAN COME TRUE.

A SPECIAL MOTHER, I CAN TELL YOU,
YOU'VE BEEN TO ALL THREE,
FOR I'VE HAD THE PRIVILEGE
OF BEING THERE TO SEE!

Thank you for being the mother of our children.

ONE LUCKY MAN

WHAT MAN IS SO LUCKY,
FIRST, TO HAVE FOUND A WIFE
THAT WAS SO LOVELY, YET
LOVED HIM ALL OF HIS LIFE;

THAT TURNED A PLAIN HOUSE
INTO A COMFY, SHOW-PLACE HOME
WHERE EVERYONE WAS WELCOME
NO MATTER WHERE THEY CAME FROM;

WHERE THREE PRECIOUS CHILDREN
WERE SIMPLY A JOY TO RAISE,
AND ALL THEIR DIFFERENT PURSUITS
GAVE ME REASON TO PRAISE;

WHERE, NOW, WHEN WE VISIT,
THEY ALWAYS HONOR AND HELP ME,
AND WE'RE ALWAYS WELCOME
AND ENJOY THEIR COMPANY;

AND, EVEN IN A MORE SPECIAL WAY,
ONE EVERY DAY I GET TO SEE
LIVING NEAR TO HELP HOW I CAN
(WHILE SHE'S REALLY TAKING CARE OF ME);

WHAT LUCKY MAN IS SO BLESSED
HIS ENTIRE LIFE SO BOUNTIFULLY
TO BE ABLE TO LIVE SUCH A
WONDERFUL LIFE? SOMEHOW, IT'S ME!

TOGETHER

A GRAVEYARD I PASSED, AND NOTICED THERE,

SIDE BY SIDE, ALMOST TOUCHING, TWO CROSSES.

I THOUGHT OF THE COUPLE THIS MUST

HAVE BEEN—THEIR LIVES, THEIR GAINS, THEIR LOSSES.

AND THEN I THOUGHT THAT I WANTED

THIS TOO, WHEN I DREW MY LAST BREATH:

AS THEY HAD WALKED HAND-IN-HAND THROUGH LIFE—

SO THEY WALK NOW IN DEATH.

PALS

THERE THEY GO, RACING AWAY,
ONE LOAFING TO MAKE IT CLOSE;
LYING IN WAIT, HE POUNCES
LION-LIKE AND GETS HIM—ALMOST;

THE HALFBACK RUNS, BUT A SURE
TACKLE BRINGS HIM TO THE GROUND,
AND THE GAME CHANGES AS HE
JUMPS ON AND THEY ROLL AROUND;

THEY ROAM ACROSS THE PRAIRIE,
OVER AND UNDER A FENCE,
THROUGH THE WOODS, OVER A LOG,
ONE A KING AND ONE A PRINCE;

WHILE CAMPING OR NOT, THEY SHARE
THE WARMTH OF ONE ANOTHER,
THE MOODS—TEARS AND LAUGHTER—MUCH
LIKE A CHILD AND HIS MOTHER;

WHERE ONE GOES, GOES THE OTHER—
HE FITTING HIM LIKE A COG;
THERE ARE MANY JOYS, BUT FEW
SURPASS A BOY AND HIS DOG!

SNOW FIGHT

SNOW GLIST'NING MIDST THE CURLS OF YOUR HAIR,

EYES TWINKLING WITH LAUGHTER—AND A DARE,

ROSY CHEEKS, FLUSHED FROM THE LONG, COLD CHASE,

MOUTH TAUNTING—YET SOFT, FRAGILE AS LACE—

THAT INSTANT, IN ALL THAT I COULD SEE,

YOU WERE IRRESISTIBLE TO ME!

SO FULL

I DON'T KNOW WHERE IN THE WORLD I'D BE
OR HOW I GOT ALONG WITHOUT YOU BEFORE,

IF LONELINESS WOULD DROWN ME LIKE THE SEA,
OR, IF SOCIALLY, I'D BE ONE BIG BORE;

I DON'T KNOW JUST WHAT IT WOULD HAVE BEEN LIKE
TO HAVE NO CHILDREN TO ENJOY AS THEY GROW,

TO HELP THEM CATCH A BALL OR RIDE A BIKE,
BY MY JOY WOULD HAVE BEEN FAR LESS, I KNOW;

I DON'T KNOW IF I WOULD HAVE SIMPLY STOPPED
RECEIVING THOSE SIGNALS THAT MAKE ME TINGLE

IF YOU DID NOT KEEP MY FEELINGS UNSTOPPED
WITH THAT SPECIALNESS WHEN OUR SOULS INTERMINGLE;

I DON'T THINK MY MOMENTS WOULD BE NEARLY SO FULL
IF YOU HADN'T COME INTO MY LONELY LIFE

AND DECIDED TO STAY, AND MAKE IT WONDERFUL,
MY ANGEL, COMPANION, LOVE OF MY LIFE—AND WIFE!

PARTY TIME

YOU'RE INVITED TO A PARTY!

JESUS IS THE HOST—

YOU'LL HAVE A GREAT TIME, I PROMISE—

IF YOU DON'T GET LOST.

YOU MAY DECLINE THE INVITATION—

IT'S TRULY YOUR CHOICE;

YOU MAY BE TOO BUSY, OR JUST

NOT IN THE MOOD TO REJOICE;

BUT IF YOU'LL ACCEPT IT AND CHRIST

COMES INTO YOUR LIFE,

IT BECOMES SPARKLING, NEW, AND

FILLED WITH JOY MIDST ALL THE STRIFE;

FOR EARTH CONTAINS NO SADNESS THAT

HEAVEN CANNOT HEAL,

SO COME TO THE PARTY CALLED LIFE

THAT ONLY GOD CAN REVEAL!

SURPRISE!

WHAT IS IT THAT WE ALL ADORE
NO MATTER AGE OR SIZE?
WE ALWAYS GET EXCITED WHEN
WE HEAR THE WORD—SURPRISE!

WHEN I WAS JUST A LITTLE LAD
I WAITED WITH WONDERING EYES
AS DADDY SEARCHED HIS POCKETS
'TIL HE'D FINALLY SAY—SURPRISE!

AS I GREW OLDER, IN MY TEENS,
ON TESTS MY HARDEST I DID TRY,
AND WHEN I WAS UNSURE, THE TEACHER
SAID, "YOU DID VERY WELL—SURPRISE!"

AND LATER STILL, WHEN I FOUND THE ONE,
UNDER BEAUTIFUL STARLIT SKIES
I GAVE HER A RING AND BREATHLESSLY
WAITED FOR HER REPLY—SURPRISE!

WHEN WE EXPECTED OUR FIRST CHILD
WE COULD HARDLY REALIZE
WHAT LAY AHEAD WHEN THE DOCTOR SAID
"ARE YOU READY FOR THREE?"—SURPRISE!

NOW THE PATTER OF LITTLE FEET
BRIGHTEN UP OUR LIVES,
AND THEY ALL WAIT FOR DAD TO BRING
THEM JUST A LITTLE—SURPRISE!

I HAD A BIRTHDAY NOT LONG AGO,
AND, IN THE MIDST OF CAKES AND PIES,
SOME OF OUR FRIENDS CAME OVER
TO GIVE ME A PARTY—SURPRISE!

AS I GROW OLDER, NONETHELESS,
I SEEK A HIGHER PRIZE:
WHEN JESUS SAYS, "YOU'VE FOLLOWED ME
THE BEST YOU CAN"—SURPRISE!

IT MAKES A DIFFERENCE HOW YOU LIVE—
THERE'LL BE NO ALIBIS—
FOR WHAT YOU DO AND WHAT YOU SAY
WILL END UP IN—SURPRISE!

"SO WELCOME INTO MY MANSION HERE—
FOREVER YOU'RE IN PARADISE
WITH SPECIAL FRIENDS AND LOVED ONES
IN PERFECT JOY—SURPRISE!"

IT'LL BE EVEN BETTER THAN I CAN DREAM—
NO MORE OF SATAN'S LIES—
JUST LIFE, AND PEACE, AND BEAUTY—
WHAT A WONDERFUL SURPRISE!

REBIRTH

WHAT AN EXPERIENCE TO BE
PRESENT AT THE TIME OF BIRTH—

IT'S A FEELING OF JOY AND FEAR
LIKE NO OTHER ON THIS EARTH;

OUR SPIRITUAL REBIRTH CAN BE
EITHER GRADUAL OR DRAMATIC,

WHERE WE GROW UP KNOWING GOD OR
HAVE A MOMENT THAT'S ECSTATIC;

THEN WE'RE ACKNOWLEDGING THAT GOD
IS IN CONTROL OF OUR LIVES,

AND HE'LL STRENGTHEN US AND QUIETEN
OUR FEARS AS WE STRIVE

TO LET HIM GUIDE US IN EVERY
DECISION OF EACH DAY,

FOR HE WILL ONLY DO GOOD THINGS
FOR US—HE LOVES US THAT WAY!

COMFORT

JESUS SAID IT WAS BEST FOR HIM TO GO,
AS HE WAS ONLY ONE,
AND THE HOLY SPIRIT WOULD BE SENT
TO BE WITH EVERYONE:

NOT A CONQUEROR, TO DESTROY
EVERYTHING IN OUR WAY,
NOR EVEN A HELPER, ALTHOUGH
HELP CERTAINLY COMES EACH DAY,

BUT A COMFORTER—TO EMBRACE
US IN ALL OUR SORROW,
TO CARE FOR US AND GIVE US
STRENGTH TO FACE WHAT COMES TOMORROW;

TO LET US REALIZE THAT WE ARE FREE
FROM ALL THE GUILT THAT WEIGHS US DOWN,
AND THAT GOD'S LOVE IS THERE FOR ALL
IN EVERY COUNTRY AND TOWN;

THAT HE LOVES US BEYOND BELIEF,
MORE THAN WE CAN EVER REALIZE,
AND IF WE CAN ONLY BELIEVE, HE WILL
WIPE ALL THE TEARS FROM ALL OUR EYES.

SO REJOICE THIS DAY, AND EVERY DAY,
THAT A COMFORTER HE SENT
TO LEAD US TO LIVING FOREVER
WITH HIM IN HEAVEN, AS HE MEANT!

THE SHEPHERD

ALL OF US STILL HAVE MANY OF
OUR CHILDHOOD FEARS—

WE JUST HIDE THEM NOW INSTEAD OF
RESORTING TO TEARS:

WHAT WE NEED IS A GOOD SHEPHERD,
FOR WE ARE LIKE SHEEP,

TO BE WITH US IN THE VALLEYS,
BUT ALSO TO KEEP

WATCH OVER US IN THE ORDINARY
TIMES OF OUR DAYS;

TO GUARD US AND DEFEND US, TO
SEEK US WHEN WE STRAY,

TO STRENGTHEN US AND LEAD US, TO
INSPIRE AND FEED US,

TO FILL OUR BORED LIVES WITH A
NEW SENSE OF PURPOSE,

TO LAY US ON HIS SHOULDERS, SO
OUR ANXIETIES CEASE

AND BRING US HOME TO HEAVEN
FULL OF JOY AND PEACE!

OUR BLESSINGS

OUR BLESSINGS ENABLE US TO DO

WHAT GOD WOULD HAVE US TO DO—

NOT FOR PAST THINGS WE'VE DONE OR SAID,

BUT TO USE FOR THINGS THAT LIE AHEAD:

TO HELP SOMEONE WHO IS IN NEED

BY SOME KIND WORD OR SMALL DEED,

TO SHARE THE BLESSINGS HE HAS GIVEN

AND GIVE OTHERS A GLIMPSE OF HEAVEN.

SO MAY WE NOT ONLY APPRECIATE AND ENJOY

ALL HIS BLESSINGS, BUT ALSO EMPLOY

THEM TO DO HIS BIDDING—DON'T YOU SEE—

"WHAT YOU DO FOR OTHERS, YOU DO FOR ME!"

STAR LIGHT

THERE IS SUCH A GLOW FROM OUR CITY'S LIGHTS,

WE ARE UNABLE TO SEE THE STARS AT NIGHT;

MILLIONS NEVER SEE THIS AWE-INSPIRING SIGHT

BECAUSE THE LIGHTS AROUND THEM ARE SO BRIGHT;

MEN TRY TO MAKE THEIR OWN LITTLE STAR-SCENE

WITH HOUSE LIGHTS STREWN ACROSS THE LANDSCAPE

BUT THE MAGNIFICENCE OF A STILL, DARK, STAR-

FILLED NIGHT IS A FACT NO ONE CAN ESCAPE.

FOR EVEN THE MOST INSPIRED AND BEAUTIFUL

WORKS OF MAN SIMPLY CANNOT STAND

IN COMPARISON TO THE MARVELOUS BEAUTY

AND MAJESTY OF GOD'S CREATIVE HAND!

HOW YOU FELT

I KNOW HOW YOU FELT, ABRAHAM, WHEN YOU PLACED YOUR SON ON THE ALTAR TO DIE—THIS SON YOU HAD WAITED FOR, WERE SO PROUD OF—THE ANGUISH OF LOSING THAT LIFE SO PRECIOUS TO YOU, NEITHER OF YOU REALLY UNDERSTANDING WHY.

I KNOW HOW YOU FELT—I HAVE A SON TOO.

I KNOW HOW YOU FELT, MAMMY, AS YOU TOLD YOUR DAUGHTER NOT TO SPEAK UP OR SIT IN FRONT OR VOTE OR WEAR YOUR STAR—THE ANGUISH OF WHAT INJUSTICE FACED HER JUST BECAUSE SHE WAS A DIFFERENT COLOR OR SPEECH OR RELIGION OR A SHE, KNOWING YOU COULD LOSE THAT LIFE SO PRECIOUS TO YOU, NEITHER OF YOU REALLY UNDERSTANDING WHY.

I KNOW HOW YOU FELT—I HAVE A DAUGHTER TOO.

I KNOW HOW YOU FELT, FATHER, AS YOU THOUGHT OF SENDING YOUR SON TO DIE, EVEN FOR THOSE WHO WOULD HATE HIM. THE PRIDE OF SEEING HIM GROW STRONG AND GOOD, FOLLOWING YOU AND HELPING EVERYONE, THEN THE ANGUISH OF WATCHING HIM RIDICULED, BEATEN, AND KILLED.

I KNOW HOW YOU FELT—I HAVE A SON TOO.

BUT YOU DIDN'T LOSE THAT LIFE SO PRECIOUS TO YOU, AND BECAUSE OF YOUR LOVE, ALL ANGUISH WILL END!

"GOD SO LOVED THE WORLD, THAT HE GAVE HIS ONLY BEGOTTEN SON, THAT WHOSOEVER BELIEVETH IN HIM SHALL NOT PERISH, BUT HAVE EVERLASTING LIFE."

WILDERNESS

EVERYONE FINDS THEMSELVES

IN A WILDERNESS SOMETIMES—

WHEN DAY-TO-DAY LIVING

IS—LET'S SAY—LESS THAN SUBLIME;

GRIEF OR FEAR OR BOREDOM,

GUILT OR LONELINESS OR PAIN

CAN BE A WILDERNESS

TO ANYONE WHO REMAINS

ENDANGERED OR FRIGHTENED

BY WHAT LIFE BRINGS HIM EACH DAY,

BUT THE "WHY" OF CHRISTMAS IS
COMFORT TO THOSE WHO'VE LOST THE WAY;

THE GOOD NEWS IS YOU DON'T

HAVE TO FIND YOUR OWN WAY OUT—

GOD'S COMING AND NOTHING

WILL STOP HIM—DON'T DOUBT—

BOTH MOUNTAINS AND VALLEYS

WILL GREET HIM AS ONE VOICE

AND PREPARE HIS WAY SMOOTHLY—

TAKE COMFORT AND REJOICE!

REMEMBERING

AS I SIT HERE, ROCKING NOW AND THEN,
MY MIND WANDERS TO 'WAY BACK WHEN:

WHERE, AS A CHILD, I WOULD RUN AND PLAY—
IT SEEMS LIKE IT WAS JUST YESTERDAY;

TO MY COURTING DAYS—HOW MUCH FUN—
AND THEN THERE WAS THAT SPECIAL ONE;

WE WORKED THROUGH TIMES BOTH TOUGH AND GAY,
BUT I WOULDN'T TRADE IT FOR THE WORLD TODAY;

CHILDREN CAME—A DELIGHT—AND HOW THEY GREW,
AND IT WAS OFF TO SCHOOL BEFORE WE KNEW;

A WONDERFUL DAY IT WAS, HAPPY AND WILD,
YET SAD—A WEDDING FOR OUR LITTLE CHILD?

THINGS SEEMED A LITTLE DIFFERENT, BUT HOW?
EXCEPT WE WERE GRANDMA AND GRANDPA NOW.

WE ENJOYED THEM MORE THAN EVEN OUR OWN,
ALTHOUGH WE KNEW THEY WERE SIMPLY ON LOAN;
THEY WENT TO COLLEGE, THEN MARRIED TOO,
LOVELY GIRLS—AND SUDDENLY I KNEW

WHY I GOT TIRED AND COULDN'T WORK AS BEFORE,
WHY I FELT SOMETIMES I COULDN'T GO MUCH MORE;

IT'S WHAT I HAD ALWAYS BEEN TOLD—
SOONER OR LATER YOU'RE GOING TO GET OLD.

WELL, I GUESS THAT I AM, BUT IT TOOK
A LONG TIME, AND WITH THE GOOD BOOK

AS MY GUIDE, THINKING BACK, I'VE GOT TO SAY,
"IT'S BEEN GREAT," AS I SIT HERE TODAY.

A WALK THROUGH THE PAST

THERE! WHAT JOY, DELIGHT I SEE,
ACCOMPANIED WITH FULL HI-FI SOUND,
OVER AND OVER AGAIN THEY FLY—
JUMPING SIX INCHES OFF THE GROUND!

AND THERE! THE SAND PACKED FIRMLY
AROUND, WITHDRAWN ARE HANDS AND TOES;
A TOWN IS BUILT FOREVER—OR UNTIL
THE FLOOD OF A GARDEN HOSE!

THE BAR GOES HIGHER, BUT SO
DO THEY, WINGS UPON THEIR HEELS;
THEY MISS, AND ONLY MORTALS NOW,
THEY'RE OFF FOR BETTER DEALS.

A MILLION BADMEN, OR MAYBE
TWO, AND ONLY WITH ONE SHELL;
A DARING ACT, AND ONCE AGAIN
THEY'LL LIVE TO TELL THE TALE!

ONE MORE RUN, A BALL TO HIT
AND CATCH, A TREE TO CLIMB;
THEY HURRY NOW, FOR IN AN HOUR
THEY'LL HEAR THAT SAD WORD—BEDTIME!

A THOUSAND TIMES I'VE DONE IT,
AND YET, IT SEEMS ONLY TODAY
I FINALLY SAW THE GLORY
IN A CHILD SIMPLY AT PLAY.

BEAUTIFUL FEET

FEET ARE NOT BEAUTIFUL—
AT LEAST NOT TO ME—
SO WHY DOES THE PROPHET SPEAK
OF ONE WITH FEET OF BEAUTY?

AH, IT'S THE GOOD TIDINGS
HE BRINGS—THAT I CAN SEE—
FOR WHEN I'M FILLED WITH JOY
EVERYTHING'S BEAUTIFUL TO ME!

THE GREAT JOY ANNOUNCED BY
ISAIAH AND GIVEN TO MARY
IS ALSO GIVEN TO US IF WE'LL
BUT BELIEVE THE GIFT IS FREE

AND RECEIVE THE GOOD TIDINGS
OF GREAT JOY TO ALL MEN,
THAT GOD LOVED US SO MUCH
HIS OWN SON HE DID SEND!

THE 12 DAYS OF CHRISTMAS
FOR LITTLE BOYS

ON THE 1ST DAY OF CHRISTMAS, SANTA GAVE TO ME
A TOY TRAIN BENEATH THE CHRISTMAS TREE.

ON THE 2ND DAY OF CHRISTMAS, MY COUSIN GAVE TO ME
TWO CANDY CANES AND . . .

ON THE 3RD DAY OF CHRISTMAS, MY AUNTIE GAVE TO ME
THREE STUFFED BEARS . . .

ON THE 4TH DAY OF CHRISTMAS, MY UNCLE GAVE TO ME
FOUR PICTURE BOOKS . . .

ON THE 5TH DAY OF CHRISTMAS, MY GRAMPA GAVE TO ME
FIVE BOUNCING BALLS . . .

ON THE 6TH DAY OF CHRISTMAS, MY GRAMMA GAVE TO ME
SIX TRUCKS AND CARS . . .

ON THE 7TH DAY OF CHRISTMAS, MY GRANDAD GAVE TO ME
SEVEN ACTION FIGURES . . .

ON THE 8TH DAY OF CHRISTMAS, MY GRANDMOM GAVE TO ME
EIGHT WOODEN PUZZLES . . .

ON THE 9TH DAY OF CHRISTMAS, MY SISTER GAVE TO ME
NINE CHOCOLATE KISSES . . .

ON THE 10TH DAY OF CHRISTMAS, MY BROTHER GAVE TO ME
TEN TOOLS AND TOOL KIT . . .

ON THE 11TH DAY OF CHRISTMAS, MY MOMMY GAVE TO ME
ELEVEN COLORED MARKERS . . .

ON THE 12TH DAY OF CHRISTMAS, MY DADDY GAVE TO ME
TWELVE MOVIE CDS . . .

THE 12 DAYS OF CHRISTMAS
FOR LITTLE GIRLS

ON THE 1ST DAY OF CHRISTMAS, SANTA GAVE TO ME
A DOLL HOUSE BENEATH THE CHRISTMAS TREE.

ON THE 2ND DAY OF CHRISTMAS, MY COUSIN GAVE TO ME
TWO SUGAR COOKIES AND . . .

ON THE 3RD DAY OF CHRISTMAS, MY AUNTIE GAVE TO ME
THREE BABY DOLLS . . .

ON THE 4TH DAY OF CHRISTMAS, MY UNCLE GAVE TO ME
FOUR STICKER BOOKS . . .

ON THE 5TH DAY OF CHRISTMAS, MY GRAMPA GAVE TO ME
FIVE HULA HOOPS . . .

ON THE 6TH DAY OF CHRISTMAS, MY GRAMMA GAVE TO ME
SIX PRETTY DRESSES . . .

ON THE 7TH DAY OF CHRISTMAS, MY GRANDAD GAVE TO ME
SEVEN BOOKS TO COLOR . . .

ON THE 8TH DAY OF CHRISTMAS, MY GRANDMOM GAVE TO ME
EIGHT PRINCESS FIGURES . . .

ON THE 9TH DAY OF CHRISTMAS, MY SISTER GAVE TO ME NINE MUSIC BOXES . . .

ON THE 10TH DAY OF CHRISTMAS, MY BROTHER GAVE TO ME TEN COLORED HAIRBANDS . . .

ON THE 11TH DAY OF CHRISTMAS, MY MOMMY GAVE TO ME ELEVEN SPARKLING BRACELETS . . .

ON THE 12TH DAY OF CHRISTMAS, MY DADDY GAVE TO ME TWELVE MUSIC CDS . . .

Despair

SLOW DEATH

SOMETHING DEEP WITHIN ME

DIED A LITTLE MORE TODAY;

IT WAS ONCE AGAIN CRUSHED,

REJECTED, HELD AT BAY;

IT WAS SMOOTHED OVER UNTIL

OUT CAME A MASK OF CLAY,

WHERE NOTHING MATTERED NOR CARED—

NOTHING WAS FELT IN ANY WAY;

I FELL CLOSER TO THE BOTTOM

AND FURTHER FROM HIM ABOVE,

FOR WHAT I LOST A LITTLE

MORE OF TODAY—WAS LOVE!

INDEPENDENT

I CAN DO WITHOUT YOU VERY WELL!

I DON'T NEED TO SEE THE GLOW FROM YOUR ANGEL'S
FACE, OR YOUR EYES THAT SPARKLE WITH THE LOVE FOR LIFE.

I DON'T NEED YOUR TOUCH, SOFT BUT SURE, TO COMFORT
WHEN I AM LOW AND TO EXCITE BEYOND BELIEF.

I DON'T NEED YOUR FEELING—KIND, GENTLE, AND UNDER-
STANDING—SO DEEP FROM THE HEART I AM OVERWHELMED.

I DON'T NEED YOUR WORDS OF ENCOURAGEMENT, TENDER AND
SWEET OR WITTY AND GAY.

I DON'T NEED YOUR SOUL TOUCHING MINE, BRING ME
BACK ALWAYS, MAKING ME MINDFUL OF GOD.

I DON'T NEED YOU! I CAN TAKE CARE OF MYSELF WITHOUT
ANYONE'S HELP. I CAN BE FREE TO DO AS I PLEASE.

SEE? I CAN DO WITHOUT YOU, MY LOVE—
BUT TO DO SO WOULD BE TO DIE!

WITHOUT

O LORD, ANSWER ME, I PRAY!

WHY DO I CRY OUT IN ANGUISH?

WHY DO I HAVE NO LOVING SPIRIT

IN MY HEART, AND, WHEN ONE TRIES TO

PUT IT THERE, WHY IS IT QUICKLY CRUSHED?

WHY DO I FAIL IN ALL I DO, WHERE

ONCE I COULD SUCCEED AT ANYTHING?

WHY DO I HOLD BACK SO THAT NO ONE

KNOWS HOW I FEEL, AND WHY IS THIS

THEN REPLACED BY UTTER UNCARING?

YOU WHO LOVES ME, PLEASE TELL ME WHY!

. . . BECAUSE I DON'T SHOW MY LOVE FOR YOU?

BEFORE AND AFTER

HER BRIGHT BLUE EYES I LOVE SO DEARLY;
THEY, UPON ONE GLANCE, HOLD ME
ENRAPTURED AND SLIGHTLY BEWILDERED;
THEY CAN LOOK SO INNOCENT, TRUSTING,
AND COMPLETELY DEPENDENT, OR HAVE THE
TWINKLE I'M SURE A SPRITELY PIXIE HAS
BEFORE DOING SOME MARVELOUSLY MISCHIEVOUS DEED;
THEY CAN LOOK SO DEEPLY, TRULY, SEARCHINGLY
INTO MINE THEY ALMOST BURST WITH THE THOUGHT:
"MY DEAREST ONE, I'LL ALWAYS LOVE ONLY YOU!"

THESE SAME BLUE EYES ARE JUST AS BEAUTIFUL
AS BEFORE. BUT NOW THEY ARE DEAD, LIFELESS,
GAZING ANYWHERE BUT INTO MINE, ALMOST AS IF
AFRAID, AND, UPON THIS HAPPENING, QUICKLY
TURN AWAY TO SOME OTHER OBJECT.
ONCE THEY HAD A VOLCANO INSIDE, BUT NOW
THE FIRE IS GONE—THEY ARE COOL, AND ALL
THAT REFLECTS IN THEM IS THE THOUGHT:
"'TIS THROUGH!"

DEAD

MY SOUL IS CHOKED;
    MY HEART HAS NO FEELING.

I AM THE SALT THAT IS TASTELESS,
    GOOD ONLY TO BE THROWN AWAY
    AS WORTHLESS.

I AM A BEACON WITH NO LIGHT,
    GOOD ONLY TO LURE OTHERS NEAR
    TO BE DASHED ON THE ROCKS.

I CAN DO NO GOOD.
    I DO NOT LIVE, O GOD—
    WHY DO I EXIST?

LIFE AFTER DEATH

AS HE LAY THERE, KNOWING
SOON WOULD COME HIS LAST BREATH,
I KNOW HIS THOUGHTS COULD NOT HELP
BUT TURN TO LIFE AFTER DEATH.

IS THIS ALL THERE IS—SOME
JOY, STRUGGLE, AND STRIFE—
OR IS THERE SOMETHING MORE—
IS THERE LIFE AFTER LIFE?

DOES NOTHING MORE LIE AHEAD
THAN TO MOLD IN A GRAVE, SLEEPING,
OR TO BE GONE, FORGOTTEN,
ERASED—NO ONE EVEN WEEPING?

OR ARE WE IN AGONY,
TORTURED BEYOND COMPARE
FOR ALL OF ETERNITY, WITH
NO HOPE—ONLY DESPAIR?

OR IS IT SOMEHOW POSSIBLE
THAT IN A BEGOTTEN BABY BOY,
WHAT LIES AHEAD IS HEAVEN
AND EVERLASTING JOY?

REBIRTH

IT'S GONE, DEAD, COMPLETELY

WORTHLESS, FINIS, KAPUT!

MIGHT AS WELL PULL IT UP

AND THROW AWAY STEM AND ROOT.

THAT LIFELESS PLANT IS NO LONGER

ANY GOOD FOR ANYTHING WORTHWHILE—

IT CAN NO LONGER BEAR FRUIT OR

PRETTY FLOWERS THAT MAKE US SMILE.

BUT WAIT—WHAT'S THIS, UNDERNEATH

THE SNOW, PEEKING OUT OF THE SOD?

A LITTLE GREEN SHOOT OF LIFE STILL THERE

JUST WAITING FOR THE NOD

TO COME FORTH IN THE SUNLIGHT

AND SHOW THE GLORY OF GOD.

WE SEE THIS EVERY YEAR, AND YET,

DON'T YOU THINK IT ODD,

WE GIVE UP ON PEOPLE TOO, WHEN

A LITTLE LIGHT FROM THE SON

CAN BRING THEM BACK FROM DEATH AGAIN—

AND A NEW LIFE HAS BEGUN!

THE MATCH

I AM LIKE A MATCH,

WAITING, WANTING SOMEONE

WITH WHICH I CAN SHARE MY WARMTH.

I LIE HERE, OF NO USE TO ANYONE,

UNTIL FINALLY I AM NOTICED, AND,

STRIKING SOMETHING DEEP WITH ME,

MY LOVE BURSTS INTO A BRILLIANT FLAME,

ONLY TO LESSEN, LINGER BUT A WHILE,

AND DIE—LEAVING ONLY THE BLACK,

CHARRED BODY TO REMAIN.

FORGETTING

FORGIVE ME, O LORD,

FOR FORGETTING YOU!

WHEN THINGS GO WRONG AND

I AM SINKING FAST

IN THE QUICKSAND THAT

COMES WITH THE FEELING

OF COMPLETE HOPELESSNESS,

MAY I REMEMBER, PLEASE,

YOUR LOVE FOR ME,

SHOWN SO MANY WAYS.

HOW COULD SOMEONE WANT

TO LIVE IN THIS WORLD

IF HE HAD NOT YOU?

SO QUICKLY

SO SLOWLY IT SEEMS TO GO AT FIRST—
WILL CHRISTMAS EVER GET HERE?
AND THEN ALL OF A SUDDEN IT'S GONE BY
SO QUICKLY—AND IT'S ANOTHER YEAR.

THE CLASSES SEEM ENDLESS, AND STILL
THERE ARE YEARS AND YEARS TO GO,
BUT, SUDDENLY, SO QUICKLY, IT'S OVER
AND MARRIAGE AND A CAREER FOLLOW.

DIAPERS, NO SLEEP—WILL IT EVER END?
AND THEN SO QUICKLY WHAT'S IN STORE
IS WALKING AND TALKING AND DRIVING
AND THEY'RE OFFICIALLY OUT THE DOOR.

AND YOU NOTICE YOU'RE NOT AS STRONG
AND HEALTHY AS YOU USED TO BE,
AND HOW, SO QUICKLY, IN YOUR JOB
YOU'VE NOW BECOME A RETIREE.

NOW, LOOKING FROM THE OTHER END,
YOU REALIZE YOUR LIFE HAS FLOWN BY
SO QUICKLY—A BLINK OF AN EYE,
A DOT OF TIME—AND THEN YOU DIE.

LIFE

LIFE IS PLAIN.

PEOPLE COME IN ALL DESCRIPTIONS. THEY ARE
SCRATCHED, OR BRUISED, OR OLD AND WRINKLED, OR
SIMPLY TIRED AND HAGGARD. THEY ARE IN CURLERS
AND BAGGY SHORTS, OR HAVE FAT STOMACHS HANGING
OUT OF UNDERSHIRTS, AND GO HOME TO HOUSES THAT
JUST SIT AND WAIT TO CRUMBLE. THEY ARE ALL ONE
LARGE MASS, AND THEY DO NOT MATTER—NOR CARE.

LIFE IS DULL.

PEOPLE GO TO THEIR JOBS AND FARM, OR DEAL, OR
SIMPLY TRUDGE ALONG, WAITING FOR THE WEEK-END
SO THEY CAN HAVE THEIR "GOOD TIME". THEY BECOME
BURDENED WITH THEIR PETTY PROBLEMS, AND, FRUSTRATED,
TRY TO FORGET WITH DRUGS OR ALCOHOL OR IMPATIENTLY
TAKE IT OUT ON ONE ANOTHER. THEY ARE ALL ONE LARGE
MASS, AND THEY DO NOT MATTER—NOR CARE.

LIFE IS CHEAP.

THERE IS NOTHING SPECIAL, NOTHING TO BE PRAISED IN PEOPLE. THERE IS ONLY WHAT THEY CAN GET FROM OTHERS. THEY ARE TO BE BOUGHT FOR AS LITTLE AS POSSIBLE, AND SIMPLY DISPOSED OF WHEN THROUGH, WITHOUT EVEN USING A LITTER BAG. THERE IS ONLY A NEON SIGN BLINKING ON AND OFF, TICKING AWAY THEIR USELESS TIME. THEY ARE ALL ONE LARGE MASS, AND THEY DO NOT MATTER—NOR CARE.

BUT SOMETIMES SOMETHING HAPPENS.

LIFE IS NO LONGER PLAIN, OR DULL, OR CHEAP. PEOPLE ARE BEAUTIFUL, THEIR HOUSE IS A HOME, THEIR JOB IS A HELP INSTEAD OF A TASK, AND OTHERS ARE OF GREAT IMPORTANCE. A REALIZATION OF GOD'S WAY TO LIVE AND SOMEONE OF TRUE BEAUTY INSIDE LETTING IT SHOW, AND THERE IS SUDDENLY BEAUTY AND EXCITEMENT AND VALUE IN LIFE. THERE IS SOMEONE WHO MATTERS—AND CARES. THERE IS SOMEONE— LIKE YOU!

WHAT DO YOU DO?

WHAT DO YOU DO WHEN
YOUR LIFE'S BEEN SHAKEN,
WHEN YOU FEEL THAT, BY
OTHERS, YOU'VE BEEN FORSAKEN,

WHEN IT'S HARD TO CONCENTRATE
ON THE TASK AT HAND
BECAUSE YOUR MIND THINKS
OF ONLY ONE THING, AND

WHAT DO YOU DO WHEN
YOU WANT TO DO RIGHT,
BUT DON'T KNOW WHETHER TO
DO NOTHING OR FIGHT,

WHEN ONE CRAZY DISTORTION
FOLLOWS ANOTHER,
AND ANGER REPLACES GOOD
FEELINGS TOWARD ANOTHER?

WHAT DO YOU DO? ONLY
THE BEST THAT YOU CAN—
STEADFASTLY ENDURE,
PRAY CONSTANTLY, AND

TRUST THAT THE RIGHTEOUS
ONE WHO'S TRULY IN CHARGE
WILL BRING US THROUGH AND
OUR FAITH IN HIM ENLARGE!

MY LOVE HAS GONE

THE MINUTES CLING, THE HOURS DRAG ON
ETERNALLY—MY LOVE HAS GONE;

I WANT TO WRITE, I WANT TO PHONE;
BUT TO SAY WHAT—MY LOVE HAS GONE;

I WANT TO SHOUT, TO CRY AND MOAN;
IT'LL DO NO GOOD—MY LOVE HAS GONE;

I CANNOT FEEL—EXCEPT ALONE;
THIS IS THE PRICE—MY LOVE HAS GONE!

FORSAKEN

I GIVE UP! I CAN'T DO IT, LORD!

I CAN'T LOVE MY FRIENDS, MUCH LESS THOSE
I HATE. LOVE THEM AS I DO MYSELF?

I CAN'T FORGIVE THOSE WHO HURT ME—I'VE
GOT TO GET EVEN! FORGIVE FOREVER?

I CAN'T BE AN EXAMPLE FOR OTHERS ALL THE
TIME, SHOWING THEM YOU! BE PERFECT?

I CAN'T GIVE UP ALL MY POSSESSIONS; I
WANT TO BE RICH! GIVE AWAY EVERYTHING?

DO ALL OF THIS, AND MORE, EVERY DAY?
FORGET IT! I'D LIKE TO, BUT THAT'S TOO MUCH!

I REALLY TRIED, BUT IT'S IMPOSSIBLE, LORD.
THERE'S NO WAY I CAN BE A CHRISTIAN!

MY CHILD, MY CHILD! WHY HAST THOU FORSAKEN ME?

ASHES

MY SON WENT TO DO WHAT HE COULD TO HELP,
AND, AT THE END OF THAT TERRIBLE DAY,
REACHED DOWN AND PRESERVED A HANDFUL OF ASHES,
CONTEMPLATING WHAT THEY MAY HAVE TO SAY:

ASHES OF A BUILDING THAT ONCE STOOD TALL—
TWIN TOWERS REPRESENTING UNLIMITED CASH—
NOW, PHYSICALLY REDUCED TO RUBBLE AND,
BY THE INTENSE HEAT AND FIRE, TO ASH.

ASHES OF MANY PEOPLE WITH HOPES AND DREAMS,
DAILY WORKING SIDE-BY-SIDE, WITH NO CLASHES—
LOVED ONES OF ALL TYPES AND AGES, IN AN
INSTANT TRANSFORMED BACK—ASHES TO ASHES.

ASHES ARE THE RESIDUE OF A FIRE—
BUT A FIRE CAN ALSO BRING US GAINS,
AS IT MOLDS AND BURNS AWAY THE DROSS,
LEAVING THE PURE, REFINED, SHINING REMAINS.

ASHES ARE PUT ON THE FOREHEAD AS A
HUMBLE ACT OF SORROW IN RELIGION,
TO REPENT AND SEEK FORGIVENESS OF OUR SINS
AND BE TRANSFORMED INTO A NEW CREATION.

THOSE WHO WOULD DESTROY LEAVE THINGS IN ASHES,
WHILE REBUILDING IS FOR WHAT IS TO BE,
KNOWING THE BATTLE HAS ALREADY BEEN WON
BY THE ONE WHO CONTROLS ALL OF DESTINY.

SO LET US RESOLVE TO RISE ABOVE THE ASHES
AND USE THE POWER FROM THAT DAY OF TRAGEDY
TO SHOW THE STRENGTH, GOODNESS, AND GIVING
THAT FREEDOM BRINGS—FOR ALL THE WORLD TO SEE!

HANG ON!

IT'S MIGHTY HARD TO KEEP ON TRYING

WHEN IT SEEMS YOU'RE NOT GETTING BETTER,

WHETHER IT'S SICKNESS, OR LOSING WEIGHT,

OR TRAINING; WHEN WE FOLLOW THE LETTER

OF THE LAW AND NOTHING SEEMS TO CHANGE,

WE GET DEPRESSED WHEN OUR EXPECTATION

DOESN'T LIVE UP TO THE REALITY

WE HAD HOPED, UPON EVALUATION.

WE CAN'T GIVE A REASON FOR THIS,

OR MANY THINGS, AND IT'S LIKE BEING

IN A PRISON, KNOWING THE DOOR HAS TO

BE OPENED FROM THE OUTSIDE, SEEING

GOD IS SUFFICIENT NO MATTER WHAT

THE TROUBLE, SO DON'T GET HATEFUL—

REMEMBER, ABOVE ALL ELSE, THAT

ONE THING IS CERTAIN—GOD IS FAITHFUL!

DELIVERANCE

WE'RE ALL SLAVES TO VARIOUS THINGS—
OF THAT THERE CAN BE NO DOUBT;

SO WE'RE IN OUR OWN LITTLE HELL,
A PLACE WHERE WE CAN'T GET OUT;

WE VOW TO BE DIFFERENT AND
KNOW THAT IT'LL BE TOUGH;

ALL OUR KNOWLEDGE IS HELPFUL,
BUT IT'S NOT NEARLY ENOUGH;

DIAGNOSIS IS GOOD, BUT
WHAT ABOUT THE CURE?

WILLPOWER IS NEEDED, BUT
STILL USELESS FOR SURE;

DELIVERANCE IS NOT EASY,
AND NEVER HAS BEEN—

WE FIRST MUST ADMIT WE ARE
POWERLESS, AND THEN,

WHEN WE'RE YOKED CLOSELY WITH CHRIST
AS A PARTNER, YOU SEE,

BOTH TRAVELING THE SAME PATH,
WE'LL FIND OUT WE'RE FREE!

WHAT DOES IT MATTER?

WHEN WE BREATHE OUR FINAL BREATH,
WHETHER IN PAIN OF QUIET REPOSE,
AND THE LIFE WE LIVED IS DONE,
DOES IT MATTER WHAT PATH WE CHOSE?

WHEN OUR EYES ARE CLOSED
FOR THE VERY LAST TIME,
WHAT DOES IT MATTER WHAT
WE DID WITH ALL OF OUR TIME?

WHAT DOES IT MATTER
IF WE HAD FORTUNE OR FAME,
IF WE LIVED OUR LIFE FULL
OF GLORY OR SHAME?

WHAT DOES IT MATTER HOW
WE DID OUR JOB EACH DAY,
IF WE WERE HELPFUL OR
KIND TO THOSE WE MET EACH DAY?

WHAT DOES IT MATTER WHAT CAR
WE DROVE OR THE HOUSE WE LIVED IN,
WHETHER WE WERE GOOD TO THE CORE
OR DEVILISHLY EVIL WITHIN?

WHAT DOES IT MATTER IF WE WERE
A GOOD PARENT—OR EVEN ONE AT ALL,
IF WE WERE ABUSIVE OR FAITHFUL
OR BEAUTIFUL OR TALL?

WHAT DOES IT MATTER WHAT WE
SAID OR DID AT ALL AT LIFE'S END,
WHETHER WE LOVED OR WERE LOVED
OR HAD MANY OR NO FRIENDS?

WHAT DOES IT MATTER WHAT
WE BELIEVED—IF AT ALL—
WHETHER GOD REALLY EXISTS OR
WE ANSWERED OUR LIFE'S CALL?

WHAT DOES IT MATTER—NOTHING AT ALL
OR A GREAT DEAL TO YOU?
IF LOVE AND LIFE ARE ETERNAL—
IT DEPENDS ON WHAT IS REALLY TRUE!

IF BEING FORGIVEN AND SHOWING
GOD'S LOVE TO ALL WE MEET EACH DAY
LEADS TO ETERNAL JOY AND PEACE,
IT MATTERS GREATLY, WOULDN'T YOU SAY?

LITTLE FAITH

O ME OF LITTLE FAITH,

AS ISRAEL WAS OF OLD,

SOON AFTER THEY WERE FREED

MADE A CALF FORMED OF GOLD.

GOD HAS SHOWED ME AGAIN

IF I WOULD BUT BELIEVE

THE LOVE AND GIFTS HE GIVES,

MORE THAT I CAN CONCEIVE.

WHEN WILL I LEARN TO TRUST

HIM AND ALL HE SAITH

HE WILL DO FOR ME,

O ME OF LITTLE FAITH?

HOPE

HOPE IS WHAT WE HAVE LEFT

AFTER WE'VE LOST EVERYTHING ELSE—

THE DAUGHTER OF JAIRUS WAS DEAD;

THERE WAS CERTAINLY NOTHING ELSE;

THE HEMORRHAGING WOMAN HAD GONE

TO THE DOCTORS, TO NO AVAIL,

BUT THEY PUT THEIR HOPE IN THE ONE

WHO DID NOT EVER FAIL;

THE SIMPLICITY OF THESE STORIES

SHOW US TRUE FAITH AND ITS MEANING—

JUST BEING IN THE PRESENCE OF GOD

BRINGS NEW LIFE AND CERTAIN HEALING!

THE POINT

WHAT'S THE POINT OF IT?" YOU SOMETIMES ASK
AS YOU GO ABOUT EACH DAILY TASK:

GET READY, GO TO WORK AND BACK, AND THEN
THE NEXT DAY YOU DO IT ALL OVER AGAIN;

THE DAYS GO BY—THEN MONTHS, SUDDENLY YEARS;
YOU'VE HAD A FEW LAUGHS AND ALSO SOME TEARS;

YOU SEE THAT YOUR LIFE WILL BE QUICKLY GONE,
AND WHAT WILL BE LEFT THAT IS YOURS ALONE?

YOUR JOB WILL BE FILLED, YOUR HOUSE WILL BE SOLD,
AND WHAT HAVE YOU DONE THAT NEEDS TO BE TOLD?

YOUR FAMILY IS GONE, AND WHAT YOU DID FOR THEM,
AND RARE IS THE MAN WHOSE GRANDSON KNOWS HIM;

THE TREES ARE CUT DOWN, THE MOUNTAINS LAID LOW—
EVEN STARS AND MOON WILL GIVE UP THEIR GLOW;

SO, WHAT'S IT ALL FOR, A REASON FOR THIS MESS?
IS THERE A WAY TO REALLY GAIN HAPPINESS?

PROBABLY NOT, IF WE GO OUR OWN WAY
FAILING TO SEE BEAUTY AROUND US EACH DAY,

REFUSING TO FORGIVE, FORGET, AND GO ON,
STRIVING FOR SUCCESS, POSSESSIONS, AND SO ON,

GOING TO PARTIES TO COMBAT LONELINESS,
OR EVEN ASKING GOD FOR HAPPINESS . . . .

WE MAY FIND REAL AND TRUE MEANING IN LIFE
BY SETTING ASIDE THE THINGS THAT BRING STRIFE,

BY SEEKING GOD WITH ALL OF OUR STRENGTH—
BY GOING TO ANY AND ALL LENGTHS

TO SEE CHRIST IN OTHERS AND TO HELP THEM—
TO DO FOR THEM AS YOU WOULD DO FOR HIM—

TO BE MERCIFUL AND KIND TO ALL THAT WE MEET,
AS HE IS WHO SITS ON THE HEAVENLY SEAT,

TO DO EACH TASK, NO MATTER HOW SMALL,
THE BEST WE CAN, AS ANSWERING GOD'S CALL,

TO BE ABLE TO TURN OUR INDIFFERENCE
INTO KNOWING WE CAN MAKE A DIFFERENCE,

TO KNOW THAT OUR LIVES ARE NOT LIVED IN VAIN—
THAT HOPE GIVEN AND PASSED ON IS GREAT GAIN—

THAT LOVE FOR EACH OTHER IS WHAT LASTS FOREVER—
THAT'S REALLY SO SIMPLE AND YET SO CLEVER;

AND THEN WE'LL BE HAPPY, CONTENT, AND FREE
TO "PRAISE GOD FOR ALL THINGS WITH ALL THAT'S IN ME,"

TO FIND PEACE AND JOY AND GRACE FROM ABOVE,
AND KNOW WE'RE ABUNDANTLY BLESSED BY HIS LOVE!

THIS CHRISTMAS

CAN ANYONE REALLY FATHOM THE INCREDULOUS IDEA THAT JESUS IS REALLY THE SON OF GOD—COMING AS A BABY, OF ALL THINGS—A MAN SHOWING US BY HIS WORDS AND ACTIONS HOW TO LIVE SO AS TO COMPLETELY CHANGE THE WORLD?

IN THE MIDST OF ALL THE DARK DEEDS THAT STILL ABOUND, TO THINK THAT THE ONE WHO CREATED EVERYTHING WOULD CARE ENOUGH TO SACRIFICE HIS SON JUST TO FREE US FROM SIN AND OFFER ETERNAL LIFE TO THOSE WHO BELIEVE IT IS TRULY UNBELIEVABLE!

JOY IS THE REALIZATION OF GOD'S LOVE BUBBLING TO THE SURFACE, OFFERING PEACE AND FORGIVENESS AND LOVE TO EVERY SINGLE PERSON. MAY IT HAPPEN TO ALL OF US THIS CHRISTMAS!

WEEPING

AS HE LOOKED OUT ON THE CITY, HOLY AND BLESSED BY GOD,

AND SAW ONLY DEBAUCHERY—GOODNESS STOMPED IN THE SOD—

AS HE TRIED TO BRING HEALTH TO OTHERS ON THE SABBATH DAY

AND WAS CRITICIZED FOR DOING WHAT THE LAW DIDN'T SAY—

AS HE TRIED TO SHOW OTHERS GOD'S GREAT LOVE FOR THEM ALL,

AND THEY DIDN'T UNDERSTAND OR TRY TO ANSWER GOD'S CALL—

JESUS WEPT!

AS HE SEES US LIVE DAILY IGNORING HIS SACRIFICE,

FORGETTING WHAT HE SHOWED US, NOT HEEDING HIS ADVICE—

AS HE SEES HOW WE DESTROY OUR WORLD AND THOSE WE LOVE,

WONDERING WHY WE WON'T ACCEPT HIS UNCONDITIONAL LOVE—

AS HE ASKS US TO BE WITH HIM IN A PARADISE ETERNALLY,

WATCHING AS WE CHOOSE TO HARDEN OUR HEARTS SO EAGERLY—

JESUS WEEPS!

THERE WILL COME A TIME WHEN HIS WEEPING WILL CEASE,

AND ALL WHO LIVE WITH HIM WILL HAVE GREAT JOY AND PEACE—

AND FOR THOSE WHO ARE LEFT IN THE DARKNESS BENEATH,

THERE WILL BE TERRIBLE WEEPING AND GNASHING OF TEETH!

PAIN

THE

GREATEST OF ALL PAIN IS TO HAVE SACRIFICED IN VAIN:

A PARENT DOES ALL THAT IS POSSIBLE
TO ERASE A CERTAIN SITUATION,

BUT THE CHILD CONTINUES
A LIFE LEADING TO THE SAME
DESTRUCTIVE CONCLUSION.

OUR SIN NAILED
CHRIST TO A CROSS,
AND FOR IT NOT
TO HAVE BEEN A LOSS

WE HAVE TO
ACCEPT THE
OFFERED
SACRIFICE
AND LIVE
LIKE IT
THE REST
OF OUR
LIVES!

EXILE

EXILE IS BEING SENT TO THE
MIDDLE OF NOWHERE WITH NO WAY

TO GET BACK, AND NOTHING TO DO
BUT SIT AND WEEP EVERY DAY;

WE'VE ALL BEEN IN EXILE SOME TIME
IN OUR LIVES, WHERE ILLNESS OR FEAR,

LOSS OF A JOB OR LOVED ONE, OR
LONELINESS LEAVES US WITH NO CHEER—

ANYTIME WE'RE CUT OFF FROM GOD
OR THOSE WHO LOVE US, WE'RE IN EXILE.

BUT IN THE MIDST OF THIS, GOD STILL
COMES TO US IN HIS LOVE, WHILE

KNOWING ALL WE'VE EVER DONE. HE
DOES NOT COME TO CONDEMN, BUT MAY

IF WE NEED TO BE, BUT HE COMES TO
SAVE US FROM OUR EXILE EACH DAY,

LIFT US FROM THE PITS OF DESPAIR,
BRING US UP TO THE LIGHT AND LIFE,

AND FILL US WITH PEACE AND JOY
THAT OVERCOMES OUR WORLD OF STRIFE!

DEAFENING SILENCE

I AM SILENT.

THE DAY BREAKS FORTH WITH SOUND: A BIRD, CLANKING

MILK BOTTLES, A COFFEE-POT PERKING; THEN MOTORS,

RUMBLINGS AND SCREECHING OF MACHINES, BLARING OF

VOICES, MUSIC, AND HORNS! THEN IT LESSENS, GIVING

WAY TO TV, AN OCCASIONAL SIREN, THE SOUNDS OF NIGHT—

CRICKETS, A FROG CROAKING, A DOG HOWLING IN THE

DISTANCE, THE WIND BLOWING GENTLY THROUGH THE TREES,

DROPS OF RAIN MAKING A PATTER ON THE LEAVES, THE

REFRIGERATOR DOOR CLOSING FOR THE LAST TIME OF THE DAY,

THE BED CREAKING ITS DISPLEASURE AT BEING AWAKENED,

A SLEEPY GOOD-NIGHT.

BUT I AM SILENT.

I AM SILENT.

MEN LOOK AND THINK (OR MAYBE NOT), AND THEN THEY

PLAN. FROM THIS SOMEONE IS HURT—ROBBED, CHEATED,

OR KILLED, FOR LIFE IS GONE WHEN A MAN IS REDUCED

TO A TOOL, AN ANIMAL, OR EVEN A VEGETABLE, DONE SO

EASILY BY A SIMPLE LACK OF HEART. OTHERS SEE AND

NOD THEIR HEADS, CLENCH THEIR TEETH, AND FISTS,

AND GO TO MAKE THEIR WAY LIKE THESE. OR MAYBE

SOMEONE NODS "NO", WAVES HIS ARMS AND STANDS TO

OBJECT, HEART STILL GIVING OFF FAINT SIGNALS, AND HE IS

CRUSHED BY THE STAMPEDE HEADED FOR THE TOP.

BUT I AM SILENT.

I AM SILENT.

LOVE COMES IN MANY FORMS: A BABY REACHING OUT FOR YOU; A HAND PLACED FIRMLY, OR MAYBE VERY GENTLY, ON YOUR SHOULDER; A MEAL PREPARED BY TOUGH, TIRED HANDS; SILENCE AS YOU WALK, SIT, OR RIDE WITH SOMEONE; AN URGENT EXCITEMENT TO SHOW YOU A BIG MOON, A SUNSET, OR A BUG; A GENTLE BREEZE ACROSS YOUR FACE; A LAUGH; A WINK; A SOFT TOUCH; KNEELING ALONE IN A DARKENED ROOM TO PRAY; A CAT, DOG, OR COLT; A HEAD LEANED ON YOUR SHOULDER; EYES FILLED WITH JOY THAT HAS NO END, WAITING FOR A WORD.

BUT I AM SILENT.

I AM SILENT.

I HEAR THESE THINGS: THE SONGS THAT NATURE SINGS;

THE SINCERE GREETING OF ONES I KNOW; THE BEAUTY THAT

COMES FROM MAN; AND ALSO THE CURSES, INSULTS, AND

LIES FROM BLIGHTED WHEAT CALLED MAN, THAT FLOW SO

FREELY WITHOUT A THOUGHT. I SEE THESE THINGS THAT

PASS BEFORE ME : THE LOOKS, THE SLY, DECEIVING WAYS;

THE TRUST, FULFILLED WITHOUT A THOUGHT. I FEEL THESE

THINGS: THE RAGE AT DECEIT, TYRANNY, AND PREJUDICE;

THE HYPOCRICY OF LEADERS AND FOLLOWERS ALIKE, THE

UNCONCERN ABOUT LIFE AND ANYTHING ASSOCIATED; THE

NEED FOR OUR GOD, ALMOST MATCHED BY THE YEARNING

FOR MY COMPLETE, PERFECT LOVE. MY HEART CRIES OUT!

BUT I AM SILENT.

SO SORRY

I'M SO SORRY I WAS SO SORRY

A HUSBAND:

I DID NOT LOVE YOU THE WAY I SHOULD HAVE. I DON'T KNOW IF I WAS SIMPLY INCAPABLE FROM CHILDHOOD, FROM MY BASIC PERSONALITY, FROM CHARACTER FLAWS, OR WHAT. BUT I WAS UNABLE TO SATISFY WHAT YOU NEEDED EMOTIONALLY AND NOT ENOUGH PHYSICALLY.

I FRUSTRATED YOU UNTIL YOU FELT CONTROLLED, WAS UNABLE TO TALK OR COMMUNICATE ENOUGH TO HAVE YOU FEEL I UNDERSTOOD OR CARED ABOUT YOUR FEELINGS, WAS UNABLE FINANCIALLY TO ALLOW YOUR CREATIVITY TO BLOSSOM INTO ITS FULLNESS IN OUR HOME, DID NOT TAKE YOU ON A 'DATE' HARDLY EVER, AND SIMPLY DID NOT LET YOU KNOW HOW LOVELY, CHARMING, GRACIOUS, AND KIND YOU WERE AND HOW MUCH YOU WERE APPRECIATED, NEEDED, AND LOVED. I'M SO SORRY.

A FATHER:

I WAS NOT THE EXAMPLE I SHOULD HAVE BEEN, ALTHOUGH I TRIED IN SOME WAYS. BUT I WAS UNABLE TO TALK TO YOU AS I SHOULD HAVE (EXCEPT TO CORRECT PERHAPS), DIDN'T SPEND ENOUGH TIME WITH YOU TO KNOW YOUR INNER THOUGHTS (WORKING OR WATCHING A GAME), OR TAKING YOU ON VACATIONS MORE TO BROADEN YOUR HORIZONS. I WAS NOT THE SPIRITUAL LEADER I SHOULD HAVE BEEN IN BRINGING GOD TO YOU PERSONALLY. I'M SO SORRY.

A PROVIDER:

I WAS NOT THE PROVIDER I SHOULD HAVE BEEN FINANCIALLY, EMOTIONALLY, SPIRITUALLY, FUN-WISE, OR PHYSICALLY TO MY FAMILY, IT BOILS DOWN TO. ANY CAUSE OR REASON FOR THIS WOULD ONLY BE AN EXCUSE—I COULD HAVE CHOSEN DIFFERENTLY AT THE TIME I DID OR DIDN'T DO WHAT I SHOULD HAVE, FOR EACH OF YOU.

I CAN ONLY ASK THAT YOU FORGIVE ME, TRY TO APPRECIATE ANYTHING GOOD, AND USE MY REGRETS TO HELP YOU NOT REPEAT THE SAME MISTAKES IN YOUR LIVES. AGAIN, I'M SO SORRY I WAS SO SORRY.

AN ANGEL CRIES

MANKIND—WHAT HAS HAPPENED TO YOU?

YOU STEAL AND KILL AND CHEAT FOR MONEY,
    AND POWER IS ALL THAT'S ON YOUR MIND;

YOU ACT ALL THE SAME IN BUSINESS SUITS
    OR REVOLTING, BECOME BOTH WITH YOUR KIND;

YOU USE YOUR GREAT MINDS TO THINK UP WAYS
    THAT MAN MAY KILL, OR RULE, OR DESTROY;

YOU SUBSTITUTE A MEDAL FOR A YOUNG FATHER
    AND SMILE UNCONCERNED AT THE LOOK OF HIS BOY;

YOU LAUGH AND SCORN ALL THAT SEEMS RIGHT
    AND ONLY REMARK, "IT USED TO BE SO."

YOU SEEK ONLY PLEASURE, AND NO FORM IS TOO LOW;
    SEX, DRUGS, AND DRINKING—SO YOU WON'T KNOW?

MANKIND, YOU THINK YOU KNOW OH-SO-MUCH,
    BUT IT LOOKS DIFFERENT WHEN SEEN FROM ABOVE;

WE'VE GIVEN UP HOPE ON YOU—ALL EXCEPT ONE;
    YOU CAN'T REMEMBER THE PROBLEM—NO LOVE!

THE FLOCK

WHO AMONG US, IN THE DEPTHS OF DESPAIR,
HAS NOT WANTED TO BE IN JESUS' CARE—

TO BE HUNTED AND FOUND, LIKE A LOST SHEEP,
THEN LOVINGLY CRADLED UNTIL WE FALL ASLEEP?

BUT THEN HE PUTS US DOWN IN A FLOCK
OF BLEATING, UNCOOPERATIVE—HEADS LIKE A ROCK—

AFRAID, WAYWARD, AND NOT-SO-BRIGHT
WANDERERS—JUST LIKE US, ALL RIGHT.

THE GOOD SHEPHERD HAS BROUGHT US TOGETHER
FOR HE KNOWS THAT WE DO NEED EACH OTHER—

THESE ARE CARING PEOPLE WHO'VE EXPERIENCED PAIN
JUST AS WE HAVE, AGAIN AND AGAIN,

WOUNDED HELPING THE WOUNDED, THE LOST
HELPING THE LOST, THE SAVED HELPING THE MOST.

HERE IN THE FLOCK WE'LL FIND SALVATION
AND HEALING, A FEELING OF ELATION

WHEN WE REALIZE HE CALLS US BROTHER
WHEN, IN HIS NAME WE HELP ONE ANOTHER!

EPIPHANY

AFTER CHRISTMAS HAS COME AND GONE

WE MAY EASILY GET DEPRESSED,

GOING BACK TO THE DAILY GRIND

INSTEAD OF THAT MUCH-NEEDED REST;

THE WISE MEN APPROACHED THE CHRIST CHILD

AND WENT AWAY DIFFERENTLY—

THEY WORSHIPPED AND OFFERED GIFTS

AND EXPERIENCED EPIPHANY—

A MANIFESTATION OF THE PRESENCE

OF THE ONE WHO SITS ON THE THRONE.

UPON THEM—AND ALSO US, IF WISE,

THE GLORY OF THE LORD SHONE!

FOLLOWING

WE RUN AWAY FROM RISK AND PAIN
AND SUFFERING, IF WE CAN,

BUT WE ALSO MAY BE RUNNING AWAY
FROM THE PATH THAT GOD HAD PLANNED;

FOR, WHEN CHRIST CALLS US TO FOLLOW
HIM, HE CALLS UPON US TO DIE

TO THE ATTRACTIONS OF THIS WORLD
AND ALL THINGS THAT DECEIVE AND LIE;

IT WON'T BE AN EASY THING TO DO—
EVEN JESUS WAS TEMPTED TO RUN AWAY—

BUT, AS HE COULD NOT DETOUR THE
CROSS, WE MUST TAKE UP OURS EACH DAY.

THE ONLY WAY THAT WE CAN SUCCEED
THROUGH THE SUFFERING THAT'LL COME OUR WAY

IF WE TRULY FOLLOW HIM IS TO
LIVE IN HIS POWER—AND OBEY!

TROUBLED WATERS

THERE ARE MANY TROUBLED WATERS THESE DAYS:

ECONOMIC WOES, A DECLINE IN ETHICAL VALUES,

WAR, AND PERSONAL TRAGEDIES LIKE DISEASE,

DIVORCE, AND DEATH ARE SOME WE CAN CHOOSE.

EVEN THE TEN COMMANDMENTS BECOME A

BARRIER TO GOD—WE MUST DO THEM TO BE WORTHY—

BUT WE'RE DOOMED TO FAIL, SO WE MUST

SEE THEM NOT AS A RIGID MORAL WAY TO BE,

BUT AS A TWO-WAY COVENANT WITH GOD—

RESPONDING TO HIS INITIATIVE.

THEY'RE NOT JUST LAWS—BUT HAVE TO DO WITH

ATTITUDE, TO SEE IF OUR WAY IS GOD'S WAY TO LIVE!

WASTED

HAS YOUR LIFE BEEN WASTED IF YOU'VE
BEEN AFRAID TO EVER TAKE A CHANCE—
OR NEVER TRAVEL AND EXPERIENCE
DIFFERENT CULTURES, FOOD, OR DANCE?

HAS YOUR LIFE BEEN WASTED IF YOU
DON'T GET MARRIED, OR, IF SO, THEN
YOU ARE UNABLE OR DECIDE
NOT TO HAVE ANY CHILDREN?

HAS YOUR LIFE BEEN WASTED IF YOU
SPEND YOUR TIME WATCHING TV
OR READING, OR YOU'RE "WASTED" EVERY
WEEKEND FROM GOING TO A PARTY?

HAS YOUR LIFE BEEN WASTED IF YOU
JUST WORK EVERY DAY WITHOUT END,
AND WHEN YOU RETIRE OR NEED HELP
YOU REALIZE YOU DON'T HAVE A FRIEND?

HAS YOUR LIFE BEEN WASTED IF YOU
LIVE WITHOUT HOPE, GOALS, OR DREAMS,
AND THERE IS NO FUTURE LIFE—
ONLY NO LONGER EXIST, IT SEEMS—

OR IF YOU STAND BEFORE THE JUDGMENT SEAT,
FACED WITH THE CHOICE OF HEAVEN OR HELL,
HAS YOUR LIFE ON EARTH BEEN WASTED?
WE <u>WILL</u> KNOW FOR SURE—TIME WILL TELL.

WAR

THEY WORK HARD TO GET READY, THEN JUST
    SIT AND WAIT FOR THE ORDER—"MOVE OUT!"

THEY LIVE IN THE MUD, TRY TO WASH FROM
    HELMETS, AND WAKE TO A SERGEANT'S SHOUT;

THEY EAT FROM CANS, LIE ON THE GROUND, TIRED
    AND TENSE WITH THE THOUGHT, "WILL I LIVE OR . . . ."

THEY GO, THOUSANDS AT A TIME, CROWDED
    TOGETHER, THE MACHINERY OF WAR;

THEY WALK AND WALK, SEARCH, SHOOT AND DESTROY,
    UNTIL THIS IS ALL THEY THINK OR KNOW;

THEY REMEMBER THEIR WIVES AND CHILDREN
    FONDLY, BUT FARAWAY, DREAMILY SO;

THEY FIGHT AND KILL AND SUFFER TO LIVE,
    AS THEIR BEST FRIENDS FALL AT THEIR SIDE;

THEY ARE TRANSFORMED QUICKLY FROM MEN WHO LOVE
    INTO CREATURES WHERE NO FEELINGS ABIDE;

THE POLITICIANS PONDER, COMMANDERS
    PLAN, AND THE SOLDIERS WANT TO SAY GOOD-BYES;

THE WIVES ACT BRAVELY, THE DEVIL LAUGHS, AND
    GOD SURVEYS THE SCENE, BOWS HIS HEAD, AND CRIES!

HIS PURPOSE

CHRIST DID NOT COME TO EARTH

TO MAKE GOOD MEN BETTER,

NOR TO GET THEM TO STICK

TO THE EXACT LETTER

OF THE LAW, BUT RATHER

TO TAKE THOSE DEAD IN SIN

AND SIMPLY RAISE US TO

ABUNDANT LIFE AGAIN!

ADVICE

"DO AS JESUS WOULD DO"

I USED TO SAY,

"AND YOU'LL DO THE RIGHT THING

COME WHATE'ER MAY";

I FEEL THAT'S GOOD ADVICE

EVEN TODAY,

BUT THERE'S SOMETHING BETTER

TO THINK EACH DAY;

WHEN THINGS ARE TOO TOUGH OR

YOU'RE DEPRESSED,

WHEN OTHERS NEED HELP OR

YOU NEED SOME REST;

TO HELP MAKE A DECISION

YOU'LL NEVER RUE,

JUST ASK "WHAT WOULD JESUS

HAVE <u>ME</u> TO DO?"

FREEDOM

WE ARE FREE TO BE AS FREE AS THE
PERSON GOD WANTS US TO BE:

FREE FROM BITTERNESS TOWARD ALL
THOSE PEOPLE WHO HAVE WRONGED US;
FREE TO FORGIVE EVERY KIND OF
TRANSGRESSION, AS DID JESUS;

FREE FROM JEALOUSY AND ENVY
OF WHAT OTHERS MAY POSSESS,
FREE TO BE CONTENT WITH ALL THE
ABUNDANCE THAT GOD GIVES US;

FREE FROM WORRY THAT DRAINS THE
HEART AND STRENGTH FROM EVERY MAN;
FREE TO BE FILLED WITH PEACE THAT WE
CAN'T BEGIN TO UNDERSTAND;

FREE FROM CRITICISM OF OTHERS
WHO DON'T DO WHAT WE THINK THEY SHOULD;
FREE TO SEE GOD'S IMAGE IN THEM
AND KNOW WHAT HE CREATES IS GOOD;

YES, WE CAN CHOOSE TO BE BOUND BY A LIFE
THAT THREATENS THE VERY SOUL OF MAN,
OR ACCEPT THE JOY OF LIVING EACH DAY
IN THE FREEDOM OF GOD'S LOVING PLAN!

HOW TO DO IT

DON'T PULL THEM UP;

DON'T PUSH THEM UP;

DON'T DRAG THEM UP;

DON'T SEND THEM UP.

BRING YOUR CHILDREN UP

IN THE WAY OF GOD'S SPIRIT,

AND WHEN THEY ARE OLD

THEY WILL NOT DEPART FROM IT.

TRUE THANKS

IN THE ABUNDANCE OF OUR LIVES,

WE FEEL WE OUGHT TO SAY "THANK YOU";

BUT HOW DO WE DO THAT? IT'S BY

CHOOSING HOW TO USE

ALL THAT HAS BEEN GIVEN US;

WE MAY SAY, "IT'S MY LIFE AND I'LL

DO WHAT I WANT"—BUT MUST LIVE

WITH THE CONSEQUENCES, WHILE

WE SHOULD BELIEVE THAT NOTHING IS

OURS, BUT HAS BEEN ENTRUSTED TO

US BY GOD, AND WE MUST USE OUR

LIFE AND TALENTS WISELY, SO TO

AVOID THE JUDGMENT OF GOD AND

RISK LOSING THEM ALTOGETHER,

WE MUST SAY, "LOOK AT WHAT WE'VE DONE

WITH WHAT YOU'VE GIVEN TO US"—AND HEAR,

"WELL DONE, GOOD AND FAITHFUL SERVANT;

YOU HAVE BEEN FAITHFUL OVER A

LITTLE; I WILL MAKE YOU OVER MUCH—

ENTER INTO THE JOY OF YOUR MASTER."

OUR PLACE

WE ALWAYS TRY TO BE
AT THE FRONT OF THE LINE,
SEATED AT THE HEAD TABLE—
"THE BEST SEAT IS MINE!"

WE PUT OTHERS IN THEIR PLACE
BY PUTTING THEM DOWN;
DOESN'T THAT MAKE US MORE
LIKELY TO GAIN GROUND?

THE CROWDS IN JERUSALEM THOUGHT
THEIR PLACE WOULD SURELY BE
WITH THE NEW KING, UNTIL
HE WAS HANGED ON A TREE.

WE'RE BORN IN OUR FORM
FROM NOTHING MORE THAN SOD,
YET WE THINK OF OURSELVES
LIKE WE'RE EQUAL TO GOD.

BUT JESUS, THOUGH TOPS,
CLIMBED DOWN THE LADDER
TO SHOW US THE WAY AND
WHAT REALLY MATTERED.

WE SHOULD START AT THE BOTTOM,
HELPING OTHERS TO CLIMB,
AND THEN WE'LL FIND,
IN ITS OWN GOOD TIME,

THAT THE LAST WILL BE FIRST,
AND OUR PLACE WILL BE
LIFTED UP WITH CHRIST
FOR ALL ETERNITY!

TREASURE

WE WANT TO PRESERVE OUR
    TREASURED EXPERIENCES—

CAPTURE THE MOMENTS OF
    OUR HEIGHTENED SENSES—

WEDDINGS, REUNIONS, AND ALL
    KINDS OF GRADUATIONS,

RECORDING EVENTS AND MOMENTS
    OF ELATION.

BUT, WITH GOD, THERE'S SO MUCH
    MYSTERY IN THE AIR

THAT WE CAN NEVER CAPTURE HIM—
    YOU HAVE TO HAVE BEEN THERE;

FOR EACH TIME WE'RE IN HIS PRESENCE
    IS A TIMELESS MOMENT,

AS HE RENEWS HIS CHARGE TO "GO
    MAKE DISCIPLES"—WE ARE SENT;

AND EVERY MOMENT IS SPECIAL,
    NOTHING COULD BE PLAINER,

FOR GOD IS ALWAYS WITH US
    AS CREATOR, REDEEMER, SUSTAINER.

MOTHERS

A MOTHER—THE BEST OF ALL THINGS
SHOWING ITSELF IN ONE PERSON!

AT THE MOMENT ONE BECOMES A MOTHER
SHE HAS A SPECIAL GLOW—A LINK WITH GOD,

AND FROM THAT TIME ON SHE AMAZES ALL
WITH HER UNDYING PATIENCE, HOPE, AND LOVE.

SHE CARES FOR HER BEAUTIFUL AND PERFECT CHILD
(AS HE IS TO HER) WITH UNBELIEVABLE TENDERNESS,

AND THEN GENTLY TEACHES, GUIDES, AND MOLDS HIM
INTO THE MAN HE WILL BECOME.

SHE FEELS HIS HURTS AND PROBLEMS IN GROWING,
BUT, BEFORE LONG, HE IS GROWN AND GONE.

SHE HAS TO STAND BY HELPLESSLY, GLADLY, AND LET
HIM GO, WONDERING IF HER GUIDANCE WERE ENOUGH,

ONLY RARELY SHOWN THANKS FOR THE LIFE SHE HAS
GIVEN TO PRODUCE AND NOURISH ANOTHER.

I OFFER THIS PICTURE OF WONDERFUL MOTHERS
AS SIMPLE THANKS AND LOVE TO A SPECIAL ONE—

THE ONE TO MY CHILDREN!

TRUE LIVING

IN THY WISDOM, O LORD, HELP ME
TO BE LIKE THE MIGHTY OAK TREE:

MY ROOTS BE DEEP AND WIDESPREAD,
REACHING ALL AREAS OF LIFE;

MY FOUNDATION BE STRONG AND FIRM, YET
FLEXIBLE, TO BEND IN STORMS AND STRIFE;

MY ARMS PROVIDE SHELTER FOR THOSE WHO
ARE WEAKER AND NEED MY LOVING STRENGTH TOO;

AND MY TOTAL BEING STRETCH UPWARD,
TRYING WITH ALL MY MIGHT TO REACH YOU!

YOU HAVE SHOWN US HOW TO LIVE LIKE THEE,
LORD, IN THE LIFE OF A MIGHTY OAK TREE.

HEIGHT AND DEPTH

ARE WE WALLOWING IN SELF-PITY, O LORD,

SITTING BACK, FEELING SORRY FOR OUR LACK OF LOVE,

AND WAITING FOR IT TO BE BROUGHT TO US,

AS JOHN'S HEAD, ON A SILVER PLATTER?

OR DO WE FORGET THIS MISDEED, AS WE DO

OUR OWN, AND EXERT OUR ENTIRE SELF TOWARD

DOING FOR AND SELFLESSLY LOVING OTHERS?

HE WHO WOULD HAVE LOVE MUST LOVE.

COMMITMENT

DIVORCES ARE AROUND US EVERYWHERE—
COMMITMENT IS THE CULPRIT;
RATHER THAN SEEING WHAT CAN BE GIVEN,
WE WONDER WHAT WE CAN GET.

CHURCH IS OFTEN THOUGHT OF THE SAME WAY—
CONSUMERS OF RELIGION ARE WE;
WE TAKE, BUT DON'T GIVE UNLESS CONVENIENT,
BUT IF IT'S NOT, "WELL, WE'LL SEE."

THINK OF GOD'S COMMITMENT TO US—
ALWAYS FAITHFUL HE SAYS HE'LL BE,
AND HE LOVES EACH OF US SO VERY MUCH
THAT HE WENT AHEAD AND DIED ON A TREE.

BUT WE MAY NOT BE ABLE TO BELIEVE IT:
"I DON'T DESERVE IT," "I'M NOT GOOD ENOUGH,"
"I'M NOT IMPORTANT IN THIS BIG WORLD,"
AND OTHER SUCH NONSENSE STUFF,

BECAUSE GOD HAS PROMISED THAT HE WILL
TAKE CARE OF US ALL OF OUR DAYS;
SO DON'T BE AFRAID—BELIEVE, REJOICE—
GOD WILL TRULY BE WITH YOU ALWAYS!

BELIEVING IS SEEING

IS GOD NOT PRESENT EVERY DAY,
OR DO WE JUST NOT SEE HIM?

FOR NO ONE HAS REALLY SEEN GOD,
AND CHANCES OF PROOF SEEM DIM;

BUT IF HE IS WITH US ALWAYS,
THEN WHAT KEEPS US FROM SEEING?

A FEAR THAT IT MAY NOT BE SO,
OR WORSE, THAT IT IS, FREEING

US TO TAKE THAT GIANT LEAP OF FAITH,
TO WHAT WE CAN'T SEE AHEAD,

TO BE ABLE TO SAY, "MY LORD",
AND TO LIVE THAT WAY INSTEAD.

FOR THEN WE'LL SEE GOD ALL AROUND:
IN NATURE, AND ITS BEAUTY,

IN OTHER'S FACES, YOUNG AND OLD,
IN OURSELVES DOING OUR DUTY;

FOR BELIEF ENABLES US TO
SEE THINGS THAT OTHERS DON'T SEE—

THAT GOD IS TRULY EVERYWHERE,
SO BELIEVE—AND THEN YOU'LL SEE!

SHAMROCK

A SHAMROCK IS A SPECIAL SIGN

THAT SHOWS GOD IS A TRINITY;

I'VE WONDERED ABOUT THE EXTRA LEAF

A FOUR-LEAF CLOVER, A RARITY,

POSSESSES—AND WHAT IT MIGHT MEAN.

IS THERE A POSSIBILITY

THAT, FOR SOMEONE WITH A SPECIAL

PURPOSE OR RESPONSIBILITY,

IT SHOWS HE WALKS AT ONE WITH GOD?

I WONDER IF I DARED TO SEE

WHAT HAPPENED IF I OBEYED GOD

COMPLETELY—IF IT COULD BE ME?

PAST OR FUTURE

AS WE LOOK BACK AT
THE "GOOD OLE DAYS",
THE EVENTS THAT SHAPED
OUR LIVES IN WAYS

WE MAY NOT REALIZE
(OR MIGHT REGRET),
WE MAY THINK OF THEM
AS THE BEST TIME YET.

OR WE MAY LOOK AHEAD
TO WHAT'S OUT THERE,
THAT "SOMEDAY" WHEN WE WILL
HAVE TIME TO CARE;

THINGS WILL BE GREAT, NO
TROUBLES OR WORRY,
AND WE WON'T DO THINGS FOR
WHICH WE'RE NOW SORRY.

BUT WE MAY BE MISSING
WHAT'S HERE FOR US NOW.
GOD'S WITH US ALWAYS
SHOWING US HOW

TO LIVE WITH GREAT JOY
AND TREMENDOUS PEACE,
IF WE'LL JUST TRUST IN HIM
ALWAYS AND CEASE

LIVING IN THE PAST OR
THE FUTURE EACH DAY;
BE AWARE OF HIM NOW—
HE'LL SHOW YOU THE WAY!

555

TO GOVERN US WE'VE CHOSEN FIVE-FIVE-FIVE
TO HELP US AMERICANS AS WE STRIVE
TODAY TO KEEP DEMOCRACY ALIVE,

BUT IT SEEMS LIKE WE'RE IN QUITE A FIX
AS ALL GOOD IDEAS THEY WANT TO NIX,
BRINGING THE WORLD CLOSER TO '666'.

OUR CONGRESS AND LEADERS MUST REALIZE
THAT IF THEY DON'T JOIN AND COMPROMISE,
THEN WE BECOME NOTHING IN THE WORLD'S EYES,

AND THE U.S. COMES CLOSER EVERY DAY
TO JOINING MIGHTY KINGDOMS NOW PASSED AWAY,
AS, FROM SEEKING GOD'S WILL, WE DID STRAY.

WE MUST REMEMBER BOTH NATIONS AND MAN
ARE PART OF AND FOLLOW HIS MASTER PLAN
AND, FINALLY, ALL THINGS ARE IN GOD'S HANDS.

LET US ALSO DO AS THEY DID OF OLD,
AND ASK THE LORD TO CHANGE OUR HEARTS SO COLD
AND ONCE AGAIN BECOME PART OF HIS FOLD.

CLICHE

"EAT, DRINK, AND BE MERRY, FOR

TOMORROW WE DIE," THEY SAY.

BUT CHRISTIANS KNOW THAT THEY WILL

LIVE "FOREVER AND A DAY."

REWARD

WE TRY FOR IT IN SCHOOL

AND JUST FORGET IT THEN.

MAY WE SHOW EVEN MORE

IN LIFE THAT WE'RE "A"-MEN!

OUR PRAYER?

THE MOST IMPORTANT, BASIC

PRAYER THAT WE SHOULD PRAY

IS TO BE RE-MADE IN HIS

IMAGE SO THAT EACH DAY

OUR WORDS, THOUGHTS, AND ACTIONS IN

THESE BODIES MADE OF SOD

ARE SUCH THAT YOU ARE NOT ASHAMED

TO STILL BE CALLED OUR GOD.

STRENGTH

MY WEAKNESS IS OVERCOME BY YOUR STRENGTH;

YOUR WEAKNESS IS COMPLEMENTED BY MY STRENGTH;

AND, WITH GOD BESIDE BOTH OF US,

TOGETHER WE STAND.

WEAKNESS

WE ARE SO WEAK, O LORD:

WE ACT STUBBORN AND REFUSE ANY HELP
OR COMPLETELY HELPLESS AND ASK FOR ALL;

WE WONDER WHO OR WHAT WE ARE
AND WHAT'S AHEAD IN THE CRYSTAL BALL;

WE WORRY ABOUT MONEY AND SECURITY
AND TRY TO KEEP OURSELVES ENTERTAINED;

WE GET BUSY WITH ALL OF OUR PETTY
BUSINESS AND FORGET HOW WE'RE REALLY SUSTAINED;

WE LOOK GOOD TO OTHERS, BUT INSIDE WE ARE NOT;
WE THINK OF OURSELVES, WANTING ALL THAT WE TOUCH;

WE ARE NOT STRONG, SO PLEASE WON'T YOU HELP,
AND GIVE US THE LOVE THAT WE NEED SO MUCH?

SEARCHING

WITH ALL MY HEART, AND SOUL, AND STRENGTH, AND MIND,

MAY I SEARCH FOR YOU, LORD, UNTIL I FIND.

AND WHEN I BEGIN TO LOVE WITHOUT BOUND,

THEN I'LL KNOW AT LAST THAT IT'S YOU I'VE FOUND!

THE QUESTION

WHAT MUST I DO TO LIVE ETERNALLY WITH YOU?

SAY "I'M SORRY, PLEASE FORGIVE ME,
I'LL TRY TO DO BETTER"

AND BELIEVE THAT JESUS PAID THE
PRICE FOR MY SIN TO THE LETTER

OF THE LAW, AND ABSOLUTELY KNOW
THAT MY SINS ARE FORGIVEN—

MY SOUL IS NOW WHITE AS SNOW?

HOW I PRAY THAT ALL OF US
WILL SEE HOW SIMPLE, HOW WILD

IT IS, IF WE WILL BUT TRUST
AND BELIEVE THIS IS TRUE, AS A CHILD.

THEN ALL OF US WILL FOREVER BE
JOYFUL TOGETHER, LOVING ETERNALLY!

LIVING

HE WHO DOES NOT LOVE REMAINS IN DEATH.

HELP ME, O LORD, TO USE

MY GREAT CAPACITY TO LOVE

EVERY DAY, IN ALL SITUATIONS,

SO THAT, WITH THE GREAT HELP

OF A WONDERFULLY LOVING WOMAN,

I MAY FIND OUT WHAT IT IS

TO LOVE, AND THEREFORE, TO LIVE.

PARADOX

IT'S FUNNY THAT HE WHO FIGHTS THE MOST

OVER ONE'S COLOR WILL BE THE ONE

WHO, FOR HOURS, ENJOYS HIMSELF THE MOST

AT THE BEACH—JUST LYING IN THE SUN!

THE ERASER

THE ERASER THAT'S SO HARD TO ATTAIN,

YET CORRECTS THE MISTAKES OF UNCLOSENESS

THAT SEPARATES BOTH NATION AND MAN

ANSWERS TO THE NAME—FORGIVENESS!

GREEN GRASS

THE GRASS IS ALWAYS GREENER
ON THE OTHER SIDE, IT SEEMS—
HOW IT USED TO BE, OR WILL BE
AFTER, OR IF WE HAD DIFFERENT DREAMS;

IF WE JUST HAD WHAT THEY HAVE . . .
WE ALWAYS ENVY OUR BROTHERS,
BUT HAPPINESS IS NEVER FOUND
IN COMPARING OURSELVES TO OTHERS.

GOD'S GRACE IS GIVEN TO ALL, A
DEEP, OVERFLOWING CHANNEL
IF WE, BY OUR SIN AND ENVY,
DON'T REDUCE IT TO A TRICKLE;

GOD'S LOVE IS GIVEN ACCORDING TO
WHAT WE NEED, NOT WHAT WE DO,
SO WE SHOULD FOCUS ON THE GIVER,
NOT WHAT HE GAVE TO WHOM;

THE REWARDS ARE NOT THE SAME
WHEN WE GET TO HEAVEN'S DOOR;
IF WE'VE LIVED OUR ENTIRE LIVES
WITH CHRIST—WE'VE GOTTEN A WHOLE LOT MORE!

IT IS HARDER

WHEN YOU'RE DOWNCAST, DEFEATED,
COMPLETELY DESTROYED,

YOUR FUTURE, IF YOU HAVE ONE,
IS SIMPLY VOID—

WHEN YOU DON'T HAVE MUCH LIFE LEFT
IT'S EASY TO GIVE IT TO CHRIST.

WHEN YOU'RE A SUCCESS, HAVE
THINGS GOING YOUR WAY,

YOUR TALENT AND CHARM POINT
ONLY TO A BETTER DAY—

WHEN YOU'VE GOT ALL OF LIFE AHEAD
WHY GIVE IT UP TO CHRIST?

IT'S MUCH HARDER TO FIND THE JOY AND
FULFILLMENT GOD CAN GIVE

WHEN YOU FEEL YOU'RE MAKING IT
ALL RIGHT IN THE LIFE YOU LIVE.

WHAT DO YOU SEE?

WHAT DO YOU SEE WHEN YOU
LOOK AT A CAMEL,

A FUNNY LOOKING CREATURE,
OR A WONDERFUL EXAMPLE

OF HOW GOD MAKES EACH OF US
PERFECT FOR THE JOB?

HOW ABOUT WHEN YOU SEE
A WORLD FULL OF SOBBING

PEOPLE FULL OF FEAR, POVERTY,
AND SICK WITH DISEASE?

DO YOU SEE EACH AS A PERSON
TO BE HELPED, AS GOD SEES?

AND WHAT DO YOU SEE WHEN YOU
LOOK AT YOURSELF?

AS A WEAK, HOPELESS NOBODY
TO BE PUT AWAY ON A SHELF,

OR AS AN INDIVIDUAL WONDERFULLY
MADE IN THE IMAGE OF GOD,

BRINGING FORTH FRUIT EVERYWHERE
IN GOD'S RICHLY PREPARED SOD?

WE MAY LOOK AND EXPECT NOTHING,
AND THAT'S WHAT WE'LL BE,

OR WE MAY SEE GOD EVERYWHERE—
IT'S UP TO US, YOU SEE.

SAINTS

EVERYONE WANTS TO BE SOMEBODY—

HONORED, IMPORTANT, RESPECTED;

BUT THE PEOPLE WE REMEMBER MOST

ARE THOSE WHO NEVER NEGLECTED

TO HELP US BY SOME KIND ACTION

AND BECAUSE OF WHAT THEY'VE GIVEN—

AND WHAT THEY'VE GIVEN US MOST IS

A GLIMPSE OF THE SAINTS IN HEAVEN.

FOR SAINTS ARE SIMPLY PERSONS WHO ARE

CALLED BY GOD TO BE HOLY,

SET APART, DIFFERENT, SEEKING TO SERVE

OTHERS FIRST, GIVING THEMSELVES WHOLLY.

WE'RE SURROUNDED BY THESE SAINTS,

CHALLENGING AND SUSTAINING US,

CHEERING US ON TO BE SAINTS ALSO—

CHILDREN OF GOD WITH JESUS!

HAPPINESS

HAPPINESS IS HARD TO DEFINE,

ALTHOUGH MANY PEOPLE DO TRY,

BUT IT'S EVEN HARDER TO FIND

AND SOME PEOPLE SEARCH 'TIL THEY DIE.

WE ARE UNHAPPY BECAUSE OF

THE WAY WE FEEL ABOUT OURSELVES;

WE SIMPLY DO NOT SHOW THE LOVE

THAT SOMEWHERE DEEP WITHIN US DWELLS.

BUT WHEN JESUS VISITS US AND

THE HOLY SPIRIT WE RECEIVE,

WE DISCOVER WE'RE SPECIAL AND

GOOD AND HAVE ONLY BEEN DECEIVED

INTO SUSPICION, SORROW, AND FEAR

ABOUT BOTH OURSELVES AND OTHERS—

WE'LL QUICKLY FIND HAPPINESS HERE

AS SOON AS WE LOVE OUR BROTHERS.

GOD IS WITH US ALWAYS, AND SO

TO BE HAPPY—ISN'T IT ODD—

WHAT TRULY COUNTS IS WHO WE KNOW—

IF THE WHO WE KNOW IS GOD!

PROOF

WE SAY THINGS THAT ARE NICE,

AND DRESS UP NICELY, TOO,

TO APPEAR TO BE GOD-LIKE

IN EVERYTHING WE DO.

BUT INSIDE WE ARE NOT—

OUR ACTIONS DO NOT SHOW

WE PRACTICE WHAT WE PREACH—

THIS WE MUST SURELY KNOW.

FOR WE ARE SO FILLED WITH

OUR OWN NEEDS AND DESIRES

THAT WE JUST HAVE NO ROOM

FOR GOD AND HIS HIGHER

WAY OF LIVING, YET WHAT WE

DO AND SAY OUGHT TO SHOW

WHAT WE BELIEVE SO FIRMLY

THAT EVERYONE WILL KNOW.

IF WE WILL LET HIM DO

HIS WORK IN US, THEN WE

CAN TRULY BE THE PEOPLE

HE CREATED US TO BE!

WRONG

SOME THINGS ARE NEVER RIGHT—
WAR, DIVORCE, ABORTION,

AND, HAVING TO LEAVE HIS PARENTS,
QUITE POSSIBLY ALSO ADOPTION;

THE BEST DECISION IN A SITUATION
MAY BE SINFUL

BUT TRAGICALLY NECESSARY—THE
LESSER OF TWO EVILS;

SO HOW DOES JESUS DEAL WITH
US, ALL OF WHOM HAVE

FALLEN SHORT OF THE GLORY OF
GOD? HE REACTS WITH LOVE,

CALLS OFF THE ATTACKERS, ASSURES
US OF FORGIVENESS,

AND ASKS US TO TRUST AND BELIEVE
AS CHILDREN, WITH THANKFULNESS,

REALIZING AS WE DO WRONG WE
WILL BE FORGIVEN,

SO WE WILL ALL HAVE A JOYFUL
TIME TOGETHER IN HEAVEN!

GOD'S STANDARD

THE TEN COMMANDMENTS ARE

A HIGH STANDARD TO KEEP,

BUT WE MAY ACTUALLY

FEEL THAT THEY'RE NOT TOO STEEP

UNTIL WE REALIZE THAT

THEY ARE ONLY THE FLOOR

AND NOT THE CEILING—WE'RE

EXPECTED TO DO MORE.

THE STANDARD GOD EXPECTS US

TO FOLLOW IS SO HIGH,

FOR OUR FORGIVENESS FOR FAILING

HE SENT HIS SON TO DIE.

BUT WE ARE FORGIVEN JUST

AS WE FORGIVE OTHERS—

HIS GRACE COMES TO US AS WE

REFLECT IT TO OUR BROTHERS.

RESOURCES

IN THE MIDST OF HARD TIMES,
GOD WITH US STILL ABIDES;

WE NEED TO TRUST IN HIM—
IN HIS GOODNESS, HE PROVIDES;

SHARING OUR RESOURCES MAY
FIRST MAKE US FEEL SORRY,

BUT IT WILL THEN TAKE US
FROM A SENSE OF WORRY,

WHERE WHAT WE HAVE IS NEVER
ENOUGH—MORE AND MORE TOYS—

BUT, WHEN OFFERED TO GOD
THEY'RE A SOURCE OF GREAT JOY,

AND IS ALWAYS ENOUGH
FOR US—AND MORE!

SO LET'S TRUST IN THEM
LESS, AND TRUST IN GOD MORE,

FOR HOW WE USE THEM SHOWS
EXACTLY WHOM WE TRUST

AND BRINGS REAL PAIN OR JOY—
IT'S EITHER HEAVEN OR BUST!

HELP!

WHEN ONE MAN CAME TO JESUS FOR HELP,
   HE ALWAYS HELPED HIM, SO WE READ;

(NOTHING IS MORE IMPORTANT TO GOD THAN
   FULFILLING ONE PERSON'S NEED;)

AND JESUS USED THE ORDINARY
   RESOURCES THAT WERE AT HAND;

(THAT MAY INCLUDE US ALSO, AS WELL
   AS EVERY OTHER MAN;)

LITTLE IS MUCH, WHEN IN THE HANDS OF
   JESUS AND THE POWER FROM ABOVE;

(IF WE SAY WE CAN'T DO IT, WE'RE NOT
   TRUSTING ENOUGH IN HIS LOVE;)

GOD IS CALLING US TO DO SOMETHING
   FOR HIM, NOT JUST HEAR THE WORD;

(IF WE SAY WE'RE TOO TIRED, TOO BUSY,
   OR TOO SMALL—ISN'T THAT ABSURD?)

GIVING

"GIVE 'TIL IT HURTS" IS WHAT THEY ALL SAY,

BUT SURELY THAT'S NOT THE BEST WAY

TO GIVE A GIFT TO SOMEONE YOU LOVE,

ESPECIALLY IF IT'S TO GOD ABOVE,

WHO GIVES TO US SO GENEROUSLY!

THE BEST WAY TO GIVE, YOU SEE,

IS NOT TO GIVE JUST WHAT YOU COULD—

BUT TO GIVE UNTIL IT FEELS GOOD!

UPLIFTING

O LORD, WE KNOW

THAT WE ARE DUST

AND CAN DO NO

GOOD UNLESS WE TRUST

IN YOU, AND HOPE THAT

HELP FROM ALL THAT YOU ARE

WILL SOMEHOW RAISE

OUR EYES TO A STAR.

SPIRITUAL LIGHT

WHEN DAYLIGHT COMES, IT CALMS OUR FEARS,

IT EASES OUR WORRIES, IT DRIES OUR TEARS;

LIGHT ALLOWS US TO SEE THINGS MORE AS THEY ARE

INSTEAD OF DARK SHADOWS WAITING TO DEVOUR;

BUT IF WE'VE BEEN IN DARKNESS, LIGHT CAN BE

PAINFUL FOR US EVEN TO TRY TO SEE;

IT ALSO EXPOSES US JUST AS WE ARE

AND ALLOWS US TO BE SEEN NOT JUST FROM AFAR;

BUT SPIRITUAL LIGHT CAN FREE US

FROM THE CONSTANT WORRY AND FUSS

OVER TRYING TO LOOK GOOD AND CALLS US TO BE

CHANGED SO WE CAN SEE OTHERS DIFFERENTLY;

WE CAN LOOK AT THE HEART—INSTEAD OF OUTSIDE—

JUST AS GOD DOES, AND SEE WHAT'S INSIDE;

SO WE CAN FORGIVE, AND HELP THOSE IN NEED;

WE BECOME SHINING EXAMPLES OF GOD'S LOVE INDEED.

SO SPIRITUAL LIGHT GIVES US SPIRITUAL SIGHT—

HE IS THE SOURCE—THEN WE ARE THE LIGHT!

ACTIVE DUTY

WE MAY WANT TO SERVE
ONLY IN THE RESERVES,

BUT GOD ONLY WANTS US, YOU SEE,
IF WE'LL BE ON ACTIVE DUTY;

WE'RE CALLED BOTH AS A CHURCH AND
EACH INDIVIDUAL MAN

TO A VOCATION BENEFITING OTHERS,
SHOWING LOVE TO OUR BROTHERS,

SHARING THE GOOD NEWS WITH ALL
WITH TALENTS GOD GIVES TO ALL.

IT CAN TAKE US TO FOREIGN
TERRITORY, EVEN BE DANGEROUS AND

INTO THE WILDERNESS WE MAY GO,
BUT IT'S SO OUR FAITH CAN GROW.

IF WE'LL GIVE OUR LIVES TO HIM,
WE'LL FIND LIFE'S TRULY A GEM,

FOR THOSE ROOTED IN CHRIST BEHAVE FAR
DIFFERENTLY THAN OTHERS—BECAUSE THEY ARE!

THE LIGHT

THE LIGHT OF THE WORLD
COMES FROM THE SON:

WE ARE LIKE THE MOON,
REFLECTING THAT LIGHT,
SO OTHERS MAY SEE
DURING THE DARK NIGHT.

WE ARE LIKE MIRRORS,
DIRECTING THAT LIGHT
SO THAT OTHERS MAY SEE
THEMSELVES SHINING BRIGHT.

WE ARE LIKE WINDOWS,
LETTING THE LIGHT THROUGH,
SO THAT OTHERS MAY SEE
GOD IN ALL THAT WE DO.

WE PRAY THAT YOUR LIGHT MAY
NOT BE SO MUCH <u>ON</u> US
AS REFLECTING <u>FROM</u> US
SO OTHERS RECEIVE YOUR FOCUS.

MAY CLOUDS NOT COVER US,
CRACKS NOT BE PRESENT,
GRIME NOT BESMUDGE US,
SO YOUR LIGHT CAN BE SENT.

RICHES

IT'S HARD FOR A RICH MAN TO ENTER
THE KINGDOM OF GOD, IT'S BEEN SAID,

BUT PERHAPS IT'S EVEN HARDER FOR
A POOR MAN WHO WANTS TO BE RICH INSTEAD;

OUR MONEY, POWER, OR ACHIEVEMENT,
OR BEING GOOD IS NOT ENOUGH, YOU KNOW,

TO HAVE ETERNAL LIFE—IT'S A GIFT—
GOODS WITH GOD LEAVE A ZERO;

IT'S NOT WHAT WE HAVE—IT'S WHAT WE DO
WITH IT THAT'S THE TRUE MEASURE—

DO WE STAY WITH JESUS, OR GO AWAY
SORROWFUL, LOSING THE GREATEST TREASURE?

FILLED

MOTHER REALLY DID KNOW BEST

WHEN SHE TOLD YOU TO EAT

THE THINGS THAT WERE GOOD FOR YOU—

FRUIT, VEGETABLES—WATCH YOUR TREATS;

FOR OUR HEALTH IS LINKED TO

WHAT FOOD IS INSIDE US,

JUST AS OUR SPIRITUAL HEALTH

NEEDS HAVING INSIDE—JESUS.

WE MAY NOT UNDERSTAND HOW

FOOD GIVES US NOURISHMENT

OR HOW BELIEVING IN CHRIST

CAN SAVE US FROM JUDGMENT,

BUT IF WE'LL THINK ABOUT CHRIST

LIKE WE AWAIT OUR NEXT MEAL,

THEN WE'LL BE FILLED COMPLETELY

WITH A SPIRIT THAT'S REAL!

GARBAGE

CHRISTIAN FAITH IS NOT LIP SERVICE,
BUT LIFE SERVICE;

WE SHOULD FOLLOW CHRIST NOT FOR OUR
BENEFIT, BUT OTHERS;

BUT WE TRY TO HAVE IT BOTH WAYS—
GOD'S AND OUR OWN!

WE WANT TO KEEP OUR PRESTIGE AND
ALL THAT WE OWN;

GOD CALLS US TO SHOW LOVE BY THE
GIVING OF OURSELVES,

BUT IF OUR LIFE IS FULL OF SIN INSTEAD
OF SERVICE,

WE MIGHT AS WELL BE GARBAGE,
UNUSABLE,

WHERE THE WORMS DON'T DIE AND THE FIRE IS
UNQUENCHABLE!

FIRST

WE'RE ALL HUNGRY FOR POWER—

MAKING PEOPLE WAIT ON THE PHONE,

BEING NUMBER ONE, OUR POWER CARS

LEAVING THE OTHERS ALL ALONE;

BUT THERE ARE THOSE WHO ARE HELPLESS—

A CHILD, THE POOR, THE ELDERLY,

THOSE LOCKED AWAY IN PRISONS,

AND THOSE WHO ARE SICK MENTALLY;

JESUS SHOWED US GREATNESS IS MEASURED

BY THOSE WILLING TO OCCUPY LAST PLACE—

HE BECAME ONE OF THE HELPLESS,

AND SUFFERED DEATH AND DISGRACE

TO SHOW US HE WHO WOULD BE

COUNTED AMONG THE HEAVENLY HOST

IS THE ONE WHO PUTS HIMSELF

LAST OF ALL—AND SERVES THE MOST!

FULL

THERE IS A WONDERFUL FEELING
   IN BEING FULL,

AND IT LASTS FOR A WHILE, AS A
   GENERAL RULE;

THE MULTITUDE WAS FILLED, AND
   WANTED MORE,

BUT FOR THINGS LASTING ONLY A WHILE,
   NOT FOREVERMORE;

WE ALSO ARE STARVING GLUTTONS—ISN'T
   THAT THOUGHT CHILLING—

WITH THINGS THAT ARE FILLING, BUT
   NOT FULFILLING;

WE NEED TO FILL THE GOD-SIZED
   SPACE WITHIN US,

AND THE ONLY ONE WHO CAN DO
   THAT IS JESUS!

LISTEN

IN THESE FRIGHTENING AND

CONFUSING DAYS THAT WE'RE IN,

WHERE NO BETTER IDEA

THAN WAR COME FROM WITHIN,

WHERE OUR LEADERS ARE LED

BY CIRCUMSTANCES ALONE,

AND THE ENEMY CLAIMS

THAT GOD THEIR SIDE IS ON;

IS THERE ANY WORD FROM

THE LORD WHEN IT'S NOW RARE?

CAN WE HEAR THE STILL, SMALL

VOICE AMIDST ALL THE BLARE?

THE ANSWER IS "YES", IF

WE'LL BUT ATTUNE OUR EARS

AND BE READY TO ANSWER

"SPEAK, LORD—YOUR SERVANT HEARS!"

LEAVING HOME

WHEN OUR CHILDREN LEAVE HOME FOR COLLEGE,

WE WONDER IF THEY'LL BE OKAY—

WILL THEY BE HAPPY, SUCCESSFUL,

REMEMBER WHAT WE TAUGHT THEM EACH DAY?

AND, LEAVING, THEY MAY FEEL INSECURE,

AWKWARD, AND MAYBE DOWNRIGHT SCARED,

AN INSIGNIFICANT NUMBER, WHILE

AT HOME NOTHING SPECIAL WAS SPARED.

GOD SEES US THIS WAY TOO—AS A

CHILD WHO'S ALSO LEFT HIS HOME ABOVE—

AND HELPS US IN EVERY WAY, FOR WE

TAKE WITH US A TREASURE—HIS LOVE!

COUNTING

HAVE YOU ALWAYS HOPED YOUR
LIFE WOULD COUNT FOR SOMETHING?

WELL, YOU CAN HAVE ALL YOU
EVER HOPED FOR IN LOSING

YOURSELF IN SHARING AND
HELPING OTHER PEOPLE.

BUT WHAT IF WHAT WE HEAR
UNDERNEATH THE STEEPLE

IS WRONG, AND WE END UP
WITH AN EMPTY ACCOUNT?

THAT'S WHERE FAITH COMES IN, AND
THE FACT THAT WE CAN COUNT

ON GOD TO ALWAYS DELIVER
ON HIS PROMISE, THAT THE

MORE WE LOSE, THE MORE WE
GAIN, AND SINCE WE'VE RECEIVED

SALVATION, WE'RE FREE TO
BE ABOUT HIS BUSINESS—

DO WHAT WE CAN TO BRING
SALVATION TO ALL, NO LESS!

KNOWLEDGE

WE'RE ALL DRAWN TO THE MYSTERIOUS,
THE UNUSUAL, THE MIRACULOUS,

AND YET WE ALSO YEARN TO KNOW
ABOUT EVERYTHING, AND WHY IT'S SO;

BUT KNOWLEDGE DOES NOT PRECLUDE MYSTERY,
AND WITH OUR RELATIONSHIP WITH CHRIST, YOU SEE,

WE CAN HAVE BOTH, AS ORDINARY EVENTS
EVERY DAY POINT TO MIRACLES, AS IF HINTS;

THE VIRGIN BIRTH, FOR EXAMPLE, SHOWS
EACH BIRTH'S MIRACLE, AS ANY MOTHER KNOWS.

FOR THE MORE WE LEARN ABOUT GOD, THE MORE
WE SEE WE DON'T UNDERSTAND, THAT'S FOR SURE;

JUST LOOK AROUND AT HIS MARVELOUS CREATION—
HE CAN CERTAINLY STRETCH OUR IMAGINATION!

TO A TEENAGER

A BULB IS COVERED, OVERSHADOWED, AND
    NOTHING IS THOUGHT OF IT;

IT GROWS INTO A SPINDLY STALK,
    FULL OF THORNS AND PLENTY OF GALL;

SLOWLY, GENTLY, UNDER THE NOURISHMENT
    OF GOD'S CARE, IT REALIZES WHAT

IT WAS MEANT TO BE, AND BLOSSOMS AS A
    ROSE—THE SWEETEST, LOVELIEST OF ALL!

LIKENESS

"LIKE FATHER, LIKE SON," THEY SAY;

SO LET IT BE WITH ME!

MAY MY LIFE BE AS MUCH AS

POSSIBLE—JUST LIKE THEE!

FLAW

MAY WE WHO ARE PERFECT

IN SPIRIT, HEART, AND MIND

HAVE THIS ONE SMALL DEFECT—

MAY WE BE COLOR BLIND!

FLAWS

THERE ARE MANY THINGS
THAT WE CANNOT CHANGE,

THAT WE HAVE TO ACCEPT—
AND THAT'S NOT TOO STRANGE—

LIKE HANDICAPS, HEIGHT,
ILLNESSES, AND FLAWS—

WE CAN'T ERASE THE
PROBLEM JUST BECAUSE

WE'D LIKE IT TO GO
AWAY, BUT SIMPLY

DO WHAT WE CAN AND
MOVE ON FAITHFULLY.

GOD MAY SAY TO US
TO LIVE WITH IT, SEE,

THAT HE SUPPLIES GRACE
QUITE SUFFICIENTLY,

FOR GOD'S STRENGTH IS MOST
CLEAR AND WE AT OUR BEST

WHEN WE DO GREAT THINGS
IN SPITE OF A WEAKNESS!

TRUST

THESE ARE DEEPLY DISTURBING TIMES—
AND IT SEEMS WE HAVE GOOD REASON—
BUT THE GREATEST DANGER WE FACE
IS NOT A WAR OR RECESSION,

BUT A LACK OF TRUST WE HAVE FOR
OTHERS, AND THOSE IN AUTHORITY;
WE FEEL "I HAVE THE RIGHT TO SAY
IF IT'S RIGHT—IF IT'S GOOD FOR ME."

ONCE ISRAEL'S MEN "DID WHAT WAS RIGHT
IN THEIR OWN EYES" AND WERE DESTROYED,
FOR THEY FAILED TO TRUST THE ONE WHO
HAD BROUGHT THEM THAT FAR, AND ONLY TOYED

WITH HIS OBEDIENCE. SO WE,
AS CHRISTIANS, MUST TRUST IN THE ONE
WHO WILL DO ANYTHING ANYWHERE
TO CARE FOR US—THAT'S THE SON.

IF WE WILL TRUST, EACH ONE OF US,
AND OBEY—WOULDN'T THAT BE NEAT—
THEN THIS TRUST WILL PROVIDE FOR A
BETTER WORLD, WHERE EARTH AND HEAVEN DO MEET!

BUSY, BUSY

WE GO ABOUT OUR BUSY LIVES

TOO OCCUPIED TO NOTICE ANYTHING,

PUTTING OFF WHAT WE MIGHT DO

UNTIL SOMETIME BETTER SUITED.

BUT THEN WE LOOK AROUND US—

OUR LOVED ONES HAVE GONE THEIR WAY,

OUR HOUSE, HEART, AND THOUGHTS ARE EMPTY—

IT'S NOW TOO LATE TO LIVE!

BIRTHDAYS

BIRTHDAYS SURELY ARE FUNNY THINGS;

GOOD OR BAD—IT'S ALL UP TO YOU!

LADIES SCREECH TO REACH TWENTY-ONE,

THEN LOUDER STILL WHEN TWENTY-TWO!

METAPHOR

AS TURKEYS STRUT

AND WON'T BE LED,

SO MAN LIKEWISE

WILL LOSE HIS HEAD!

CHANGE

WHAT IMPACT DOES CHANGE REALLY HAVE ON US?

IT MAKES IT STRESSFUL ON US, TO BE SURE;

SO ALSO, WHEN JESUS INTRODUCED NEW RULES—

A WORLD ORDER FROM THE PHYSICAL TO THE PURE—

THE PEOPLE DIDN'T UNDERSTAND HIS WAY,

AND, UNLESS WE ACT WITH FAITH, NOR WILL WE;

WE MUST LET GO, TRUST, AND ALLOW GOD TO

SHAPE US INTO THE ONE HE WANTS US TO BE!

SEARCHING

WHY DO WE SEEK ONLY PLEASURE

ALL THROUGH THE DAY AND NIGHT,

AS IF THAT WERE ALL THAT MATTERED?

WHY DON'T WE SEEK WHAT'S RIGHT?

WALKING IN DARKNESS

AS WE TURN FROM THE SOURCE

OF A VERY BRIGHT LIGHT,

WE SEE OUR OWN SHADOW

STRETCHING BLACK AS THE NIGHT;

DARKNESS AHEAD, BUT WE

IGNORE WHAT'S INSIDE US;

WE KNOW THE WAY! WHY HAVE

ANYONE ELSE GUIDE US?

WE STEP ON OURSELVES AND,

UNSURE, FEAR FILLS OUR MIND—

WE'RE WALKING IN DARKNESS

WHEN WE LEAVE GOD BEHIND!

OUR PROBLEM

MOST OF OUR RACIAL PROBLEMS NOW ARISE

FROM FEELINGS IN WHICH WE CATEGORIZE

THEIR RACE AS LOWER, AND THEY, I SURMISE,

HAVE JUST HEARD TOO MANY LITTLE WHITE LIES!

THE LESSON

I SEE THE TREES, WITH BARE ARMS LIFTED HIGH,

THEIR FINGERS STRETCHED IN AGONY ABOVE,

PLEADING THAT LIFE MAY RETURN IN THE SPRING—

AND SO THEY BLOSSOM AGAIN THROUGH HIS LOVE.

I SEE MEN IN AGONY TOO, SEARCHING

FRANTICALLY FOR LIFE IN THEIR MAN-MADE HELL;

WHY DON'T THEY TURN THEIR EYES THE OTHER WAY

AND LEARN THE LESSON THE TREES KNOW SO WELL?

WITNESSES

WE ARE SO CONCERNED WITH HOW WE APPEAR;
WE WORK OUT, DRESS RIGHT, AND BLOW DRY OUR HAIR.

BUT SHOULDN'T WE BE MORE CONCERNED WITH WHO WE REALLY ARE?
APPEARANCES ARE DECEIVING; ISN'T THIS MORE IMPORTANT BY FAR?

OUR ACTIONS REVEAL US AS WE REALLY ARE, AND
REPRESENT OUR WITNESS OF LOVE TO EVERY MAN;

FOR A WITNESS SEES, THEN THE TRUTH ONLY HE TELLS;
IF WE'VE EXPERIENCED THE PRESENCE OF CHRIST, WELL,

THE TRUTH OF HIS SELF-GIVING LOVE, FORGIVENESS OF SINS,
THE ASSURANCE OF ETERNAL LIFE IS WHERE WE BEGIN,

AND OUR ACTIONS BACK UP OUR WORDS SO BOLD,
FOR EVERYONE NEEDS TO HEAR THE GREATEST STORY EVER TOLD!

REST

ONE OF THE BASIC LAWS OF CREATION

IS THAT ALL LIVING THINGS NEED SOME REST—

EVEN PLANTS TAKE A BREAK FROM ACTIVITY,

AND MAY EVEN LOOK THEIR LOVELIEST;

SO ALSO, WE, WHEN FEELING ALL WORN OUT,

NEED A LONELY PLACE TO REST A WHILE;

WE MAY NOT BECAUSE OF FALLING BEHIND,

WE'RE BUSY ADULTS—WE'RE NOT A CHILD;

BUT GOD SAYS, "COME AWAY"—NOT <u>GO</u>, WHERE

WE MUST STRUGGLE WITH THINGS ALL ALONE,

FOR HE IS WITH US, ACCEPTS US, STRENGTHENS

US, LOVES US, AND LIFTS US TO HIS THRONE!

RESOLUTION

AS A NEW YEAR BEGINS
WE RESOLVE TO CHANGE, OR

WIPE THE SLATE CLEAN, MAKE
WHO WE WERE A STRANGER.

AS WE MAKE A NEW START,
SHOWING DISSATISFACTION

WITH WHO WE ARE, WE MAY
HAVE A STRANGE REACTION

AS WE BRING ALL OUR GUILT
AND SELF-PITY, FRUSTRATION,

AND ANGER, CRIPPLING OUR BID
FOR A NEW CREATION.

BUT AS WE RENEW OUR
COVENANT WITH GOD, WE

ARE BOUND TOGETHER WITH
HIM IN A COMMUNITY;

HE PROMISES TO MAKE
ALL THINGS NEW—AND THAT

INCLUDES US, SO AS WE
ASK FOR A NEW LIFE THAT

BRINGS PEACE AND JOY, HE WILL
GRANT IT AND SAY, AS HE SMILES,

"I FORGIVE YOU ALL THAT'S PAST—
DO BETTER NOW, MY CHILD."

THOUGHTS

SIMPLY NICE THOUGHTS DIRECTED OUR WAY,

WHEN WE'RE HURTING OR NEED HELP IN SOME WAY,

END IN DOING NOTHING AND THUS COULD

BE MEANINGLESS AS FAR AS DOING ANY GOOD;

GOD COMMANDS US TO LOVE IN A WAY

THAT'S DIFFICULT—TO ACT RATHER THAN JUST SAY—

WITH ALL OF OUR HEART, BODY, STRENGTH, AND MIND,

TO EACH AND EVERY NEEDY ONE OF MANKIND,

SO THAT NEITHER GOD NOR OTHERS WILL

EVER HAVE CAUSE TO WONDER JUST HOW WE FEEL

ABOUT HIM, AS WE ACTIVELY, LAVISHLY

LOVE THOSE AROUND US CONTINUALLY.

WE LOVE OURSELVES THIS WAY—

WE RECEIVE IT FROM HIM EACH DAY;

JESUS SHOWED IT TO ALL WHO

WERE IN NEED—AND WE CAN TOO!

PREPARE

PREPARE TO MEET YOUR GOD—

THE WORDS ECHO, FILLED WITH GLOOM,

BUT THEY SHOULD SPEAK OF A NEW

BEGINNING, AND GREAT JOY—NOT DOOM;

EVEN IF IT INCLUDES OUR DEATH

AND THE WORLD AS WE KNOW IT NOW,

IT OPENS THE DOOR TO SO MUCH MORE

OUR ONLY REACTION WILL BE "WOW!"

SO WHETHER YOUNG OR OLD, IN DEFEAT

OR VICTORY, PAIN, DEATH, OR NEW LIFE,

ON A MOUNTAINTOP BRIGHT, OR IN A

DARK VALLEY OF SHADOWS AND STRIFE,

KNOW THAT WHEREVER, WHATEVER

THE CIRCUMSTANCES MAY BE,

GOD HAS BEEN THERE AND IS THERE STILL

AND WITH YOU GOD ALWAYS WILL BE.

SO HAVE CONFIDENCE AND FAITH AS

YOU HEAR THE WHISPER OF GOD SAY

THE ETERNAL ASSURANCE OF LOVE—

PREPARE TO MEET YOUR GOD TODAY!

ENOUGH

WE DOUBT THAT WE HAVE ENOUGH
TO DO ALL THAT NEEDS TO BE DONE;

HOW ARE WE GOING TO SAVE THE LOST,
FEED THE HUNGRY, OR TEACH THE YOUNG?

WE FORGET THAT WE DON'T HAVE TO
DO ALL THESE THINGS ALL ALONE—

GOD IS ABLE TO DO FAR MORE
THROUGH US THAN WE CAN IMAGINE;

JESUS SHOWED A POWER THAT ALWAYS
SUSTAINED, NO MATTER THE NEED,

AND HE WILL SEE IT TO HARVEST—
WE JUST HAVE TO PLANT THE SEED!

CALLING

SOME PEOPLE THINK OF

BEING A MISSIONARY—

HELPING SOME NATIVE TRIBE

SOMEWHERE ACROSS THE SEA—

BUT IF WE'RE DOING

WHAT GOD WANTS US TO DO

IT'S OUR CALLING, NO MATTER

WHERE OR WHAT—IT'S TRUE!

JUNK MAIL

THOSE PIECES OF MAIL WE GET

THAT ARE NOT JUNK MAIL WE KNOW

BECAUSE THE ADDRESS IS WRITTEN

BY HAND TO US, NOT ANY OLD JOE;

BUT HOW DO WE RECOGNIZE

WHEN WE'VE RECEIVED SOMETHING OF

IMPORTANCE IN OUR SPIRITUAL

MAILBOX, IF IT'S FILLED WITH LOVE?

IF THE MESSENGER HAS INTEGRITY,

IF IT'S CONSISTENT WITH SCRIPTURE,

IF DISCIPLESHIP WILL BE DIFFICULT—

THEN IT'S FROM GOD, YOU CAN BE SURE!

HYPE

WE OFTEN GET CAUGHT UP IN THE HYPE

OF SOME GREAT PERSON OR EVENT—

SEE ONLY HOW ONE APPEARS TO BE,

BUT THE TRUE PERSON HAVE NOT A HINT;

SO IT WAS WITH JESUS, EVEN THOUGH

HE SAID HE'D BE REJECTED AND DIE,

PEOPLE TRIED TO MAKE HIM INTO THE

KIND OF KING HE WASN'T, THAT HE'D DENY;

FOR HE DIDN'T COME TO BE THEIR KING,

BUT THEIR GOD, TO FREE ALL THE GUILTY.

WHEN THEY YELLED, "COME DOWN AND SAVE YOURSELF,"

HE HAD COME DOWN—TO SAVE YOU AND ME!

THE ULTIMATE PRICE

THE PROBLEM FACING OUR NATION
TODAY IS SPIRITUAL!
CERTAIN WAYS OF THINKING HAVE
NOW BECOME HABITUAL:

WE WANT GOOD THINGS, LIKE
CHILD CARE AND NICE ROADS,
TO HELP THE POOR, FEED THE
HUNGRY BY THE BUCKET-LOADS,

BUT WE WANT ALL OF THIS
AT NO COST TO US—
IT SHOULD BE DONE, BUT BY
SOMEONE ELSE, WE TRUST.

WE, AS STEWARDS OF GOD'S EARTH,
CAN'T DO WITH IT AS WE PLEASE;
HE HOLDS US ACCOUNTABLE FOR
WHAT WE ONLY OVERSEE,

FOR IT ALL BELONGS TO HIM
AND HE'S PAID THE ULTIMATE PRICE
FOR OUR UNDESERVED FORGIVENESS—
HE GAVE THE LIFE OF CHRIST!

TOMBS

WE STRUGGLE EACH DAY
WITH OUR OWN KINDS OF TOMBS:

DISAPPOINTMENT, DEFEAT,
DESPAIR EVERWHERE LOOMS;

BUT A TOMB THAT WAS EMPTY
DIDN'T CAUSE MARY TO BELIEVE,

BUT SEEING THE RISEN CHRIST
HER FEARS DID RELIEVE.

SO ALSO WITH US, EACH
EASTER SO SUBLIME—

IF IT ONLY COMES ONCE,
IT BECOMES "ONCE UPON A TIME . . ."

WE HAVE TO CELEBRATE
EASTER EACH AND EVERY DAY,

REALIZE THAT WE'RE ALIVE
AND LIVE EACH MOMENT THAT WAY;

BECAUSE CHRIST LIVES, AND
EACH DAY AGAIN FORGIVES,

WE'RE EQUIPPED TO FULLY LIVE
AND DIE—AND LIVE!

VISION

EVERYONE HAS HAD A VISION FROM GOD,

WHEN HE'S SPOKEN TO ONLY YOU—

YOU MAY NOT BE ABLE TO EXPLAIN IT,

BUT YOU CERTAINLY KNOW IT'S TRUE.

OTHERS PROBABLY WON'T UNDERSTAND

UNLESS THEY'VE EXPERIENCED IT TOO—

HOW ONE MOMENT IN TOUCH WITH THE

ETERNAL MAKES SUCH A CHANGE IN YOU.

YOU SEE, YOU NEVER CAN BE THE SAME

ONCE GOD HAS SPOKEN TO YOU—

YOU HOPED THERE WAS MORE TO LIFE THAN

YOU SAW, AND HEAVEN WAS REALLY TRUE.

BUT NOW YOU KNOW YOU HAVE A GREAT TASK

WHEREVER YOU GO, WHATEVER YOU DO,

TO WHOMEVER YOU MEET, WHENEVER THEY ASK—

GIVE A REASON FOR THE HOPE THAT'S IN YOU.

FOR A VISION OF GOD CHANGES YOU INTO A

CREATION WHERE WITHIN YOU'RE ENTIRELY NEW—

THERE'S A PROMISE OF HEAVEN IN THE BACK OF

YOUR MIND, AND YOU KNOW IT'S ETERNALLY TRUE!

FORGETTING

WE CONVENIENTLY FORGET
THE PAIN AND VIOLENCE OUTSIDE,

THE HUNGER AND HOPELESSNESS
OF THE WORLD'S PEOPLE, WE ABIDE;

THE WORLD JUST GOES RACING BY,
ANXIOUS AND FIGHTING EACH OTHER—

WHAT DOES IT MEAN TO HAVE TO
TENDERLY CARE FOR MY BROTHER?

HAVE WE FORGOTTEN SO SOON
WHAT GOD HAS DONE FOR US, AND WHY?

AS HE WAS BRUISED FOR US, AND
SUFFERED SO EVEN TO DIE,

SO WE NOW JUST CAN'T FORGET
THE CRUEL SUFFERING OF OTHERS,

THEIR NEEDS AND THE INJUSTICE
DONE BY ONE MAN TO ANOTHER,

BUT WE MUST SHARE THEIR SUFFERING,
CARE FOR THEM AND PLANT THE SEED

OF HIS LOVE TO ALL, LOVING NOT
JUST IN WORD, BUT TRULY IN DEED!

BUILDING

BUILDING IS BOTH A
   VERB AND A NOUN;
IT'S WHAT WE LIVE IN
   ALL OVER TOWN,
OR IT'S WHAT WE'RE DOING—
   EITHER UP OR DOWN.

GOD WANTS US TO BUILD
   FOR THE FUTURE AHEAD;
NOT JUST KEEPING THE RAIN
   OFF OUR HEADS,
BUT MAKING SURE THAT ALL HIS
   SHEEP ARE FED,

FOR WE ARE THE CHURCH
   AND WE BUILD AND GROW
AS LIVING STONES WHERE-
   EVER WE GO;
SO LET'S BUILD FOR GOD
   TRUE BUILDINGS WHERE NO

INJUSTICE IS DONE, NO
   POVERTY FOUND,
WHERE MERCY IS COMMONPLACE,
   CHARITY'S ALL AROUND,
WHERE WE'RE SAFE AND SECURE,
   FOR GOD'S LOVE ABOUNDS.

DEAD BUT NOT BURIED

WE MAY BE, OH, SO FULL OF LIFE

WITH ALL OUR WORK AND FESTIVITIES,

BUT INSIDE WE MAY BE HOLLOW AND DEAD,

GOING THROUGH THE MOTIONS OF OUR ACTIVITIES;

SOMETIMES WE FEEL, THOUGH WE'RE FLESH AND BLOOD,

AND IT'S TOO HARD TO HIDE,

NO MATTER HOW MUCH WE LOOK ALIVE

GOD KNOWS WE'RE DEAD INSIDE.

BUT GOD CAN DO A MARVELOUS THING,

IF WE WILL BUT BELIEVE;

HE'LL BRING NEW LIFE TO OUR VERY SOUL—

BETTER THAN WE COULD EVER CONCEIVE!

GOD ACTS IN UNEXPECTED, SURPRISING WAYS

(AND WE DO NOTHING IN THIS RESURRECTION);

HIS SPIRIT REVIVES AND REMOLDS US

AND WE BECOME A NEW CREATION.

EACH OF US MAY DIFFER IN MORE WAYS

THAN WE COULD EVER CONTRIVE,

BUT IF WE'RE DOING GOD'S WORK EACH DAY

WE'LL KNOW WE'RE TRULY ALIVE!

SEASONS

WHAT CAN A SEED SAY TO THE SOIL THAT CRADLES IT,
KEEPS IT WARM,
GIVES OF ITS SECRETS AND SUSTENANCE?
WHAT CAN A SEED SAY TO ITS EARTH
WHEN IT COMES TIME TO PUSH AGAINST HER
AND SHE NUDGES BACK, CAREFULLY, FORCEFULLY,
    LOVINGLY. PUSHES
UNTIL SEED MEETS THE SUN AND THEN WHAT CAN BE SAID
    TO THE SUN?
THE SUN WHO MOVES HIS HEAD SLOWLY TO SMILE.
THEY GIVE EVERYTHING
AND IT'S NOTHING
AND IT'S EASY AND IT'S THE MOST ANGUISHING AND
    ARDUOUS ENDEAVOR
THEY WILL EVER TAKE PART IN.
IT'S WHAT THEY'RE LIVING FOR AND WHAT'S MORE . . .
IT'S PERFECT.

AND THEN IT RAINS.
WHAT JOY.
AND IT BATHES.
AND THE SEED, NOW SAPLING, BECOMES FULL AND IT
    GROWS.
REACHING. HIGHER. GOING AND GOING.

BUT THE WATER DOESN'T STOP.
IT COMES TOO HARD, TOO FAST, TOO LONG, TOO MUCH.
AND THE ONCE SEED, ONCE SAPLING, NOW TRYING TO BE
    TREE IS IN TROUBLE.
IS IN NEED.

AND THERE IS THE SOIL AND THERE IS THE SUN.
ONCE AGAIN.
AND SHE DRINKS OF THE WATER AND HE HEATS UP THE SKY.
AND THE TREE GETS BY.

AND BY AND BY THERE COMES A TIME WHEN SEEDS FALL
    FROM ITS LIMBS.
THEY FALL THROUGH THE SUN LIGHT TO THE SOIL'S SWEET
    BED.
AND WHAT CAN BE SAID?
WHAT CAN A TREE SAY TO A SEED?

THEY SIMPLY LET BE.

Jason Downs

OPEN YOURSELF

FEEL YOUR EYES SHUTTING, AND FEEL YOUR MIND OPENING;
FEEL YOUR MIND FLOATING THROUGH A ROSY SEA OF
    RAINDROPS;
FEEL YOUR HAND RIPPLE OVER THE WRINKLED FACE OF
    EARTH;
FEEL YOUR HEART DIVE INTO AN ENDLESS BLUE WORLD OF
    CURRENTS;
FEEL YOUR FACE EMBRACED BY WAVES OF WARM LIGHT;
FEEL YOUR BODY TICKLED AS IT'S TACKLED BY FRIENDLY
    BLADES;
FEEL YOUR FINGERS REACH TO FEEL ANOTHER PERSON;
FEEL YOUR BLOOD SCREAM AS IT SCURRIES TO SMOLDER
    THE FIRE;
FEEL YOUR SPINE SHIVER AS IF TOUCHED BY HANDS OF
    FREEZING FLAMES;

NOW . . .

FEEL YOUR CONSCIENCE WEEP WHEN REMINDED OF
    WORLDLY WAYS;
FEEL YOUR PRIDE PIERCED BY THE SWORD OF SELFISHNESS;
FEEL YOUR STOMACH FULL OF KNOWLEDGE, WHILE
    HUNGER SITS OUTSIDE;
FEEL YOUR GUT GOUGED WITH GUILT FOR PAVING THE WAY
    TO LIES;
FEEL YOUR HEALTH DISEASED BY ESCAPE ROUTES AND
    IDLENESS;
FEEL YOUR LIFE WASTED WITH ENERGY TOSSED AND LOST
    TO UNKNOWNS;

NOW . . .

FEEL YOUR HOPE, WHICH SHATTERS THE GLASS OF OUR
   POLLUTED VISION;
FEEL YOUR SALVATION, WHICH SURPASSES OUR
   UNDESERVED EXPECTATIONS;
FEEL YOUR NAME REWRITTEN WITH BRIGHT COLORS,
   ERASED OF BLACK TAR;
FEEL YOUR EYES OPEN TO THE SIGHT OF TRUE LIGHT;
FEEL YOUR HEART OPEN, YOUR MIND OPEN, YOUR SOUL
   OPEN TO THE LOVE OF JESUS CHRIST!

Jason Downs

TREASURE

WE WANT TO PRESERVE OUR
   TREASURED EXPERIENCES—

CAPTURE THE MOMENTS OF
   OUR HEIGHTENED SENSES—

WEDDINGS, REUNIONS, AND ALL
   KINDS OF GRADUATIONS,

RECORDING EVENTS AND MOMENTS
   OF ELATION.

BUT, WITH GOD, THERE'S SO MUCH
   MYSTERY IN THE AIR

THAT WE CAN NEVER CAPTURE HIM—
   YOU HAVE TO HAVE BEEN THERE;

FOR EACH TIME WE'RE IN HIS PRESENCE
   IS A TIMELESS MOMENT,

AS HE RENEWS HIS CHARGE TO "GO
   MAKE DISCIPLES"—WE ARE SENT;

AND EVERY MOMENT IS SPECIAL,
   NOTHING COULD BE PLAINER,

FOR GOD IS ALWAYS WITH US
   AS CREATOR, REDEEMER, SUSTAINER.

MEMORY

MEMORY CAN BE A BLESSED THING—
ENJOYING PRECIOUS MOMENTS AGAIN,
KEEPING US ALIVE AND HOPEFUL,
ALLOWING US TO BE YOUNG AGAIN;

MEMORY CAN BE A CURSED THING—
IF WE CANNOT FORGET AND FORGIVE,
KEEPING US HATING SOMEONE FOREVER,
BEING JOYLESS EACH DAY THAT WE LIVE;

MEMORY CAN BE A FURTIVE THING—
COMING AND GOING AS IT PLEASES,
KEEPING A NAME OR FACE OR DATE AT BAY,
KNOWING THIS BUT NOT THAT, IT TEASES

UNTIL OUR MEMORY MAY BE NO MORE—
EVERYTHING WE EVER DID FORGOTTEN—
BUT NOT TO OTHERS ALONG OUR PATH,
AND NOT TO GOD IN HEAVEN.

AUTUMN LEAVES

IN THE AUTUMN OF THE YEAR
THE LEAVES SHOW DIFFERENT COLORS,
AS IN THE AUTUMN OF ONE'S LIFE
WE MAY BE BRIGHTER OR DULLER:

MAY WE BE THE TREES WITH
ALL SORTS OF DIFFERENT-COLORED LEAVES—
STILL GREEN AND FULL OF ENTHUSIASM
FOR LIFE, INSTEAD OF PET PEEVES;

BRIGHT CRIMSON RED, STILL FULL OF
PASSION AND JOY AND LOVE—
IDEALISTICALLY DOING GOOD
INSTEAD OF IGNORING SIGNS FROM ABOVE;

SHADES OF YELLOW AND ORANGE,
INDICATING TRANQUILITY AND PEACE,
CONTENTMENT WITH LIFE LIVED
AND, WITH THE FUTURE, AT EASE.

MAY THE BEAUTY THAT SURROUNDS US—
EVEN MORE BRIGHTLY IN THE SUN—
REFLECT IN OUR LEAVES BEFORE
THE WINTRY DAY IS DONE.

AND MAY OUR LEAVES BE SO PRECIOUS
AND BEAUTIFUL TO ANOTHER'S MIND
THAT THEY ARE PRESSED BETWEEN THE PAGES
OF THEIR MEMORY FOR ALL TIME!

AT ONE

GOD'S GREATEST WISH FOR EVERY ONE OF US
IS TO BE AT ONE WITH ALL, AS WAS JESUS:

TO BE AT ONE WITH NATURE MEANS
WE ARE PART OF ITS HARMONY
AND NEED TO APPRECIATE AND
PRESERVE, FOR ALL, ITS GREAT BEAUTY.

TO BE AT ONE WITH OURSELF MEANS
WE KNOW THE GOOD AND EVIL WITHIN,
BUT ARE ABLE TO MOLD THEM
INTO ACTIONS THAT DO NOT MAKE US SIN.

TO BE AT ONE WITH OTHERS MEANS
WE KNOW GOD LOVES EACH ONE OF THEM
AS MUCH AS US, AND FORGIVES THEM TOO—
AND THUS WE TREAT EACH ONE LIKE HIM.

TO BE AT ONE WITH OUR GOD MEANS
WE KNOW WHO HE IS—AND OBEY
HIS DESIRE THAT WE LOVE HIM WITH
ALL OUR STRENGTH AND MIND EACH DAY.

IF WE CAN BE AT ONE WITH THESE,
THEN WE WILL TRULY BE WHOLE,
AND PEACE AND JOY AND CONTENTMENT
AND LOVE WILL FILL EACH HEART AND SOUL!

AWARENESS

WE WALK ALONE ON A MISTY MORN,

THE DAY AS YET UNBORN,

THINKING THE WAY AHEAD IS CLEAR,

NEVER SEEING THE FOG THAT'S NEAR;

SUDDENLY WE'RE GROPING OUR WAY,

SEARCHING FOR ANY HELP TO STAY

SAFE AND SECURE! THEN WE REALIZE

THAT FOG DOESN'T COVER HIS EYES,

SO WE STRETCH FORTH OUR HAND

TO GRASP HIS, AND WE UNDERSTAND

THAT HE DOES SEE A SPARROW FALL

AND TRULY LOVES US ABOVE ALL.

WHY DOES ONE ENGULFED BY

DARKNESS AND CLOUDS OF DESPAIR,

FEELING HELPLESS AND HOPELESS,

REALIZE HE'S IN GOD'S CARE?

WHEN ONE HAS WALKED THIS PRECIOUS PATH

HE BECOMES UNCOMMONLY WISE,

AND, AS THE GLOOM LIFTS OVERHEAD,

CLEARLY SEES THE SON-RISE!

SUCCESS

WHAT IS IT THAT MAKES A PERSON A SUCCESS?
WHAT ALL DO YOU CONSIDER WHEN YOU ASSESS?

IT'S NOT A BIG HOUSE, FANCY CAR, OR BEING THIN.
IT'S NOT FAME, FORTUNE, OR POWER—BUT WHAT'S WITHIN:

DO YOU TRY YOUR BEST IN ALL THAT YOU DO,
IN BOTH THE IMPORTANT AND INSIGNIFICANT THINGS TOO?

ARE YOU HELPFUL AND FRIENDLY AND TREAT PEOPLE NICE?
ARE YOU KIND AND GENEROUS WITHOUT THINKING TWICE?

ARE YOU PLEASED WITH YOUR JOB—WHAT YOU DO EVERY DAY?
ARE YOU HAPPY WITH THOSE YOU LIVE YOUR LIFE WITH EACH DAY?

ARE YOU CONTENT WITH WHO YOU ARE, AND WHERE, AND WHEN?
ARE YOU ABLE TO RELAX WHEN YOU MESS UP, AND JUST GRIN?

ARE YOU ABLE TO ENJOY THE BEAUTY ALL AROUND YOU?
ARE YOU FORGIVING TO ALL WHO MAY MISTREAT YOU?

ARE YOU FILLED WITH THE PEACE, THE JOY, AND THE LOVE
THAT COMES TO THOSE WHO KNOW THEY'RE LOVED FROM ABOVE?

THESE ARE THE KEYS TO A LIFE THAT'S SATISFYING—
ONE WITH NO REGRETS WHEN IT'S TIME TO FACE DYING.

TO DO THE BEST YOU CAN, EACH AND EVERY DAY—
TO LIVE AS YOU'D WANT TO, WITH GUIDANCE AS YOU PRAY.

YOU CAN'T REALLY DO ALL THESE THINGS, IS MY GUESS,
BUT TRYING TO—YOU'LL FIND YOUR LIFE IS A SUCCESS!

THE ANSWER?

WHAT IF EVERY CHILD SHOULD ASK

HIS FATHER NOT TO FIGHT,

IF EVERY WOMAN ASKED HER

SWEETHEART, EACH MOTHER HER SON?

WHAT MAN WOULD STILL MAKE WAR?

WHAT IF MAN TOLD THEIR LEADERS

TO WORK IT OUT—

THE PROBLEMS OF WANTING MORE,

NEEDING MORE, CORRECTING THE WRONG—

THAT THEY WOULD NOT MAKE WAR?

WHAT IF MAN DECIDED HE WOULD

USE HIS STRENGTH AND MIND

TO HELP INSTEAD OF DESTROY,

TRUSTING, WITH NO TRACE OF FEAR?

WHAT MAN COULD HARM ANOTHER?

WHAT IF EVERY MAN, THROUGHOUT

THE WORLD, SAW THE SORROW

AND SHAME IN VIOLENCE AND WAR,

IF HE REFUSED TO FIGHT?

GOD WOULD SMILE.

TO MOTHERS

BECAUSE JESUS FIRST LOVED US AND SHOWED US HOW,
HE COMMANDED US TO LOVE ONE ANOTHER, KNOWING AS
WE ARE SHOWING LOVE TO OTHERS, WE ARE LOVING HIM.

WE ARE COMMANDED TO LOVE, NOT BECAUSE OR WHEN WE
FEEL LIKE IT; LOVE IS NOT A FEELING, BUT AN ACTION,
DOING WHAT HE DID AND WOULD HAVE US DO—
    BEING HELPFUL, CONSIDERATE, KIND, PATIENT,
    FORGIVING, SEEKING WHAT IS GOOD FOR OTHERS,
    AND MEETING THEIR NEEDS THE BEST WE CAN.

THIS KIND OF LOVE OVERCOMES ALL OBSTACLES, AND THIS
KIND OF LOVE IS TYPIFIED BY MOTHERS EVERYWHERE TOWARD
THEIR CHILDREN. MOTHERS ARE LOVE IN ACTION, AND GOD
APPROVES AND EMPOWERS THEM TO DO THEIR IMPOSSIBLE TASK!

LOVE AND REPENTANCE

LOVE IS NOT A PARTICULAR WAY OF FEELING,

FOR HOW WE FEEL CHANGES AND IS
DIFFERENT AT DIFFERENT TIMES,

BUT IT IS A WAY OF DOING,

A COMMITMENT
THAT YOU ARE GOING TO ACT IN A CERTAIN
WAY,
NO MATTER WHAT—

THEN WE TRULY LOVE.

REPENTANCE IS NOT A PARTICULAR WAY OF
FEELING,

FOR BEING SORRY CAN FADE
OR MEANS NOTHING
IF NOTHING CHANGES.

BUT IT IS A WAY OF DOING,

AN ACTION
THAT REQUIRES A SPECIFIC, MEASURABLE,
ATTAINABLE GOAL—

THEN WE TRULY REPENT.

PAST, PRESENT, FUTURE

THE PAST IS JUST THAT—TO BE FORGOTTEN,
BUT MISTAKES MADE ALONG THE WAY
ARE TO BE LEARNED FROM, SO THAT WE
SERENELY, FULLY, LIVE EACH DAY.

THE GREATEST REMEMBRANCE OF THE
PAST, AS WE EMPLOY THIS GAME
OF SELECTIVE REMEMBERING,
IS THE FACT THAT JESUS TRULY CAME!

THE PRESENT IS JUST THAT—A HOLY
GIFT FROM OUR CREATOR, OF TODAY—
TO USE AS BEST WE CAN—TO WORK
AND HELP AND ENJOY IN EVERY WAY.

THE GREATEST THING TO REMEMBER
IN THE PRESENT, BE IT NINE OR FIVE,
IS THAT IN OUR MIDST TODAY
JESUS CHRIST IS STILL ALIVE!

THE FUTURE IS JUST THAT—TO BE
PLANNED FOR, BUT NOT PROMISED AT ALL—
TO FULFILL OUR DREAMS OF WHAT WE
CAN BE, WITH TALENTS GIVEN US ALL.

THE GREATEST HOPE—AS THE PAST, PRESENT,
AND FUTURE ARE BLENDED TOGETHER
AND INTERTWINED TO BECOME OUR LIVES—
IS THE PROMISE OF . . . . FOREVER!

THE ABCs

ALL AROUND US IS YOUR HANDIWORK, DONE
BEAUTIFULLY.
COULD WE BUT FOLLOW YOUR EXAMPLE
DUTIFULLY.
EVERYWHERE WE CAN FIND YOU,
FOR YOU ARE IN ALL THINGS.
GOD, YOUR STRENGTH AND POWER
HELPS THE SMALLEST WEAKLING.
I AM ABLE TO DO ANYTHING,
JESUS, WITH YOUR AIDE,
KNOWING YOU ARE WITH ME,
LEADING ME IN YOUR WAY.
MAY I ALWAYS FOLLOW YOU,
NEAR TO YOU,
OPEN TO THE GREAT
POWER FROM YOU.
QUIETLY MAY I LISTEN TO YOU,
RISKING ALL IF YOU BUT
SAY THE WORD,
TRUSTING AS I MUST.
UNDER YOUR SHELTERING ARMS
VIEWED FROM BELOW
WE HAVE NOTHING TO FEAR
'XCEPT OUR FAITH TO SHOW.
YOU PROVIDE THE HOPE AND THE
ZEST FOR MY LIFE!

UNDESERVED

WHY GIVE THEM A GIFT?
      THEY DON'T DESERVE IT!

LIFE IS PRECIOUS, BUT
      THEY DON'T PRESERVE IT!

THEY CHEAT AND THEY STEAL,
      THEY LIE AND THEY KILL,

THEY'RE UNWORTHY OF
      ANYTHING, AND STILL

YOU WANT TO DO SOMETHING
      THAT WILL HELP THEM, IT SEEMS—

GIVE THEM A GIFT THAT
      WILL SAVE AND REDEEM!

THE ANGELS MARVELED
      AT GOD'S SPECIAL PLAN

TO GIVE TO MANKIND
      THE ONE PERFECT MAN—

A GIFT, UNDESERVED,
      AS ONLY HE COULD CONCEIVE—

FOR YOU AND FOR ME,
      IF WE BUT BELIEVE!

LABOR OF LOVE

IT WAS NOT WHAT WE IMAGINE—
THE NIGHT THAT DEAR MARY GAVE BIRTH—
'MIDST ALL THE BUSTLE AROUND,
IT WAS HARDLY NOTICED ON EARTH.

SHE WAS TRAVELING A HARD JOURNEY,
DESPERATELY NEEDING A REST,
BUT HIS FIRST REJECTION CAME,
SO A STABLE WAS WHAT GOD BLESSED.

JOSEPH GATHERED UP SOME LOOSE STRAW
AND MADE READY A MANGER-BED
SO THAT THE SON OF MAN WOULD HAVE
AT LEAST ONE PLACE TO LAY HIS HEAD.

IN AWE, THE ANIMALS GOT QUIET,
LOOKING UPON THE TEEN MOTHER,
WAITING EXPECTANTLY FOR THIS
BABY WHO WAS LIKE NO OTHER.

THEY SHARED IN THE PAIN AND FEAR
ON THE FACE OF ONLY A GIRL
IN ANTICIPATION OF THE BIRTH
OF THE SAVIOR OF THE WORLD.

SHE CRIED ALOUD AND SQUEEZED HIS HAND
AS JOSEPH DID WHAT HE COULD
TO HELP HER WHILE HAVING FAITH,
UNSURE HE FULLY UNDERSTOOD.

MARY BEGAN TO GIVE BIRTH,
AND STRUGGLING THROUGH PAIN AND JOY
REMEMBERED GOD WAS WITHIN HER—
IMMANUEL IN A BABY BOY.

AS LIGHT FINALLY BROKE THE DARKNESS
FROM A BRIGHT STAR SHINING ABOVE,
MARY BROUGHT FORTH THE SON OF GOD
AND FINISHED HER LABOR OF LOVE.

THE SWAP

GOD DECIDED HE WOULD MAKE A SWAP:

HE WOULD SWAP A HEAVENLY HOME—FOR EARTH;
FOR MAJESTY AND POWER—A HELPLESS BABY'S BIRTH;

FOR THE COMPANY OF ANGELS—INSTEAD
HE WOULD HAVE NOWHERE TO LAY HIS HEAD;

FOR A COMPLETE LOVE THAT NEVER FAILS—
HE WOULD FACE LONELINESS AND BETRAYAL;

FOR THE ONE WHO GIVES TO ALL THE BREATH
OF LIFE—AN AGONIZING, HUMILIATING DEATH;

FOR A COLD TOMB WHERE ALL DREAMS END—
A RESURRECTION AND HOPE FOR ALL MEN;

FOR STRICT LAWS THAT BOUND LIKE A THIEF—
A GIFT FREELY GIVEN THOSE WITH BELIEF;

FOR A SPOTLESS LIFE FULLY SACRIFICED—
MAN'S GUILT AND PUNISHMENT SATISFIED;

FOR WALKING WITH GOD AND EVERLASTING LIFE—
MAN'S WILLFUL WAY OF MISDEEDS AND STRIFE;

FOR HIS BELOVED SON TO DO THIS AND SUFFER—
FORGIVENESS FOR ALL WHO ACCEPT HIS OFFER.

BUT, TO ACCEPT THIS AND BECOME A PART—
YOU HAVE TO SWAP YOUR HEART!

THE HEART OF GOD

THE HEART OF GOD IS TREMENDOUSLY LARGE—

TO SEPARATE US FROM OUR SINS AS FAR AS
THE EAST IS FROM THE WEST,

TO REMEMBER THEM NO MORE, AND THEN

TO LOOK UPON US AS WHITE AS SNOW.

THE HEART OF GOD IS MARVELOUSLY KIND—

TO WANT FOR US NOW A LIFE SO ABUNDANT AND
BEAUTIFUL THAT HE GIVES US WHATEVER WE
ASK FOR OUR GOOD—AND MORE—AND THEN

TO PREPARE A PLACE FOR US TO BE WITH HIM FOREVER.

THE HEART OF GOD IS INCREDIBLY SOFT—

TO SEND HIS ONLY SON TO TEACH AND HEAL AND
SHOW THE WAY TO HIM,

TO SUFFER MISERABLY, AND THEN,

AS A SACRIFICE FOR US, TO DIE OF A BROKEN HEART!

SCENE OF LOVE

SEE HOW HE STILL STANDS TALL,
THOUGH BEATEN UNTIL HE MUST FALL.

HEAR HOW HIS VOICE SOUNDS STRONG,
THOUGH THE LEADERS SAY HE'S WRONG.

SEE HOW HIS EYES LOOK KIND,
THOUGH HIS FRIENDS LEFT HIM BEHIND.

HEAR AGAIN HIS WORDS SO TRUE,
"THIS IS MY BLOOD, WHICH IS SHED FOR YOU."

KNOW THAT THE GIFT FROM ABOVE
IS HIS EVERLASTING LOVE.

DISCIPLE

COME! COME AND FOLLOW ME!

COME AND WORK; BE WEARY,

BE SCORNED, THREATENED, ALONE;

BE STARVED, BEATEN—CRY AND MOAN;

BE HOPELESS—NONE WILL TRY;

BE HATED—COME AND DIE!

JESUS CALLS.

IT IS FINISHED!

WHEN JESUS UTTERED "IT IS FINISHED" FROM THE CROSS,
EVEN TODAY, WE MAY STILL BE AT A LOSS

AS TO WHAT WAS COMPLETED AND DONE—
WHAT WAS IT EXACTLY THAT THE SON

OF GOD HAD PROPHETICALLY ACCOMPLISHED?
IT WAS NOT WHAT THE PEOPLE HAD WISHED.

IT WAS THE PERFECT SACRIFICE—
THE ONLY THING THAT WOULD SUFFICE.

JESUS PAID THE PRICE FOR MAN'S SIN—
"PAID-IN-FULL" IS WHERE WE BEGIN

WITH THE REDEEMING FORGIVENESS OF SIN
FOR THOSE WHO BELIEVE, AND THEN,

AS FAR AS THE EAST IS FROM THE WEST,
THEIR SIN IS REMOVED FOR THOSE WHO CONFESS

THAT JESUS IS THEIR SAVIOR AND KNOW
GOD NOW REGARDS THEM AS WHITE AS SNOW.

HOW SIMPLE IT IS—JUST BELIEVE IT'S TRUE;
THIS FREE GIFT IS OFFERED TO ME—AND YOU!

BLESSED

WHEN JESUS GAVE THE BEATITUDES—
THOSE WHO HAD FOUND GOD'S FAVOR—

NOT INCLUDED WERE THOSE ITEMS
THAT WE NORMALLY SEEK AND SAVOR:

FAME AND FORTUNE, A LIFE OF EASE
AND PLEASURE—WHAT THE WORLD THINKS BEST.

NO, INSTEAD THEY WERE THE TRAITS
THAT WE DON'T THINK OF AS BLEST:

BLESSED ARE THE POOR IN SPIRIT,
THE MEEK, MERCIFUL, THOSE WHO MOURN,

THE PURE IN HEART, PEACEMAKERS, THOSE
WHO THIRST FOR JUSTICE AND SUFFER SCORN.

TWO BLESSINGS INCLUDE THE KINGDOM
OF HEAVEN, ONE WHO WILL SEE GOD,

OBTAIN MERCY, BE COMFORTED,
FILLED, AND CALLED THE CHILDREN OF GOD.

HE TOLD US THESE WERE THE BLESSED ONES,
AND HE GAVE, FOR EACH, THE REASON WHY.

SO LET US LIVE IN SUCH A WAY
THAT WE ARE BLESSED AS GOD COMES NIGH

AND HE LOOKS UPON EACH MAN'S HEART,
THAT HE WILL TRULY SEE OUR WORTH

AND GIVE US ALL HE HAS TO OFFER,
AS WELL AS INHERIT THE EARTH.

LOST FAITH

WHAT DO YOU DO, AND
WHERE ON EARTH DO YOU GO
WHEN ASKED, "WHERE'S YOUR FAITH?"
AND YOU SAY, "I DON'T KNOW!"?

WHEN YOU'RE PARALYZED WITH FEAR
AND ONLY FEEL DREAD,
HOW DO YOU FIND MEANING IN LIFE
AND NOT WISH YOU WERE DEAD?

WHEN FACED WITH A TASK
THAT'S IMPOSSIBLE TO DO,
HOW DO YOU START TO BEGIN
TO MAKE IT COME TRUE?

WELL, FIRST YOU START PRAYING—
AND NEVER STOP THAT—
YOU QUOTE BIBLE VERSES, ANY
UNDER YOUR HAT;

YOU PRAISE AND FORGIVE,
SPEAK HUMBLY AND SOFTLY;
YOU LET GOD WORK MIRACLES
AND WATCH AWE-FULLY;

YOU BELIEVE AND YOU TRUST,
AND ACT LIKE YOU DO,
AND SLOWLY FAITH IN GOD
WILL SURELY CONSUME YOU,

AND YOU'LL KNOW FOR SURE
THAT GOD IS ALWAYS NEAR,
AND THE FAITH THAT YOU'D LOST—
WELL, IT'S STILL HERE!

EVIDENCE

WHERE IS THE EVIDENCE TO THE
RESURRECTION—THAT HE REALLY DID RISE?

THERE WERE NO WITNESSES TO THE EVENT,
AND AN EMPTY TOMB WILL NOT SUFFICE;

THE EVIDENCE IS IN THE HEARTS AND MINDS
OF PEOPLE TO WHOM JESUS MAKES HIMSELF KNOWN;

THE EVIDENCE IS IN THE CHANGED LIVES IN
WHICH LOVE GROWS WHERE BITTERNESS WAS SOWN;

IN RENEWAL OF LIFE IN A CHURCH OR MARRIAGE,
IN PEACE AT THE TIME OF DEATH, IN HEALING,

IN BEING AT THE RIGHT PLACE AT THE RIGHT TIME,
IN ADDICTIONS BEING NO LONGER APPEALING,

IN WEARINESS TURNING TO STRENGTH, FAILURE
TO HOPE, GUILT TO FEELING FREE,

PAIN TO THE ENDURANCE TO OVERCOME,
AND SORROW TO JOY EVERLASTINGLY!

WE NEED NO SCIENTIFIC EVIDENCE—ALL
ARGUMENTS PRO AND CON SEEM LAME

TO THOSE WHO KNOW FOR SURE THAT HE DOES LIVE
AND WHOSE LIVES CAN NEVER BE THE SAME!

ALPHA AND OMEGA

EVEN AS THE STAR PROCLAIMED CHRIST'S BIRTH,
IT FORMED A CROSS SHOWING HIS DEATH ON EARTH;

AS MARY HELD HIM GENTLY WHEN BORN,
SO SHE HELD HIM LATER WHEN TORN;

AS HE WAS LAID IN A STABLE OF STONE,
SO HE WAS LAID IN A TOMB LATER ON;

AS MYRRH WAS BROUGHT BY THOSE WHO WERE LED,
IT WAS LATER USED TO ANOINT THE DEAD;

AS, AT BIRTH, HE HAD ONLY SWADDLING CLOTHES,
AT HIS DEATH THEY WERE TAKEN BY HIS FOES;

AS HE WAS BORN AWAY FROM HOME,
SO HE WOULD DIE WHERE HE HAD ROAMED;

AS PEOPLE CAME AND GAZED THAT FIRST NIGHT,
SO THEY LATER CAME AND WATCHED IN FRIGHT;

AS HE RODE A DONKEY TO EGYPT TO HIDE
SO HE RODE TO JERUSALEM BEFORE HE DIED;

AS THE STAR INDICATED GOD WAS THERE,
A STORM OVER THE CROSS SHOWED HIS CARE;

AS HE WAS REJECTED BY A KING WHEN SO SMALL,
AT HIS DEATH HE HAD BEEN REJECTED BY ALL;

AS HE WAS BORN ESPECIALLY FOR US,
HE BLED AND DIED ESPECIALLY FOR US;

GOD SHOWED HIS LOVE WHEN HE SENT HIM HERE—
HOW VERY MUCH HE HOLDS US DEAR;

GOD GAVE US CHRISTMAS TO OPEN THE DOOR
AND EASTER TO SHOW HIS LOVE EVEN MORE!

SLEEP, HOLY BABE, SLEEP

SLEEP, HOLY BABE, SLEEP!

BEFORE YOU BECOME AWARE
OF THE ROLE YOU WILL PLAY;

BEFORE YOUR MESSAGE EXHAUSTS
YOU AT THE END OF EACH DAY;

BEFORE YOU FACE ALONE
THE CROSS FOR US ALL;

BEFORE WE, EVEN NOW,
LISTEN FOR YOUR CALL, SO

SLEEP, HOLY BABE, SLEEP!

MORNING PRAYER

IF LEFT TO MYSELF TODAY, O GOD,

I WILL SEEK ONLY MY OWN GOOD, NEVER THINKING OF OTHERS;

I WILL HURT OTHERS TO HELP MYSELF;

I WILL NOT THINK OF OTHERS AS HUMANS HAVING FEELINGS;

I WILL WANT OTHERS TO DO THINGS ONLY MY WAY;

I WILL HAVE A GREED AND LUST FOR ALL THINGS;

I WILL GET ALL THAT I CAN, ANY WAY I CAN;

I WILL HOLD FAST TO ALL THAT I GET, NEVER SHARING WITH OTHERS;

I WILL THINK OF MYSELF AS A KING—OR EVEN, A GOD;

I WILL DO ALL OF THIS, O GOD, IF LEFT TO MYSELF TODAY,

SO PLEASE HELP ME REMEMBER THAT YOU ARE ALWAYS WITH ME AND

I AM NEVER LEFT TO MYSELF.

CHRISTMAS GIVING

CHRISTMAS IS A TIME FOR GIVING GIFTS:

GOD

GIVES US

LIFE, BEAUTY

LOVE, SERENITY

PEACE, FORGIVENESS

GRACE, PATIENCE, HOPE

KINDNESS, ENDURANCE, JOY

CONTENTMENT, FAITH, PURITY

CHARITY, SALVATION, E T E R N I T Y.

WE GIVE GOD OUR CHANGED LIVES—

OUR PROMISE TO FOLLOW HIM

THE BEST WE CAN

FOREVER!

AN EASTER REMEMBRANCE

AS JESUS PITIFULLY HUNG THERE ON THE CROSS,

RACKED WITH PAIN, ENDURING THE MOST GROSS

THINGS BEING DONE TO HIM THAT MAN COULD CONCEIVE,

WORDS SUCH AS "SAVE YOURSELF AND WE WILL BELIEVE",

HOW TEMPTING IT MUST HAVE BEEN TO ATTACK THOSE

WHO WERE BETRAYING HIM, BUT INSTEAD HE CHOSE

TO IGNORE THE HORRID TAUNTS AND EXCRUTIATING PAIN

AND REMEMBER THE WAY HE TAUGHT US TO LIVE TO GAIN;

HIS WILL TO LOVE WAS SO MUCH STRONGER

THAN HIS WILL TO LIVE, WHETHER WRONG OR

RIGHT, SO HE FORGAVE—WE KNOW NOT WHAT WE DO—

(AND GOES FURTHER TO FORGIVE EVEN WHEN WE DO);

WHAT A GRACIOUS GIFT TO US—AND CHALLENGE TOO—

(FOR US TO TRY TO FOLLOW HIS EXAMPLE TOO),

KNOWING NOTHING ON EARTH BELOW OR HEAVEN ABOVE

CAN EVER SEPARATE US FROM HIS UNDYING LOVE!

THERE IS NO GOD

"THERE IS NO GOD," THE WICKED SAITH,
"AND TRULY IT'S A BLESSING.
FOR WHAT HE MIGHT HAVE DONE WITH US,
IT'S BETTER ONLY GUESSING."

"THERE IS NO GOD," A YOUNGSTER THINKS,
"OR REALLY, IF THERE MAY BE,
SURELY HE DID NOT MEAN A MAN
ALWAYS TO BE A BABY."

"THERE IS NO GOD, OR IF THERE IS,"
THE TRADESMAN THINKS, "'TWERE FUNNY
IF HE SHOULD TAKE IT ILL IN ME
TO MAKE A LITTLE MONEY."

"WHETHER THERE BE," THE RICH MAN SAYS,
"IT MATTERS VERY LITTLE,
FOR I AND MINE, THANK SOMEBODY,
ARE NOT IN WANT OF VITUAL."

SOME OTHERS, ALSO, TO THEMSELVES,
WHO SCARCE SO MUCH AS DOUBT IT,
THINK THERE IS NONE, WHEN THEY ARE WELL,
AND DO NOT THINK ABOUT IT.

BUT COUNTRY FOLKS WHO LIVE BENEATH
THE SHADOW OF THE STEEPLE,
THE PARSON AND THE PARSON'S WIFE,
AND MOSTLY MARRIED PEOPLE,

YOUTHS GREEN AND HAPPY IN FIRST LOVE,
SO THANKFUL FOR ILLUSION,
AND MEN CAUGHT UP IN WHAT THE WORLD
CALLS GUILT AND VAST CONFUSION,

AND ALMOST EVERYONE WHEN AGE, DISEASE,
OR SORROWS STRIKE HIM,
INCLINES TO THINK THERE IS A GOD,
OR SOMETHING VERY LIKE HIM.

EASTER TODAY

AS HE WAS FALSELY ACCUSED,
ALL FINGERS POINTING HIS WAY,
EVERYONE WILLING TO BETRAY HIM,
SO IT STILL IS TODAY.

AS HIS FRIENDS ALL DESERTED HIM,
LEFT HIM ALONE THAT TRAGIC DAY,
AND HE HAD NO ONE TO TURN TO,
SO IT STILL IS TODAY.

AS HE WAS LAID BARE AND MOCKED,
SCORNED, BEATEN, AND LEFT TO PAY,
TAUNTED UNTIL THE VERY END,
SO IT STILL IS TODAY.

AS ALL THIS WAS DONE TO JESUS,
AND TO OTHERS STILL—DON'T YOU SEE—
"AS YOU DID IT UNTO MY CHILDREN,
"YOU HAVE DONE IT UNTO ME."

AND HOW DID HE RESPOND
TO ALL THE HATE SHOWN TO HIM?
HE LOOKED AT THEIR IGNORANCE IN
PITY AND SAID, "FATHER, FORGIVE THEM."

THEN HE DIED FOR US AND
WAS RAISED FOR US,
SO THAT OUR SINS MAY BE FORGOTTEN
AND EACH ONE BE PURE LIKE JESUS.

AND SO IT IS THIS EASTER MORN
THAT THE HATE THAT TEARS APART
IS REPLACED BY SHINING, EVERLASTING
LOVE IN EACH ONE'S SOUL AND HEART.

PRAISE GOD ALMIGHTY, ALL-WISE,
WHO KNOWS WHAT'S REALLY BEST,
AND THEN GENTLY LEADS US TO
THE WAY THAT'S TRULY BLESSED!

DID HE KNOW?

"SON, I'VE GOT A JOB FOR YOU,"
THE FATHER SAID ONE DAY,
"IT'LL BE TOUGH—AND IT'LL BE ROUGH
EACH AND EVERY DAY;

THIS IS THE ONLY WAY LEFT TO TRY,
BUT I'LL BE WITH YOU THROUGH IT."
"IT MUST BE IMPORTANT FOR YOU TO ASK—
WHATEVER THE TASK—I'LL DO IT."

SO THE SON DID GO, AND DID THE JOB
AS PERFECTLY AS COULD BE DONE;
HE SERVED OTHERS AND HEALED AND TAUGHT
AND SUFFERED AND DIED—NO FUN.

I'VE WONDERED SINCE IF JESUS KNEW
WHEN HE LEFT HIS HEAVENLY HOME
WHAT REALLY LAY AHEAD OF HIM—
WHAT ACTUALLY WAS TO COME;

I GUESS IT DOESN'T MATTER, AND
WE'LL REALLY NEVER KNOW,
BUT I'D LIKE TO THINK HE DID—
AND STILL HE CHOSE TO GO;

HE WAS WILLING TO GIVE EVERYTHING
HE HAD—SAVING US, YOU SEE—
JUST TO SHOW US WHAT TREMENDOUS LOVE
GOD HAS FOR YOU AND ME!

HEAVEN-WORSHIP

ONE OF THE THINGS THAT WE'LL

BE DOING IN HEAVEN

IS WORSHIPPING CHRIST,

WHO'S A PERFECT SEVEN,

THE ONE WHO IS WORTHY

TO OPEN THE PAGES

OF THE BOOK OF LIFE—GOD'S

PLAN FOR ALL THE AGES;

HE IS OUR SAVIOR AND

TRUE RECIPIENT OF

ALL PRAISE, RICHES, SONG,

GLORY, POWER, AND LOVE;

FOR WHAT HE HAS SURELY

DONE FOR EACH ONE OF US—

WHAT CAN WE DO BUT LOVE

HIM AND SPEAK OF JESUS?

THREE TREES

THREE TREES ARE LINKED, THROUGHOUT ALL TIME,
TO THE HISTORY OF MAN, MIDST GLORY AND GRIME:

THE FIRST TREE IS IN THE GARDEN OF EDEN,
THE KNOWLEDGE OF GOOD AND EVIL,
WHERE, MAN'S CHOICE LED TO ALL MEN'S DEATH,
DECEIVED IN THEIR THINKING BY THE DEVIL.

THE SECOND TREE IS THE ONE HE DIED ON,
WHEN, FOR SINS, IT WAS SUPPOSED TO BE US—
BUT, INSTEAD, HE CHOSE TO LOVE AND FORGIVE AND
REDEEM EVERYONE WHO BELIEVES IN JESUS.

THE THIRD TREE IS THE TREE OF LIFE,
AFTER CHOICES ARE MADE AND DEATH IS NO MORE—
WHEN GOD HIMSELF WALKS AMONG US AGAIN,
AND, EATING ITS FRUIT, ALL LIVE FOREVERMORE!

DARKNESS AND LIGHT

AS THE CLOUD OF SMOKE AND ASHES,
DEBRIS AND DESTRUCTION, DESPAIR
AND DEATH OVERTOOK THEM, RUNNING
AND STUMBLING IN PANIC AND FEAR,

FALLING AND CRAWLING, REALIZING
THIS DARKNESS WAS DELIBERATE, WAS HATE—
AS ALL HATE AND EVIL IS DARKNESS—
TOWARD LIGHT, BEFORE IT WAS TOO LATE.

DARKNESS—UNABLE TO SEE ANOTHER'S
FACE, WAYS, EYES, SOUL—AND THUS
SUSPICION, HATE, AND VIOLENCE
BLACKEN OUT THE FACE OF JESUS.

LIGHT—PIERCING THE DARKNESS, WITH
EVEN A TINY, BABY BEAM BEING
SEEN FROM A GREAT DISTANCE, AND,
UNLESS SNUFFED OUT, GROWING

UNTIL THERE ARE NO MORE SHADOWS,
NOWHERE TO HIDE, WHERE ALL BECOMES CLEAR,
WHERE THERE IS NO PAIN NOR DEATH NOR FEAR—
DEAR FATHER—LET US ALL DRAW NEAR!

LIFE GOES ON

THE LAND BECOMES PARCHED AND DRY,
THE GREENERY TURNS BROWN AND DIES—
OR SO IT SEEMS—UNTIL RAIN FALLS UPON
THE PLANTS AND BLOSSOMS APPEAR—LIFE GOES ON.

DROUGHTS AND PLAGUES AND FLOODS ABOUND
THROUGHOUT HISTORY, LEAVING NO PEOPLE AROUND—
BUT A FEW SURVIVE, A NEW SEED IS SOWN
AND THE POPULATION GROWS—LIFE GOES ON.

A TRAGEDY OCCURS—TOO HORRIBLE TO CONCEIVE—
AND WE FEEL THERE WILL NEVER BE RELIEF,
BUT, SLOWLY, THROUGH TIME WE LESSEN OUR MOANS
AND TAKE A STEP FORWARD—LIFE GOES ON.

THEN DEATH OVERTAKES US, OR A LOVED ONE,
AND WE FEEL EVEN NO WARMTH FROM THE SUN,
UNTIL WE REALIZE THAT DEATH IS OVERTHROWN
BY ETERNAL LOVE—THAT LIFE GOES ON.

THE FUTURE MAY BRING WHAT IT WILL—
PLEASANT DAYS AND WINTRY CHILL—
BUT GOD HAS PROMISED TO EACH HIS OWN
THAT THEY WILL LIVE WITH HIM—LIFE GOES ON!

UNDERSTAND?

HOW CAN GOD POSSIBLY UNDERSTAND
WHAT ALL WE HUMANS GO THROUGH,
WHEN HE'S AN ALL-POWERFUL SPIRIT?
HE DOESN'T HAVE TO LIVE AS WE DO!

HOW CAN HE UNDERSTAND HAVING NO FOOD,
OR BEING SICK, OR LONELINESS?
HOW CAN HE UNDERSTAND THE TEMPTATIONS
WE FACE, OR THOSE WHO ARE HOMELESS?

HOW CAN HE REALIZE THE AWFUL SHAME
THAT REJECTION AND NAME-CALLING BRINGS,
AND WHAT ABOUT PAIN AND DEATH ITSELF,
IF HE'S ONLY WHERE ANGELS SING?

BUT, WAIT—WHAT IF HE CHOSE TO COME
TO EARTH AS A TOTALLY HUMAN MAN
AND TO FACE ALL THOSE TERRIBLE THINGS
HIMSELF—WOULDN'T HE UNDERSTAND?

FINAL ANSWER

HE WAS CERTAINLY ON THE HOT SEAT,
ANSWERING QUESTIONS OF ALL KINDS;
BUT, INSTEAD OF TAKING THE OFFERED PRIZE,
HE RISKED IT ALL, BAFFLING OUR MINDS.

HE GOT NO HELP FROM LIFELINES, AS
OTHERS, INSTEAD, TURNED AWAY—
AND WHEN THE CRITICAL QUESTION CAME,
WHAT WAS HE GOING TO SAY?

FOR HE WAS PLAYING FOR US, REALLY—
TO MAKE US "MILLENIUM-HEIRS"—
TO RULE WITH HIM AT HIS KINGDOM-COME—
AND NO SACRIFICE WAS TOO GREAT TO BEAR.

AND THEN HE LOST, OR SO IT SEEMED,
AND THE DREAM ALL SHATTERED TO BITS—
BUT THREE DAYS LATER HIS FINAL ANSWER
CONFIRMED THE VICTORY WAS HIS!

SO WE, THE AUDIENCE, SAT TRANSFIXED
AT THE DRAMA UNFOLDING BEFORE US;
NOW LET US STAND AND CHEER AND SING
PRAISE TO THE WINNER NAMED JESUS!

CELEBRITY

THE BEST-KNOWN MAN IN THE ENTIRE REGION,
HE WAS TRULY A CELEBRITY—
PEOPLE LISTENED TO ALL HE HAD TO SAY
AND BASICALLY GAVE HIM THE KEY TO THE CITY!

HIS NAME AND FAME GREW FAR AND WIDE,
WITH NOT EVEN A HINT OF A SCANDAL—
WELL, MAYBE THAT WOMAN, OR WHAT HE DID THERE . . .
BUT SURELY NOTHING HE COULDN'T HANDLE.

AN ACCUSATION—THE FRENZIED CROWD
WAS ENOUGH TO GIVE YOUR HEART A CHILL—
AND, BEFORE THE WEEK WAS THROUGH, HE HAD
BEEN CRUCIFIED UPON A HILL!

BUT TRUE CELEBRITY DOES NOT DIE—
EVEN WHEN FACED WITH LIES AND HATE—
AND NOW FOR OVER TWO THOUSAND YEARS
THIS CELEBRITY WE CELEBRATE!

CONTRAST

HE WENT FROM A PARADE IN HIS HONOR
TO A PROCESSION FOR HIS DISHONOR;

HE WENT FROM THE CROWD CHEERING A KING
TO THE CROWD JEERING THE STILL-NAMED-KING;

HE WENT FROM BEING TOLD HE WAS THE CHRIST
TO BEING LEFT ALONE AND DENIED THRICE;

HE WENT FROM RIDING WITH PALM LEAVES SPREAD BEFORE
TO CARRYING HIS OWN CROSS, WITH DEATH AT THE DOOR;

HE WENT FROM BEING PRAISED AND ADORED
TO BEING BEATEN FOR BEING CALLED "LORD";

HE WENT FROM BEING THE MOST WONDERFUL WINNER
TO BEING A LOSER, CRUCIFIED WITH TWO SINNERS;

BUT HE WENT FROM GREAT SUFFERING AND DEATH
INTO EVERLASTING GLORY WHEN HE DREW HIS LAST BREATH,

AND, BECAUSE HE DID, SUCH SINNING LOSERS AS WE
BECOME WINNERS WITH HIM FOR ALL ETERNITY!

MILLENNIUM

WE'RE APPROACHING A NEW CENTURY,
A BRAND NEW MILLENNIUM,
AND MANY PEOPLE ARE CONCERNED
ABOUT WHAT EVENTS WILL COME.

WE WORRY ABOUT Y2K AND
WHAT DISASTERS WE MAY SEE,
BUT ARE WE CONCERNED ABOUT
WHAT HAPPENS FOR ETERNITY?

WE HABITUALLY WORK ON AND ON
UNTIL WE BECOME NUMB,
WHEN WE SHOULD BE REJOICING—
THE LORD HAS COME!

THE FUTURE IS SIMPLE, WITH
NO NEED TO BE VEXED—
IT'S SIMPLY WHATEVER GOD
WANTS US TO DO NEXT!

TRAVEL AGENT

DO YOU WANT TO TRAVEL?
WANTING PEACE OR EXCITEMENT OR PLEASURE?
FOLLOW THIS TRAVEL POSTER TO A
LAND THAT'S JUST WHAT YOU TREASURE!

YOU MAY BE TIRED AND BEAT DOWN
OR SIMPLY OVERCOME BY STRESS;
JUST LISTEN TO YOUR TRAVEL AGENT
AND HE WILL BRING YOU REST!

READ THE TRAVEL BROCHURE AND
IT WILL TELL YOU HOW TO GET THERE—
WHERE GOD'S WILL IS DONE ON EARTH
AS IT HEAVENLY IS ELSEWHERE.

YOU'LL BE TRANSFORMED INTO WHAT
HE REALLY HAS IN MIND FOR YOU—
A CLOSE, LOVING RELATIONSHIP
THAT WILL MAKE YOUR DREAMS COME TRUE!

SO, COME JOIN THE EXCITING JOURNEY—
JUST GIVE JESUS THE NOD—
AND YOU'LL BE ON YOUR WAY TO
THE WONDERFUL KINGDOM OF GOD!

LIGHT

WE TURN ON THE LIGHTS
BUT THEY'RE ARTIFICIAL,
AND WITH NO POWER SOURCE
THEY'RE NOT BENEFICIAL.

THE TRUE LIGHT TURNS US ON
AND WE REFLECT THIS LIGHT
TO LIGHT THE WAY FOR OTHERS
AND MAKE DAYLIGHT OUT OF NIGHT.

GOD SENT HIS LIGHT—
THE LIGHT OF THE WORLD—
AND WE ARE THE CHILDREN OF
THE LIGHT, EACH BOY AND GIRL.

HIS LIGHT SHINES EVERYWHERE,
CUTTING THROUGH DARKNESS LIKE A KNIFE,
AND, IF WE WILL ONLY LOOK UP,
HE WILL LIGHT UP OUR LIFE!

THE PURPOSE OF LIFE

THE PURPOSE OF LIFE IS A LIFE OF PURPOSE:

TO DO ALL THINGS TO THE GLORY OF GOD,
WHETHER PLANTING A SEED IN THE SOD

AND WATCHING IT WONDROUSLY GROW,
OR IN THE MIND—RESULTS YOU MAY NEVER KNOW;

WHETHER MOWING A YARD OR TYPING A LETTER,
DOING IT FOR GOD MAKES YOU DO IT BETTER;

A JOB DONE COMPLETELY, THE BEST THAT YOU CAN,
IS SMILED UPON BY GOD AGAIN AND AGAIN,

FOR YOU'VE USED TALENTS GIVEN YOU BY HIM
AND YOUR LIFE ISN'T JUST BASED ON A WHIM;

THE VARIETY OF JOBS THAT ONE CAN DO
PROVIDES A PURPOSE TO LIFE IF DONE IN TRUE

SERVICE AND OBEDIENCE TO GOD'S WILL,
AND YOU'LL FIND YOURSELF TOTALLY FULFILLED,

FOR THERE IS NO TASK THAT IS LOWLY OR SMALL
IF IT IS DONE TO HONOR GOD ABOVE ALL!

MARY'S CALLING

"GREETINGS, FAVORED ONE"—
THE WORDS COME JOYFULLY,
BUT THE RESPONSE IS ALWAYS
THE SAME—"WHO, ME?"

"THE LORD IS WITH YOU"—
WE SHOULD SEE THAT A LOT,
BUT THE RESPONSE IS ALWAYS
THE SAME—"UH, WHAT?"

"DO NOT BE AFRAID"—
AND WE MIGHT GIVE IT A TRY,
BUT THE RESPONSE IS ALWAYS
THE SAME—"TELL ME WHY!"

"YOU WILL DO GREAT THINGS"—
IF WE ONLY BELIEVED IT NOW,
BUT THE RESPONSE IS ALWAYS
THE SAME—"TELL ME HOW!"

"NOTHING IS IMPOSSIBLE WITH GOD"—
WHAT A RELIEF IT WOULD BE
IF WE COULD ONLY BELIEVE THAT
AND SET OURSELVES COMPLETELY FREE.

MARY'S CALLING WAS TO BRING CHRIST
INTO THE WORLD FOR ALL—
AND SO IT IS FOR EACH OF US
WHENEVER WE HEAR HIS CALL!

MARTYR

TO BE WILLING TO DIE FOR WHAT ONE BELIEVES
IS A LOFTY THOUGHT BY MAN OVER THE CENTURIES;

TO DIE FOR OUR GOD IS THE ULTIMATE SACRIFICE—
BUT THE REWARD FOR DOING SO IS WORTH THE PRICE;

JESUS SET THE EXAMPLE, AS HE DIED FOR US ALL—
AND WE, AS HIS FOLLOWERS, MAY HAVE TO HEED THIS CALL;

BUT WHAT OF THE BOMBER, WHO THINKS IT A SMALL PRICE
TO KILL ENEMIES OF GOD AND BE REWARDED WITH PARADISE?

SO IT IS MORE THAN TO BE WILLING TO DIE FOR WHAT WE SAY,
BUT, IF JESUS IS THE TRUTH, THE SACRIFICE, THE ONLY WAY,

AND IF THE CHARACTER OF GOD IS NOT ONE OF VENGENCE
    AND DEATH,
BUT ONE OF LOVE AND GOODNESS, JOY AND PEACE WITH
    EACH BREATH;

THE MORE IMPORTANT QUESTION THAT REMAINS MUST BE,
    THEN,
ARE WE WILLING TO <u>LIVE</u> FOR HIM, EACH DAY LOVING ALL
    HIS CHILDREN?

THE BIBLE

THE BIBLE IS THE STORY OF GOD
CREATING ALL THERE IS—AND MEN;

ORIGINAL SIN IS MAN'S TENDENCY
TO WANT TO BE LIKE GOD, SO THEN

HE DISOBEYS OR REPLACES GOD WITH
SOMETHING THAT'S CREATED INSTEAD;

SO GOD DECIDED ON A PLAN BY
WHICH ALL PEOPLES COULD BE LED

BACK TO HIM—A CHOSEN PEOPLE
WITH A SPECIAL JOB TO DO—

HE WOULD BLESS THEM IF THEY FOLLOWED
HIM, SO THEY COULD BE A BLESSING TOO.

HE USED ORDINARY PEOPLE TO LEAD THE WAY,
SO EVERYONE COULD SEE IT WAS HE,

AND WHEN THEY FAILED HE ALWAYS FORGAVE
AND ATONED FOR THEIR SIN UPON A TREE.

BUT IF THE "CHOSEN PEOPLE" DIDN'T WORK
WHAT MORE CAN HE DO IF WE FAIL TOO?

HE MAY SIMPLY SAY, "IT'S NOW JUDGMENT DAY"
AND CREATE HEAVEN AND EARTH ANEW!

GOD'S GRACE

WE MAY TRY TO TAKE ALL WE CAN
AT ONE TIME,

AND SAVE IT TO USE WHEN WE
NEED IT MOST,

OR WE MAY JUST TOUGH IT OUT
ON OUR OWN,

AND REALIZE TOO LATE
THAT WE'RE LOST.

WHEN WE SUFFER ENOUGH WE MAY
RECOGNIZE AT LAST

THAT THE GOODNESS OF GOD DOESN'T DEPEND
ON US BEING GOOD,

THAT HE'S RICHLY BLESSED US ALREADY
SO VERY MUCH,

AND THAT HE'LL CONTINUE TO PROVIDE
AS ONLY HE COULD,

THAT ALL OUR NEEDS ARE MET,
LARGE OR SMALL,

IF WE'LL BUT TRUST HIM
DAY BY DAY,

WE'LL SEE THAT ALONG WITH
ALL THE REST

OUR BIGGEST NEED—RECONCILIATION—
HE PROVIDES TODAY.

BORN ANEW

IF WE'RE NOT BORN FROM ABOVE

WE'RE NOT MINDFUL OF GOD'S LOVE;

WE'LL THEN SIN WITHOUT MEASURE

AND FORGET OUR TRUE TREASURE;

WE'LL SEEK OUR OWN PLEASURE,

FAME, FORTUNE, OR LEISURE

INSTEAD OF FLYING LIKE A DOVE

INTO GOD'S OUTSTRETCHED PALM OF LOVE.

IF WE ARE BORN FROM ABOVE

THEN WE'RE AWARE OF GOD'S LOVE;

WE'LL HAVE FAITH WITHOUT MEASURE

AND REMEMBER GOD'S TREASURE;

WE'LL TRUST HIM AND OBEY

EVEN THOUGH SUFFERING EACH DAY

UNTIL WE, LIKE A GLOVE,

ARE ENVELOPED BY HIS LOVE.

THE RIGHT WAY

LORD, HELP ME FIND THE RIGHT WAY;
MAY I FOLLOW YOU EVERY DAY;
YOU'LL BE WITH ME ALL THE WAY
IF I'LL ONLY SEEK THE RIGHT WAY!

I SEE THE PATH AHEAD OF ME
BUT I DON'T KNOW WHICH WAY TO GO—
THE NICE, WIDE PATHWAY SEEMS TO BE
THE WAY, BUT I DON'T KNOW;

ALL THE PEOPLE RACING BY
ARE BOUND FOR—WHO KNOWS WHERE?
THEY'RE ALL PRESSURING ME TO GO—
TO GO DOWN WITH THEM THERE;

I LOOK AT THEM AND I SEE
NO ONE SEEMS TO BOTHER;
THEY'RE ONLY INTERESTED IN THEMSELVES
AND DON'T CARE FOR ONE ANOTHER;

I SEE AN EXIT COMIN' UP!
IT LOOKS SO NARROW AND SMALL;
SHOULD I TAKE A CHANCE AND SEE
WHERE IT LEADS, BEFORE I FALL?

I TURN OFF ON EXIT SEVEN—
IT'S SUDDENLY PEACEFUL AROUND;
I FEEL LIKE I'M ALMOST IN HEAVEN;
MY FEET ARE ON SOLID GROUND;

I NOW KNOW I MADE THE RIGHT CHOICE;
I FEEL IT EVERY DAY;
WHEN YOU WALK ON GOD'S PATHWAY
THEN YOU'VE FOUND THE RIGHT WAY!

JACOB

WE WRESTLE WITH OUR FEARS,

ANXIETIES, AND SHAME EACH DAY;

TRYING TO GO IT ALONE,

WE SEND ALL OTHERS AWAY.

BUT THERE IS ONE WHO KNOWS

WE'RE SIMPLY NOT THAT STRONG,

WHO'S FAITHFUL EVEN WHEN

WE DON'T WANT HIM ALONG.

WE MAY KNOW GOD, BELIEVE

IN HIM—BUT THAT WON'T DO

UNLESS WE REALIZE THAT

WE ALSO NEED HIM TOO.

THEN, EVEN WITH SCARS OR LIMPS,

WE'LL KNOW WE'VE BEEN BLESSED STILL,

AS HE BRINGS OUR LIVES INTO

CONFORMITY TO HIS WILL.

'TWAS THE NIGHT BEFORE JESUS CAME

'TWAS THE NIGHT BEFORE JESUS CAME AND ALL THROUGH THE HOUSE
NOT A CREATURE WAS PRAYING, NOT ONE IN THE HOUSE.
THEIR BIBLES WERE LAID ON THE SHELF WITH CARE
IN HOPES THAT JESUS WOULD NOT COME BY THERE.

THE CHILDREN WERE DRESSING TO CRAWL INTO BED,
NOT ONE EVER KNEELING OR BOWING A HEAD,
AND MOM IN HER ROCKER WITH BABY ON HER LAP
WAS WATCHING A LATE SHOW WHILE I TOOK A NAP.

WHEN OUT OF THE EAST THERE AROSE SUCH A CLATTER
I SPRANG TO MY FEET TO SEE WHAT WAS THE MATTER;
AWAY TO THE WINDOW I FLEW LIKE A FLASH,
TORE OPEN THE SHUTTERS, AND THREW UP THE SASH.

WHEN, WHAT TO MY WONDERING EYES SHOULD APPEAR,
BUT ANGELS PROCLAIMING THAT JESUS WAS HERE!
WITH A LIGHT LIKE THE SUN SENDING FORTH A BRIGHT RAY
I KNEW IN A MOMENT THIS MUST BE THE DAY!

THE LIGHT OF HIS FACE MADE ME COVER MY HEAD.
IT WAS JESUS, RETURNING, JUST LIKE HE HAD SAID.
AND THOUGH I POSSESSED WORDLY WISDOM AND WEALTH,
I CRIED WHEN I SAW HIM IN SPITE OF MYSELF.

IN THE BOOK OF LIFE WHICH HE HELD IN HIS HAND
WAS WRITTEN THE NAME OF EVERY SAVED MAN;
HE SPOKE NOT A WORD AS HE SEARCHED FOR MY NAME;
WHEN HE SAID "IT'S NOT HERE" MY HEAD HUNG IN SHAME.

THE PEOPLE WHOSE NAMES HAD BEEN WRITTEN WITH LOVE
HE GATHERED TO TAKE TO HIS FATHER ABOVE;
WITH THOSE WHO WERE READY, HE ROSE WITHOUT A SOUND,
WHILE ALL THE REST WERE LEFT STANDING AROUND.

I FELL TO MY KNEES, BUT IT WAS TOO LATE;
I HAD WAITED TOO LONG AND THUS SEALED MY FATE;
I STOOD AND I CRIED AS THEY ROSE OUT OF SIGHT;
OH, IF ONLY I HAD BEEN READY TONIGHT!

IN THE WORDS OF THIS POEM THE MEANING IS CLEAR—
THE COMING OF JESUS OUR SAVIOR IS NEAR.
THERE'S ONLY ONE LIFE AND WHEN COMES THE LAST CALL
WE'LL FIND THAT THE BIBLE WAS TRUE AFTER ALL!

A TEMPLE

A TEMPLE IS A BEAUTIFUL PLACE:
LIGHTED SPIRES STRETCHING UPWARD SO TALL
AND STAINED GLASS WINDOWS—A FACE
REVEALING GOD'S BEAUTY TO ALL;

A TEMPLE IS A PEACEFUL PLACE:
THE QUIETNESS IGNORING THE MESS
AND HUBBUB OF THE OUTSIDE WORKPLACE—
ASSURED THAT GOD'S IN CHARGE, NO LESS.

A TEMPLE IS A JOYFUL PLACE:
SINGING AND FELLOWSHIP ABOUND;
HOPE AMIDST HARDSHIP SHOWS ON THE FACE,
BEYOND THE UNDERSTANDING OF THOSE AROUND.

A TEMPLE IS A HOLY PLACE:
RIGHTEOUS, MERCIFUL, JUST, AND PURE;
REALIZING IT COMES FROM GRACE
AND NOTHING WE DID, FOR SURE.

A TEMPLE IS A HELPFUL PLACE:
WHERE PEOPLE'S SPECIAL NEEDS ARE MET;
GOODS AND COMFORT GIVEN TO EASE
SUFFERING THAT CONTINUES YET.

A TEMPLE IS A LOVING PLACE:
SHARING, CARING FOR OTHERS ALWAYS,
HUGGING DEAR FRIENDS UPON MEETING,
PRAYING FOR EACH EVERY DAY.

A TEMPLE IS A SPECIAL PLACE:
PEOPLE COME FROM ALL AROUND
SEARCHING FOR ANY SORT OF TRACE
THAT GOD'S LOVE DOES ABOUND.

OUR BODIES ARE A LIVING SACRIFICE
UPON THE ALTAR EVERY DAY—
WE ARE GOD'S TEMPLE IN THE WORLD
TO HELP OTHERS ALONG THE WAY.

THE EXAMPLE

IT'S NOT JUST AN IDEA,

NO MATTER HOW FINE AND TRUE,

THAT WE CAN TRY TO LIVE BY,

BUT ONE WHO SHOWS US WHAT TO DO.

WE DON'T HAVE TO BE SO SMART

OR WISE BEYOND OUR YEARS

TO FOLLOW SOMEONE WHO SHOWS

US HE CARES ABOUT OUR TEARS.

WE DON'T HAVE TO FEEL ALONE,

OR THAT NO ONE SEEMS TO CARE—

WE HAVE SOMEONE IN EVERY TRIAL

THAT WE KNOW HAS ALREADY BEEN THERE.

YES, OUR RELIGION IS DIFFERENT,

AND IT'S NICE TO HAVE SOMEONE

TO SET THE EXAMPLE OF HOW TO LIVE—

ESPECIALLY IF IT'S GOD'S SON!

RESPONSIBILITY

THE CHURCH IS AN ARMY—

YOU MIGHT THINK THIS ODD—

IN A LIFE-AND-DEATH STRUGGLE,

ON A MISSION FROM GOD;

SO EACH ONE OF US REPRESENTS

GOD IN THE WORLD

AND ARE HELD ACCOUNTABLE

FOR EACH BOY AND GIRL

THAT MAY SEE US AND FOLLOW

WHAT WE DO EVERY DAY—

WE ARE RESPONSIBLE IF WE

CAUSE ANYONE TO STRAY;

SINNERS ARE TREATED WITH

FORGIVENESS AND GRACE,

ENABLING THEM AGAIN TO

SEE GOD FACE TO FACE;

HOW DO WE DO IT? IT'S

IMPOSSIBLE, YOU SAY?

GOD BEING IN OUR MIDST

IS THE ONLY POSSIBLE WAY!

KNOWING GOD

WE CAN NEVER FULLY KNOW GOD

OR, CERTAINLY, ALL ABOUT HIM,

BUT TO KNOW WHAT WE CAN,

AND THE KNOWLEDGE NOT BE SLIM,

WE NEED TO TALK TO HIM THROUGH PRAYER,

TO STUDY ABOUT HIM IN THE BIBLE,

TO WORSHIP HIM REGULARLY AND TO LOOK

FOR HIM IN THE LIVES OF MODERN DISCIPLES.

THEN WE'LL KNOW THAT GOD LOVES US COMPLETELY,

MORE THAN WE CAN EVER UNDERSTAND,

AND PROMISES US PEACE AND JOY AND LOVE

IF WE'LL BUT WALK WITH HIM HAND IN HAND;

WE'LL BE ABLE TO LOOK BEYOND OUR

GUILT AND SIN TO SEE HOW GOD SEES US

AND MAKES US FREE TO SPREAD THE GOSPEL

AND MINISTER TO OTHERS, AS JESUS.

KINDOM

CHRIST IS REALLY KING—

THE RULER OF OUR LIVES.

ALL THAT WE HAVE, OR

ARE, AND ALL THAT WE STRIVE

TO BE BELONG TO HIM,

AND, IF WE WANT IT BADLY,

WE CAN HELP USHER IN

THE KINGDOM, BUT SADLY,

WE USUALLY DON'T REALIZE

THAT WE'RE REALLY ALL KIN—

WE'RE ALL BROTHERS AND SISTERS

NO MATTER RELIGION OR SKIN,

AND WE'RE TO DO ALL WE CAN TO

MAKE HIS KINGDOM THUS—

REMEMBER, FOR THIS GOD GAVE

HIS BEST AND ALL—JESUS!

EXCLUSIVE

IS THE CHURCH AN EXCLUSIVE CLUB?

FOR THOSE TO WHOM COMMUNION IS DENIED,

OR ACCEPTED ONLY IF THEY HOLD CERTAIN BELIEFS,

IT DOESN'T MATTER WHETHER OR NOT CHRIST DIED.

FOR WE ARE CALLED TO BRING ALL TO GOD,

AND NOT TO KEEP PEOPLE AWAY

JUST BECAUSE THEY DON'T THINK JUST LIKE US

OR ACT LIKE THEY SHOULD IN EVERY WAY.

FOR "CHOSEN" MEANS BEING GIVEN A SPECIAL

JOB TO DO, TO COMMUNICATE

GOD'S LOVE TO ALL, NOT TO JUDGE

IF ONE'S ABLE TO PARTICIPATE

IN RECEIVING GOD'S FREE GIFT OF MERCY

AND SALVATION, FOR, YOU SEE,

IF WE EXCLUDE OTHERS IN CHURCH, THE ONES

EXCLUDED FROM HEAVEN MAY BE WE!

CHRISTMAS PRAYER

FATHER,

HELP US TO BE LIKE MARY AND JOSEPH—
WILLING TO DO WHATEVER YOU ASK,

IGNORING WHAT OTHERS MAY THINK OR SAY,
NO MATTER HOW DIFFERENT THE TASK;

HELP US TO BE LIKE THE SHEPHERDS—
SIMPLE AND PURE-HEARTED ENOUGH

TO BELIEVE THE MESSAGE GIVEN THEM
AND SEEK GOD IN A PLACE SO ROUGH;

HELP US TO BE LIKE THE ANGELS—
PRAISING GOD IN WHAT WE SAY,

JOINING WITH OTHERS LIKE-MINDED
TO GLORIFY HIM IN EVERY WAY;

HELP US TO BE LIKE THE WISE MEN—
TO STUDY AND SEARCH TO FIND

THE TRUE KING AND SAVIOR OF THE WORLD,
THEN ACT UPON WHAT'S ON OUR MIND;

AND, HELP US TO BE LIKE JESUS,
IN THE MIDST OF EACH DAY SO STARK—

TO BRING PEACE AND JOY AND FORGIVENESS
TO THOSE WHO DWELL IN THE DARK.

QUESTIONS

WHERE DO YOU GO TO FIND GOD?

NOWHERE—HE'S ALREADY FOUND YOU AND

HAS BEEN WAITING FOR YOU TO RECOGNIZE IT.

WHAT DO YOU SAY TO PLEASE GOD?

NOTHING BUT "I BELIEVE." ALL ELSE IS

UNNECESSARY AND FOLLOWS THIS.

WHAT DO YOU DO TO HEAR GOD?

NOTHING BUT WANT TO—HE'S ALREADY HERE

SPEAKING TO YOU IF YOU WILL BUT LISTEN.

WHERE DO YOU GO TO SEE GOD?

ANYWHERE—HE'S ALL AROUND YOU

IN THE BEAUTY OF THE EARTH, THE GLORY OF

THE SKY AND PEACE, JOY, AND LOVE OF PEOPLE.

HOW DO YOU LIVE TO PLEASE GOD?

HOWEVER HE WANTS YOU TO—

A MYRIAD OF DIFFERENT WAYS—

JUST BE WILLING TO PLEASE HIM IN WHATEVER YOU DO.

TURNAROUND

ONE REASON WE MAY LOVE CHRISTMAS

IS THAT IT BRINGS BACK MEMORIES

OF CHILDHOOD JOYS AT CHRISTMAS-TIME—

TOYS AND COOKIES AND BRIGHTLY-LIT TREES;

BUT CHRISTMAS IS ABOUT CHANGE, NOT

THE PAST—A CALL TO REPENTANCE.

BUT WE MAY LIKE THINGS THE WAY THEY

ARE, AND GIVE UP GOD'S ACCEPTANCE

BY OUR WISH TO BE RIGHT, NOT

FORGIVEN, FOR THAT CALLS FOR A

COMPLETE TURNAROUND—GIVING GOD

PERMISSION TO RE-SHAPE US LIKE CLAY,

PUTTING HIM IN CHARGE, NOT US—

AND LETTING HIM CHANGE US THE WAY

HE WANTS TO, SO THAT WE ARE MORE

LIKE JESUS EACH AND EVERY DAY!

SPECIAL DELIVERY

HOW DID GOD SEND TO US
HIS EMBODIMENT CALLED JESUS?

AS A HUMAN, JUST LIKE WE,
INSTEAD OF APPEARING MYSTERIOUSLY;

AT JUST THE RIGHT TIME AND
CONDITIONS, SO WE WOULD UNDERSTAND,

WHEN WE NEEDED HIM MOST,
FEELING HELPLESS AND LOST,

TO EVEN THOSE THAT NO ONE
ELSE CARED ABOUT AND WERE SHUNNED,

WHEN NOTHING ELSE WAS GETTING
THROUGH TO US, HE KEPT PERSISTING,

AT AN AWFUL, TREMENDOUS COST,
BUT WORTH IT TO SAVE THE LOST,

AS A REMINDER FROM ABOVE
THAT NOTHING SEPARATES US FROM HIS LOVE;

THAT IS HOW HE NOW SENDS US
IN BEHALF OF HIS BELOVED JESUS!

EPIPHANY

AFTER CHRISTMAS HAS COME AND GONE

WE MAY EASILY GET DEPRESSED,

GOING BACK TO THE DAILY GRIND

INSTEAD OF THAT MUCH-NEEDED REST;

THE WISE MEN APPROACHED THE CHRIST CHILD

AND WENT AWAY DIFFERENTLY—

THEY WORSHIPPED AND OFFERED GIFTS

AND EXPERIENCED EPIPHANY—

A MANIFESTATION OF THE PRESENCE

OF THE ONE WHO SITS ON THE THRONE—

UPON THEM—AND ALSO US, IF WISE,

THE GLORY OF THE LORD SHONE!

ENOUGH

WE DOUBT THAT WE HAVE ENOUGH

TO DO ALL THAT NEEDS TO BE DONE;

HOW ARE WE GOING TO SAVE THE LOST,

FEED THE HUNGRY, OR TEACH THE YOUNG?

WE FORGET THAT WE DON'T HAVE TO

DO ALL THESE THINGS ALL ALONE—

GOD IS ABLE TO DO FAR MORE

THROUGH US THAN WE CAN IMAGINE;

JESUS SHOWED A POWER THAT ALWAYS

SUSTAINED, NO MATTER THE NEED,

AND HE WILL SEE IT TO HARVEST—

WE JUST HAVE TO PLANT THE SEED!

OPPORTUNITY

WE ALL HAVE OUR FAMOUS STORIES
OF MISSED OPPORTUNITY,

AS THE RICH YOUNG RULER DID,
IN THAT WELL-KNOWN BIBLE STORY;

AS HE MISSED THE OPPORTUNITY
OF HIS (ETERNAL) LIFE

BY HIDING BEHIND HIS MONEY—
ALL WAS WELL—NO STRIFE IN HIS LIFE;

GOD DOESN'T SELL—HE GIVES
TO ALL WHO WILL RECEIVE,

IN SPITE OF WHAT WE DO—
JUST ACCEPT IT AND BELIEVE,

CLIMB ON BOARD GOD'S BUS, LEAVING
OTHER THINGS THAT RULE BEHIND,

AND GO WITH GOD INTO HIS
KINGDOM—THE BEST DEAL YOU'LL EVER FIND—

INTO A RELATIONSHIP WHERE GOD
REIGNS, WHERE HIS WILL IS DONE,

AND WE'LL FIND NOW AND FOREVER
WE'LL SHINE IN THE LIGHT OF HIS SON!

KING

IN AMERICA
ONE OF THE THINGS

WE'RE THANKUL FOR IS
NOT HAVING A KING.

BUT A KING REPRESENTS
ALL THAT IS BEST

IN A PEOPLE, ONE
WHO CAN STAND THE TEST

OF BEING THEIR MORAL
LEADER, ONE WHO

CARES ABOUT THEM,
WHOM THEY LOOK TO

FOR GUIDANCE AND HELP,
WHOM THEY REVERE

AND TRUST IN TIMES BOTH
GOOD AND SEVERE.

BUT, WHETHER WE LIKE
IT OR NOT, WE DO

HAVE A KING—A
SPECIAL ONE WHO

WALKS WITH US WHERE
WE LIVE EACH DAY—

THE KINGSHIP OF CHRIST
WE CELEBRATE TODAY!

DYING

WE THINK THAT THE KINGDOM OF GOD
WILL COME WHEN WE CLEAN UP OUR ACT,

WHEN WE BECOME GOOD ENOUGH—
BUT WE CAN'T, AND THAT'S A FACT;

SO A SAVIOR WHO WAS WILLING
TO WORK AT THE BOTTOM OF THE DRAIN

CAME TO SHOW US HOW TO LIVE,
THEN DIED TO REDEEM US AGAIN;

SO WE CAN TRY TO SAVE OURSELVES
AND END UP ETERNALLY IN HELL,

OR WE CAN TRUST IN GOD AND END
UP IN HEAVEN WITH HIM, AS WELL,

FOR, IN DYING TO THINGS ON EARTH,
WE'LL FIND, IS TRIUMPH, NOT TRAGEDY;

WE THEN CAN BE RESURRECTED BY
HIS GRACE AND LIVE WITH HIM ETERNALLY!

WEEDS

WE MAY LIVE IN THE MIDST OF A DROUGHT,

BUT WEEDS STILL SEEM TO FLOURISH THROUGHOUT;

CHURCHES, ALSO, MAY EITHER WITHER AND DIE,

OR GROW LIKE A WEED TOWARD THE HEAVENLY SKY;

THEY GROW INWARDLY THROUGH STUDY AND PRAYER,

AND OUTWARDLY BY SHOWING OTHERS THEY CARE;

FOR MORE PEOPLE HAVE A LARGER VOICE IN CARING

FOR THE HOMELESS, ENVIRONMENT, AND SHARING;

AS THERE MUST SURELY BE A PURPOSE FOR WEEDS—

SO ALSO FOR THE CHURCH—TO PLANT THE SEEDS

THAT WILL EVANGELIZE, BAPTIZE, AND TEACH

OTHERS, SO EVENTUALLY HEAVEN THEY'LL REACH!

THE LAMB

BEHOLD, THE LAMB OF GOD!

AN IMAGE OF GENTLENESS

EMERGES, SIGNIFYING

A CHANGE WROUGHT BY KINDNESS;

BUT A PURE, SPOTLESS LAMB

IS ALSO THE SYMBOL OF

SACRIFICE—ALL OUR SINS

BLOTTED OUT BY HIS LOVE;

THE LAMB BECOMES THE SHEPHERD,

GATHERING ALL OF THOSE

WHO ARE WANDERING AND LOST—

THE ONES WHOM GOD HIMSELF CHOSE!

CHURCH

WE COME TO CHURCH TO
GAIN INSIGHT FROM PREACHING;

WE COME TO CHURCH TO
LEARN MORE OF GOD'S TEACHING;

WE COME TO CHURCH TO
EXPERIENCE AND KNOW GOD BETTER,

BUT WE COME TO CHURCH
MOSTLY TO BE TOGETHER

WITH LIKE-MINDED ONES WHO
ARE CARING, HELPFUL PEOPLE—

THAT'S WHO YOU'LL FIND
UNDERNEATH A CHURCH STEEPLE—

TO SHARE THE MOST SIGNIFICANT
TIMES OF OUR LIVES AS SUCH,

WHEN WE CAN REALLY FEEL
THROUGH THEM THE SAVIOR'S TOUCH,

WHERE ONE-ON-ONE WE CAN SHARE
WHAT GOD'S DONE FOR US

AND GROW TO ENORMOUS NUMBERS
IN HEAVEN WITH JESUS!

ABIDING

ISRAEL WAS GOD'S VINEYARD IN THE WORLD,
TO BEAR THE FRUIT OF RECONCILIATION,
BUT, IT'S PLAIN, THAT THOSE WHO DON'T ARE
CUT OFF, AND, THOSE WHO DO ARE STRENGTHENED;

WE ARE NOW THE NEW ISRAEL, AND THE
KEY IS TO ABIDE IN HIM, TO KEEP IN TOUCH—
WE DO THIS BY REGULAR BIBLE STUDY, PRAYER,
WORSHIP, WORKING FOR HIM, AND SUCH;

AND IF WE ABIDE IN HIM, WE WILL ASK
FOR GOD'S WILL TO BE DONE, AND HE WILL
GIVE US WHATEVER WE NEED, HIS PURPOSE
OF RECONCILIATION TO FULFILL;

THE PRIMARY PURPOSE GOD HAS PLANTED
US IN THIS WORLD IS THAT WE
SHOULD BEAR FRUIT AND GLORIFY HIM, AND
WE CAN, IF WE'LL ABIDE IN HIM CONTINUALLY!

STRENGTH

YOU ARE OUR HELP IN ALL WE DO,

GIVING US STRENGTH TO SEE US THROUGH;

YOU NEVER FAIL; YOU'RE ALWAYS THERE.

HELP US KNOW IT, O GOD—OUR PRAYER!

COMMUNION

O COME, PLEASE COME, IMMANUEL, TO ME!
MAY MY LIFE AFTER BIRTH BE OF THEE.

YOU GIVE YOUR BODY TO ME, BECOMING A PART
OF ME, AND I TAKE IT. MAY OTHERS SEE YOU
IN ME WHEREVER I AM, DOING AS YOU WOULD DO.

YOU GIVE YOUR BLOOD TO ME, AS YOU DID
ONCE BEFORE, AND I TAKE IT. MAY YOU FLOW
IN MY LIFE-STREAM WITH EVERY HEARTBEAT—FOREVER.

YOU GIVE YOUR LIFE, AND LOVE, AND SPIRIT TO
ME, AND I TAKE IT. MAY I NOW GIVE IT TO OTHERS,
MAKING ME TRULY WITH YOU AND OF YOU—A CHRISTIAN.

DRY BONES

AS GOD MADE NEW CREATURES
OF ALL THE DRY BONES,

SO HE STILL CAN AND DOES
TO EACH AND EVERYONE

WHO LIVES JOYLESS, LIFELESS,
DRAB LIVES EVERY DAY—

THAT MAKE US EVER NEAR
THAT VALLEY PER SE;

BUT IF WE KNOW GOD
WE'RE NOT ONE OF THOSE—

WE DREAM DREAMS AND HAVE
FAITH, NOT ONE WHO CHOSE

TO LIVE JUST FOR FRIDAY;
FOR GOD TOOK SCARED MEN

AND FILLED THEM WITH THE
HOLY SPIRIT, AND THEN

THEY BECAME WITNESSES
FOR CHRIST IN EVERY WAY—

THAT'S WHAT WE'RE CALLED TO
DO ALSO TODAY!

HOMELESS

CHRISTMAS IS COMING AND HE'S AWAY FROM HOME;

HIS PARENTS DISLIKE IT, BUT THEY HAVE NO SAY;

THE CITY'S BUSTLING—TOO CROWDED WITH PEOPLE—

SO THAT HE'S HOMELESS, WITH NO PLACE TO STAY;

CHRISTMAS IS OVER, AND HE'S STILL ON THE ROAD;

NOW HIS PARENTS ARE MOVING, LEAVING ALL THEY

HAVE, FEARFULLY HEADING FOR A FOREIGN LAND,

SO THAT HE'S HOMELESS, WITH NO PLACE TO STAY;

HE NOW WANDERS AROUND, DOING WHAT HE CAN;

A FEW PEOPLE BEFRIEND HIM, MOST IGNORE HIM, SOME

TREAT HIM CRUELLY, BUT ALL LEAVE HIM ALONE

IN THE END, SO HE HAS NO PLACE TO CALL HOME;

RIGHT NOW THERE ARE MILLIONS FAR AWAY FROM HOME,

IN A FOREIGN LAND, FEARING DEATH EACH DAY;

DO THEY KNOW THAT JESUS UNDERSTANDS, THAT HE

ALSO WAS HOMELESS, WITH NO PLACE TO STAY?

JESUS IS NOW HOME, AND STILL BUSY EVERY DAY

SUMMONING ALL OF US, "COME, COME THIS WAY."

IF WE WILL BUT LISTEN AND BELIEVE, THEN WE'LL SEE

THAT HE HAS A PLACE FOR US ALWAYS TO STAY!

LIGHTS

WHY ARE TWINKLING LIGHTS PUT UP

THIS SEASON OF THE YEAR?

IT'S MORE THAN JUST A WISH TO

ALL A TIME OF GOOD CHEER:

IT'S A WAY OF CELEBRATING

A SPECIAL ONE WHO CAME

AS A LIGHT INTO THE DARKNESS—

THAT WAS HIS SPECIAL AIM;

THAT SHOULD ALSO BE OUR ROLE—

IT'S NOT OPTIONAL, I'M AFRAID;

IT MAY NOT BE A GREAT DISPLAY,

BUT SIMPLY GIVING AID,

SO OTHERS SEE THE LIGHT OF

GOD'S LOVE IN WHAT WE DO,

AND, IN THE DARKNESS ALL AROUND,

OUR LITTLE LIGHT SHINES THROUGH!

JUDGES AND KINGS

THERE WAS A TIME WHEN ISRAEL
HAD NO CENTRAL AUTHORITY,
BUT EVERY MAN DID WHAT HE THOUGHT
WAS RIGHT, AS FAR AS HE COULD SEE;

ANARCHY AND CHAOS THEREFORE
RAGED THROUGHOUT THE LAND,
SO JUDGES—REALLY MILITARY LEADERS—
WERE SENT TO BE GOD'S RIGHT HAND;

BUT THE PEOPLE THEN CLAMORED
FOR A KING TO LEAD THEM,
BUT ABSOLUTE POWER CORRUPTED THEM
ALL, LEADING FURTHER AWAY FROM HIM

WHO HAD LED THEM ALL THIS WAY,
THEIR FOCUS ON THE POLITICAL
RATHER THAN THE RELIGIOUS THAT
HAD OVERCOME EVERY OBSTACLE.

TODAY WE'RE NO DIFFERENT, PUTTING
OUR FAITH IN MANY OTHER THINGS,
WORSHIPPING OTHER IDOLS
RATHER THAN THE ONE TRUE KING!

AFTER EASTER

A CHRISTIAN IS NOT JUST ONE WHO BELIEVES,

BUT ONE WHO IS A WITNESS THAT HE LIVES:

BY WHAT WE SAY EVERY DAY,

BY HOW WE LISTEN AND HOW MUCH WE CARE,

BY WHAT WE DO IN EVERY WAY,

BY OUR PRAISE AND BY OUR PRAYER;

WE CAN UNDERSTAND HOW TO FORGIVE BY

REALIZING HOW FORGIVEN WE ARE;

WE CAN FEEL THE PEACE HE ONLY CAN GIVE BY

TRUSTING HIM TO FIGHT ALL OUR WARS;

WE CAN HAVE THE HOPE THAT HE BRINGS BY

SEEING THE ETERNAL AND NOT BEING DECEIVED;

WE CAN THEN UNDERSTAND THE BOUNDLESS JOY

THAT HE ALONE OFFERS TO ALL WHO BELIEVE!

PRAYER

PRAYER IS IMPORTANT:

IT PUTS US IN TOUCH WITH THE CONTINUING
CREATOR OF ALL THINGS;

IT ALLOWS US TO MAKE REQUESTS THAT CAN
TRULY CHANGE THINGS;

IT ALLOWS US TO BE CHANGED OURSELVES
IF THAT IS WHAT IS NEEDED ALSO;

IT ALLOWS A CHANNEL TO OPEN THROUGH WHICH
THE HOLY SPIRIT CAN FLOW;

IT CAN CLARIFY OUR THINKING ON EXACTLY
WHAT GOD WOULD HAVE US DO IN THIS LIFE;

IT CAN REASSURE US OF HIS FORGIVENESS AND
UNDYING LOVE AND PROMISE OF ETERNAL LIFE!

BUT PRAYER IS NOT ENOUGH:

IF IT DOES NOT LEAD TO ACTION ON OUR PART,
THEN WE HAVE NOT RECOGNIZED WE'VE BEEN
SENT TO SERVE THOSE WE CAN, EMPOWERED
BY THE HOLY SPIRIT TO DO SO, AND
OUR PRAYER DRIES UP
LIKE WATER ON
THE DESERT
SAND!

CONSTRUCTION WORKERS

I'M SURE THE THING THE DEVIL HATES,

WHEREVER HE MAY LURK,

IS THE SIGN SAYING "CONSTRUCTION AHEAD;

DANGER, FOR CHRISTIANS ARE AT WORK".

CHRISTIANS ARE CONSTRUCTION WORKERS—

TEARING DOWN WALLS BETWEEN EACH OTHER

THAT SATAN BUILDS TO PREVENT US

FROM SEEING EACH OTHER AS A BROTHER

AND BUILDING BRIDGES ACROSS A CHASM

THAT DIVIDES US FOR SOME REASON,

THAT LOOKED UPON FROM GOD'S VIEWPOINT

CAN ONLY BE THOUGHT OF AS TREASON.

FOR JESUS CAME TO SAVE US ALL—

ALL WHO BELIEVE IN HIM—

SO LET US WORK OUR JOB EACH DAY

TO BUILD HOPE AND FAITH WHERE IT IS DIM.

THE GIFT

IT MIGHT BE NICE TO PONDER,

AT THIS TIME OF THE BIRTH OF CHRIST,

JUST WHAT IT WAS THAT GOD DID

AND FELT AND THOUGHT AND SACRIFICED

AS HE GAVE HIS ONLY SON,

THE ONLY THING THAT WOULD SUFFICE,

TO THOSE WHO WOULD BUT BELIEVE,

NO MATTER HOW NAUGHTY OR NICE.

CONSIDER THIS TRUE SHOW OF

LOVE, AS A PIECE OF PIE YOU SLICE,

AND PRAISE GOD FOR THE GREATEST

POSSIBLE CHRISTMAS GIFT—OF CHRIST!

CLEANSING

"CHRISTENING" IS GIVING A CHRISTIAN NAME TO ONE—

"BAPTISM" IS THE CHRISTIAN CLEANSING OF ONE:

THAT WE HAVE BEEN NAMED,

THAT WE HAVE BEEN CLAIMED

BY GOD, CHOSEN BY HIM TO BE ONE

OF HIS CHILDREN, ORDAINED TO BE ONE

OF HIS MINISTERS IN ALL WE DO,

EMPOWERED BY THE HOLY SPIRIT.

WATER IS A SYMBOL OF THIS CLEANSING—

THAT WE HAVE ACCEPTED GOD'S FORGIVENESS

AND HAVE, IN HIS EYES, BECOME SINLESS.

EACH OF US BECOMES HIS BELOVED CHILD,

AND HE LOVES US MORE THAN WE CAN IMAGINE!

BAPTISM

BAPTISM IS A GIFT FROM GOD—

HIS CHOOSING US TO BE FAMILY—

THE WATER ASSURING US OF HIS

CLEANSING US OF SIN ETERNALLY.

BAPTISM NAMES US AND CLAIMS US

AS ONE OF HIS OWN CHILDREN—

THEN ORDAINS US WITH THE SPIRIT

TO SERVE HIS PEOPLE AS FRIEND.

SO, REPENT, BE BAPTIZED, AND REJOICE

IN ALL HE HAS DONE FOR YOU—

KNOW THE GOOD WORK HE HAS BEGUN

YOU CAN COUNT ON HIM TO DO!

THE MAGIC OF CHRISTMAS

WHAT IS THE MAGIC OF CHRISTMAS—

THAT MAKES US THRILL EACH TIME

WE HEAR AGAIN THE SAME OLD STORY;

THAT MAKES US SING A SONG

WE'VE SUNG SO MANY TIMES BEFORE;

THAT MAKES US GIVE UP ALL

IDEAS OF BEING A SCROOGE;

THAT HAS US LOOKING FORWARD

TO THE COMING OF SANTA CLAUS,

AND THE LOOK IN A CHILD'S EYES?

WHAT IS THE MAGIC OF CHRISTMAS?

IT'S THAT ON THIS DAY OF BIRTH

WE TOO ARE REBORN WITH THE

OVERWHELMING LOVE OF GOD!

NO ROOM

THERE WAS NO ROOM FOR YOUR BIRTH

OR YOUR LIFE—YOU WERE APART;

IS THERE NO ROOM IN THIS WIDE WORLD

FOR YOU—NOT IN ONE SINGLE HEART?

WORSHIP

LIGHTS ARE ON IN THE SMALL COUNTRY CHURCH;

THERE IS WARMTH ALTHOUGH THE HEATING FAILS.

A CHILD'S SOFT VOICE BLENDS WITH THE OFF-KEY

TONES OF AN OLD MAN—GOD IS LISTENING!

THE GREAT JOY OF CHRISTMAS

THOUGH OUR MAKER, ALL-POWERFUL—RULER HE COULD BE,

OUR GOD LOVED US SO THAT HE MADE US ALL FREE;

HE SENT US HIS SON TO SHOW US AND SAY,

"I AM YOUR FATHER AND LOVE YOU THAT WAY."

JOHN THE BAPTIST

WHAT WAS THE CROWD'S ATTRACTION TO JOHN—
HE WHO ATE LOCUSTS AND HAD SHEEPSKIN ON?

IT WAS THE INVITATION TO HEAVEN HE GAVE,
AND HE BAPTIZED PEOPLE TO SHOW THEY WERE SAVED;

FOR BAPTISM IS AN OUTWARD SIGN OF GOD'S GRACE,
THAT WE ARE NOW CLOTHED WITH RIGHTEOUSNESS;

IT IDENTIFIES US AS CHRISTIAN TO ALL,
SO REMEMBER, THE NEXT TIME YOU SEE A BABY SQUALL

AT HIS BAPTISM, THAT HE IS NOW PART OF
THE FAMILY OF GOD AND HIS SPECIAL LOVE,

AND REMEMBER YOUR OWN BAPTISM, HOW SPECIAL
THAT GOD WOULD CARE THIS MUCH FOR YOU—AND BE THANKFUL!

JESUS

WHEN WE SEE ALL THAT GOD
HAS DONE FOR US,

WE CAN ONLY LOVE HIM AND
SPEAK OF JESUS.

FOR HE ONLY IS GOD'S PLAN
FOR THE AGES,

WORTHY TO TAKE THE BOOK AND
OPEN THE PAGES;

HE IS THE LORD OF ALL
OUR HISTORY,

OUR SAVIOR—FROM SIN AND DEATH
WE'VE BEEN SET FREE—

AND SO ALL RICHES AND
GLORY AND PRAISE,

ALL HONOR AND SONGS OF
JOY THAT WE RAISE

GO TO HIM WHO IS WITH US
IN ALL OF OUR STRIFE—

OUR EXAMPLE AND GUIDE TO
EVERLASTING LIFE!

CALLED

WE ARE ALL CALLED TO BE

FISHERS OF MEN, ALTHOUGH

WE FEEL INADEQUATE

WHEN CALLED BY GOD SO;

BUT PEOPLE ARE HURTING

AND SEARCHING FOR SOUL FOOD,

IN BARS OR IN CHURCHES,

WHATEVER THE MOOD;

WE WHO HAVE RECEIVED THAT

WHICH SATISFIES THE SOUL

MUST TELL OTHER STARVING

BEGGARS OUT IN THE COLD

ABOUT THE GOD THAT SEEKS

THOSE WHOSE FUTURES ARE DIM

AND OFFERS THEM FREELY

TO LIVE FOREVER WITH HIM!

LIFE-SAVERS

DO WE, AS A CHURCH, ACT
AS A LIFE-SAVING STATION?

DO WE RECOGNIZE EACH PERSON'S
WORTH, AND GREET THEM WITH ELATION?

WE MUST INVITE ALL, OR GO OUT
AND GET THEM, EVEN IF POOR

OR DISTURBED, ANGRY, OR SICK;
WE CAN'T SHUT THE DOOR,

FOR ALL HAVE SINNED AND ARE
SAVED ONLY BY CHRIST.

THERE'S NO SUBSTITUTE FOR BEING
PART OF GOD'S WORK—IT'S NICE,

IT'S HARD HELPING OTHERS, BUT IT'S
GOOD WORK, DON'T FEAR;

WE REALLY HAVE NO CHOICE—
FOR THAT'S WHY WE'RE HERE!

THE OLD TESTAMENT

IN <u>GENESIS</u> THE WORLD BEGAN—
    'TWAS THEN THAT GOD CREATED MAN,
IN <u>EXODUS</u> THE LAW WAS GIVEN
    AS ISRAEL'S GUIDE FROM EARTH TO HEAVEN.
<u>LEVITICUS</u>—FROM LEVI'S NAME,
    THE TRIBE FROM WHICH THE PRIESTHOOD CAME.
THEN <u>NUMBERS</u> TELLS ABOUT THE WAY—
    WHAT GOD WOULD HAVE US DO AND SAY.
<u>DEUTERONOMY</u>, WHICH MEANS "TWICE TOLD",
    THE TRUTH ONCE HEARD MUST NE'ER GROW OLD.
THEN <u>JOSHUA</u> CAME IN MOSES' PLACE—
    WHEN LAW HAD FAILED, GOD BROUGHT US GRACE.
HE NEXT BY <u>JUDGES</u> ISRAEL RULED,
    HIS LOVE TOWARD THEM NEVER COOLED.
AND THEN THE STORY SWEET OF <u>RUTH</u>,
    FORESHADOWS VERY PRECIOUS TRUTH.
IN <u>FIRST SAMUEL</u> WE READ OF SAUL,
    THE PEOPLE'S KING—HIS RISE AND FALL.
IN <u>SECOND SAMUEL</u> THEN WE HEAR
    OF DAVID, MAN OF GOD SO DEAR.
IN <u>FIRST KINGS</u> THE GLORY FILLED
    THE TEMPLE SOLOMON DID BUILD.
AND <u>SECOND KINGS</u> RECORDS THE LIVES
    OF PROPHETS, KINGS, THEIR SONS AND WIVES.
IN <u>FIRST CHRONICLES</u> WE'RE SHOWN
    THE HOUSE OF DAVID AND HIS THRONE,
AND <u>SECOND CHRONICLES</u> RECORDS
    KING SOLOMON'S GOOD DEEDS AND WORDS.

THEN EZRA BUILDS GOD'S HOUSE AGAIN
    WHICH HAD FOR LONG IN RUIN LAIN,
AND NEHEMIAH BUILDS THE WALL
    'ROUND JUDAH'S CITY GREAT AND TALL.
THEN ESTHER, JEWISH MAID AND WIFE
    RAISED UP TO SAVE HER PEOPLE'S LIFE,
AND JOB, HIS PATIENCE SORELY TRIED,
    AT LAST GOD'S DEALINGS JUSTIFIED.
THEN CAME THE PSALMS, WHOSE SACRED PAGE
    IS FULL OF TRUTH FOR EVERY AGE,
THE PROVERBS WHICH THE WISE MAN SPAKE
    FOR ALL WHO WILL THEIR TEACHING TAKE.
ECCLESIASTES SHOWS HOW VAIN
    THE VERY BEST OF EARTHLY GAIN.
SOLOMON'S SONG SHOWS HOW MUCH WE NEED TO PRIZE
    THE TREASURES SET ABOVE THE SKIES.
ISAIAH, FIRST OF THE PROPHETS WHO
    FORETELLS THE FUTURE OF THE JEW,
THEN JEREMIAH, SCORNED BY FOES,
    YET WEEPS FOR FAITHLESS ISRAEL'S WOES.
THE LAMENTATIONS TELLS IN PART
    THE SADNESS OF THEIR PROPHET'S HEART.
EZEKIAL TELLS IN MYSTIC STORY
    DEPARTING AND RETURNING GLORY,
THEN DANIEL FROM THE LION'S DEN
    BY POWER DIVINE IS RAISED AGAIN.
HOSEA SHOWS THE FATHER'S HEART
    SO GRIEVED OF SIN ON EPHRAIM'S PART,
AND JOEL TELLS OF JUDGMENT NEAR,
    THE WICKED NATIONS QUAKE AND FEAR.

THEN AMOS FROM THE HERDSMEN SENT,
  CALLED HARDENED SINNERS TO REPENT.
IN OBADIAH EDOM'S FALL
  CONTAINS A WARNING WORD TO ALL.
JONAH, A PROPHET OF THE LORD,
  YET FLED TO TARSHISH FROM HIS WORD.
THEN MICAH SINGS IN SWEETEST LAYS
  THE GLORY OF MILLENIUM DAYS,
AND NAHUM TELLS THE FEAR AND GLOOM
  OF NINEVAH AND OF HER DOOM.
HABAKKUKK THOUGH THE FIG TREE FAIL,
  HIS FAITH AND TRUST IN GOD PREVAIL.
ZEPHANIAH TELLS OF GRACE
  AND LOVE THAT COMES IN JUDGMENT'S PLACE.,
AND HAGGAI IN THE LATTER DAYS
  REPEATS: CONSIDER WELL YOUR WAYS.
IN ZECHARIAH'S WONDROUS BOOK
  WE FIND EIGHT VISIONS IF WE LOOK,
THEN MALACHI, THE LAST OF ALL,
  SPEAKS SADLY STILL OF ISRAEL'S FALL.

(WITH APOLOGIES TO THE UNKNOWN AUTHOR)

THE NEW TESTAMENT

IN <u>MATTHEW</u> THE LIFE OF JESUS IS SHOWN,
HIS TEACHINGS GIVEN TO MAKE OUR OWN;

WHILE <u>MARK</u> EMPHASIZES THE DEEDS HE DID,
SHOWING HIS WORKS AND SIMPLY HOW SPLENDID;

<u>LUKE</u> SHOWS US HOW MUCH HE CARES,
HOW FULLY HUMAN YET WITHOUT ERRS,

AND <u>JOHN</u> EMPHASIZES HIS DIETY,
THE GOSPEL'S GOOD NEWS FOR ALL TO SEE;

IN <u>ACTS</u> THE SPIRIT GIVES SCARED APOSTLES REBIRTH
SO THEY CAN SPREAD THE WORD OVER ALL THE EARTH;

IN <u>ROMANS</u> GENTILES WHO BELIEVE ALSO WIN,
AS PAUL SETS FORTH SOME CENTRAL DOCTRINE;

IN <u>1ST CORINTHIANS</u> PROBLEMS ARE LIKE A SIEVE
AS PAUL INSTRUCTS US ON HOW TO LIVE;

AND <u>2ND CORINTHIANS</u> IS FULL OF LOVE
AS WE SET OUR MINDS ON THINGS ABOVE;

IN <u>GALATIONS</u> CHRIST SETS US FREE, TO BOOT,
BUT WE SHOULD USE IT TO PRODUCE FRUIT;

IN <u>EPHESIANS</u> WE HAVE WEALTH ABOVE ALL,
BUT WE MUST REMEMBER THAT IT'S SPIRITUAL;

<u>PHILIPPIANS</u> TELLS US TO REJOICE IN ALL SITUATIONS,
EVEN IN THE MIDST OF PERSECUTIONS;

FROM COLOSSIANS WE LEARN THAT CHRIST IS PRE-EMINENT
IN EVERYTHING IN THE WORLD, FOR HE WAS GOD-SENT;

1ST THESSALONIANS ASSURES US THAT, AS CHRIST ROSE ANEW,
WE WHO BELIEVE IN HIM WILL RISE AGAIN TOO;

2ND THESSALONIANS WARNS US GOD'S JUDGMENT COMES
    TO ALL MEN
AND TELLS US TO KEEP WORKING DILIGENTLY UNTIL THEN;

PAUL'S 1ST LETTER TO TIMOTHY IS A PERFECT EXAMPLE
OF WHAT IS CONSIDERED A PASTORAL EPISTLE,

AND 2ND TIMOTHY TELLS US TO BE A LEADER,
THEN GIVES ADVICE ON CONDUCT BECOMING A MINISTER;

TITUS OFFERS US, IN THE MIDST OF STRIFE,
TRAINING CONDUCIVE TO THE CHRISTIAN LIFE;

PHILEMON REMINDS US NO ONE IS TOO MUCH BOTHER—
GOD CAN CHANGE A SLAVE INTO A CHRISTIAN BROTHER;

HEBREWS IS A CALL TO A FAITH SO FINE
IN CHRIST, WHO IS BOTH HUMAN AND DIVINE;

JAMES GIVES US PRACTICAL RELIGION, WITH NO BOTHER,
WE OUGHT TO TAKE HEED—IT'S FROM JESUS' BROTHER;

1ST PETER EMPHASIZES A CALL WE HAVE
TO BECOME CHRISTIANS OURSELVES AND OTHERS HELP SAVE;

WHILE 2ND PETER GIVES US A REMEDY FOR DOUBT—
A FAITH SO STRONG WE CAN'T DO WITHOUT;

1ST JOHN IS A RECALL TO THE FUNDAMENTALS
THAT MAKE LIVING WITH GOD SO INSTRUMENTAL;

2ND JOHN BIDS US TO WALK IN THE LOVE
AND TRUTH THAT COMES ONLY FROM ABOVE;

3RD JOHN CALLS US TO HOSPITALITY,
KEEPING OUR FAITH FULL OF VITALITY;

JUDE WARNS US OF THE DANGER OF FALSE BELIEF,
WHICH CAN LEAD US TO THE POINT OF NO RELIEF;

AND REVELATION GIVES US A GLIMPSE OF THE FUTURE,
WHICH OFFERS US HOPE FOR TODAY TO NURTURE.

THE ENTIRE BIBLE WE'VE NOW GONE THROUGH—
IN POETIC SEQUENCE TO HELP RECALL—
MAY IT BE OF SERVICE TO YOU
AND BRING ETERNAL LIFE TO ALL!

MARY WAS THE ONLY ONE

WHEN GOD WAS PLANNING JESUS' BIRTH, TO SPREAD HIS
   LOVE ACROSS THE EARTH,
HE CHOSE A LADY FAIR AND MEEK AND TALKED WITH HER
   THROUGHOUT THE WEEK.

SHE WOULD NOT LISTEN, NOT AT ALL, TO THE STRANGE
   VOICES THAT WOULD CALL;
INSTEAD SHE SIMPLY TURNED HER BACK, NOT SEEING WHAT
   SHE'D ONE DAY LACK.

SO GOD CHOSE A WOMAN WHO DISPLAYED WHAT MAN ON
   EARTH SHOULD DO,
BUT WHEN HE KNOCKED ON HER FRONT DOOR, ALL SHE DID
   WAS JUST IGNORE.

THEN, WALKING ONE DAY, GOD DID SEE A WOMAN WORKING
   DUTIFULLY,
AND SO HE CALLED HER BY HER NAME—BUT AS HE CALLED,
   NO ONE CAME.

SADLY SITTING DOWN TO REST, GOD PUT HIS HAND AGAINST
   HIS BREAST,
HE HELD HIS HEART AND WONDERED WHY NOT A SOUL
   WOULD HEAR HIS CRY.

WHEN, AS A TEAR RAN DOWN HIS CHEEK, HE HEARD A VOICE
   SOFT AND WEAK
OF SOMEONE PRAYING TO BE WISE AND HEAR THE
   DESPERATE SINNERS' CRIES.

GOD FOLLOWED THIS VOICE AND THE SAME DAY SAW A
WOMAN KNEELING TO PRAY;
GOD TALKED WITH HER ABOUT HIS PLAN—JESUS BECOMING
AN EARTHLY MAN.

THE WOMAN, UNMARRIED, WONDERED HOW SHE'D
CONCEIVE RIGHT HERE AND NOW;
THEN, WITHOUT A WORD, SHE SIMPLY KNEW GOD'S PLAN
WOULD TELL HER WHAT TO DO.

A MAN WHO LOVED HER FROM HER TOWN AWAITED HER
DRESSED IN A GOWN
AND KNEW SHE WAS TO BEAR A SON NOT OF THIS WORLD—A
HEAVENLY ONE.

AS THE TIME OF BIRTH GREW NEAR, THEY HAD TO TRAVEL
FAR IN FEAR;
THEY HAD A PROMISE TO FULFILL THAT JESUS NOT A SWORD
WOULD KILL.

THEY FOUND A BARN, THE ONLY PLACE AVAILABLE TO HAVE
HIS GRACE,
SO, LATE AT NIGHT, AMONGST A CROWD—ANGELS, ANIMALS,
SHEPHERDS BOWED.

A SINGLE CRY AND STAR SO BRIGHT WAS PROOF A KING WAS
BORN THAT NIGHT.
MARY LOOKED UP IN THE SKY AND KNEW GOD WAS PLEASED
AND RIGHT NEARBY.

LATER THAT SAME FATEFUL NIGHT, BENEATH THE STAR THAT
    SHONE SO BRIGHT,
MARY WALKED CLOSELY BY GOD'S SIDE AND ASKED, AS SHE
    HAPPILY CRIED,

"MY DEAR FATHER, WHY DID YOU CHOOSE ME? THERE'S NOT
    A REASON I CAN SEE!
I'M NOT THE FAIREST ONE IN TOWN OR ROYALTY WHO
    WEARS A CROWN.

I'M JUST A SINNER, AS YOU KNOW, WHO'S YOUNG AND HAS A
    LOT TO GROW;
I'M NOT THE WOMAN I WOULD SEE BEARING A CHILD SO
    HEAVENLY."

GOD THEN REPLIED, "MY DEAR SWEET ONE, YOU DON'T
    REALIZE WHAT YOU HAVE DONE.
WHEN I QUESTIONED WHO IT COULD BE, IT WAS YOUR
    PRAYER THAT ANSWERED ME.

I CALLED OTHERS SO FAITHFULLY, BUT THEY WOULDN'T
    TRUST WHAT THEY DIDN'T SEE.
BUT YOU, DEAR MARY, PRAYED ONE THING—FOR THE
    WISDOM AND MERCY THAT I BRING

SO I KNEW THAT I COULD PICK YOU TO TRUST MY PLAN AND
    FOLLOW THROUGH,
FOR WHAT YOU PRAYED IS WHAT I GAVE—JESUS THROUGH
    YOU IS HERE TO SAVE!

Jillian Downs

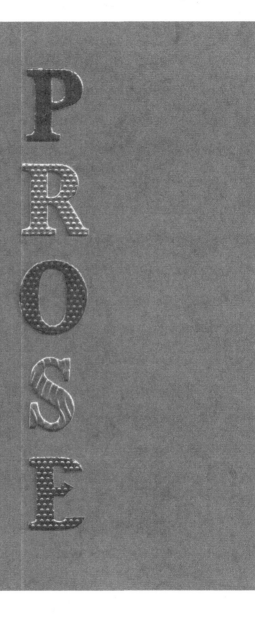

A STUDENT'S LITTLE INSTRUCTION BOOK

STUDY—THAT'S THE DEFINITION OF A STUDENT.

STUDY TO BE APPROVED BY GOD, NOT JUST YOUR TEACHER.

TRY TO DO A LITTLE MORE THAN THE TEACHER REQUIRES.

REMEMBER THAT THE TEACHER IS A PERSON TOO.

DON'T CHEAT—EVER.

TEACH SOMEONE ELSE THE IDEAS YOU'RE LEARNING.

ALWAYS RESPECT YOUR FELLOW STUDENTS.

ALWAYS RESPECT YOUR TEACHER.

LISTEN CAREFULLY IN CLASS.

WRITE DOWN WHAT YOU NEED TO—NOT EVERYTHING SAID.

KEEP YOURSELF ORGANIZED.

DO EVERY ASSIGNMENT.

SHOW YOUR WORK—NEATLY AND COMPLETELY.

WORK HARD—THEN RELAX.

DO YOUR BEST IN EVERY SUBJECT—YOU NEVER KNOW WHAT YOU MAY USE LATER IN LIFE.

DO YOUR MOST DIFFICULT HOMEWORK FIRST, IF POSSIBLE.

MAKE FRIENDS WITH OTHERS HAVING DIFFERENT CULTURES AND LEARN FROM THEM.

DON'T SAY OR FEEL YOU DON'T LIKE SOME SUBJECT.

LEARN TO TYPE.

TAKE A COMPUTER COURSE.

TAKE AN ART, DANCE, THEATER, OR MUSIC COURSE.

RAISE YOUR HAND WHEN YOU KNOW THE ANSWER.

VOLUNTEER TO PRESENT SOMETHING TO THE CLASS.

QUESTION THE TEACHER IF YOU FEEL A MISTAKE HAS BEEN MADE IN YOUR GRADE.

GO TO CLASS—ON TIME.

DRESS REASONABLY AND COMFORTABLY.

EAT BREAKFAST AND LUNCH.

MEMORIZE WHAT YOU NEED TO, BUT USE GIMMICKS TO HELP AND TRY TO MAKE SENSE OF IT, SO YOU REALLY UNDERSTAND IT.

DON'T DRINK OR USE DRUGS—YOU NEED ALL THE BRAIN CELLS YOU HAVE.

RECOGNIZE HOW MUCH TIME EACH HOMEWORK ASSIGNMENT MAY TAKE—AND PLAN ACCORDINGLY.

DON'T WAIT UNTIL THE LAST MINUTE TO DO HOMEWORK.

KEEP UP EACH DAY.

WHILE DOING HOMEWORK, LISTEN TO MUSIC YOU LIKE, BUT SOFT ENOUGH FOR YOU TO CONCENTRATE.

HAVE A GOOD LIGHT TO SEE BY WHEN STUDYING.

HAVE ALL YOUR MATERIALS HANDY.

DON'T ANSWER THE TELEPHONE WHILE DOING HOMEWORK.

USE YOUR TIME WISELY DURING A TEST.

GET PLENTY OF SLEEP THE NIGHT BEFORE A TEST.

BRIEFLY REVIEW THE MORNING OF THE TEST.

BE CALM AND CONFIDENT OF YOUR PREPARATION AND KNOWLEDGE ON A TEST.

ALWAYS BRING TWO PENCILS—AND PAPER—TO CLASS AND TO TESTS.

READ THE QUESTION.

ANSWER THE QUESTION.

GET SOME EXERCISE EACH DAY.

REMEMBER THAT NO ONE CAN TAKE AWAY WHAT YOU LEARN.

FOLLOW SCHOOL RULES CONTENTEDLY.

GET HELP FROM THE TEACHER OR ANOTHER STUDENT WHEN YOU NEED IT.

IT'S SMART TO REALIZE WHEN YOU NEED A TUTOR AND GET ONE.

DON'T LET OTHERS COPY YOUR WORK.

KEEP SCHOOLWORK IN PERSPECTIVE WITH LIFE.

REMEMBER THAT NEXT YEAR YOU PROBABLY WON'T EVEN REMEMBER THIS TEST.

ACT FRIENDLY AND INTERESTED—SO YOU MAY BECOME THAT WAY.

DO A RESEARCH PAPER ASSIGNMENT AS SOON AS POSSIBLE—DON'T PUT IT OFF.

LEARN HOW TO USE A CALCULATOR.

SIT NEAR THE FRONT OF THE CLASSROOM.

DON'T SIT NEXT TO THE BEST-LOOKING PERSON IN CLASS.

ALWAYS KNOW HOW YOU'RE DOING GRADE-WISE IN EACH CLASS.

REMEMBER YOUR GOAL—BE PURPOSEFUL IN ACHIEVING IT.

TAKE PRIDE IN STUDYING HARD AND DOING YOUR BEST.

ASSOCIATE WITH OTHER STUDENTS WHO ARE INTERESTED IN DOING WELL.

REMEMBER THAT YOU HAVE THE RIGHT TO FAIL AS MUCH AS YOU HAVE THE RIGHT TO PASS.

REMEMBER THAT THE TEACHER IS ON YOUR SIDE.

IN EACH CLASS, UNDERSTAND EXACTLY WHAT THE TEACHER EXPECTS AND HOW IT IS TO BE DONE.

USE THE RESOURCES AVAILABLE FROM A COMPUTER, BUT DON'T COPY.

LOOK AHEAD TO THE NEXT LESSON IF POSSIBLE—YOU'LL UNDERSTAND THE NEXT PRESENTATION MUCH MORE.

BE FACTUAL AND PRECISE WHEN NEEDED—CREATIVE WHEN NEEDED.

TRY TO DO ALL EXTRA CREDIT WORK GIVEN.

DO REVIEW FOR FINAL EXAMS TO REFRESH YOUR MEMORY.

MARVEL AT ALL YOU REALLY HAVE LEARNED IN SO SHORT A TIME.

PARTICIPATE IN EXTRA-CURRICULAR ACTIVITIES.

GO TO GAMES, PLAYS, AND DANCES AT SCHOOL.

DO SOME TYPE OF VOLUNTEER WORK AT SCHOOL OR IN THE COMMUNITY.

VISIT A NURSING HOME AND CHILDREN'S HOSPITAL.

WRITE A NOTE TO YOUR TEACHER THE LAST DAY OF SCHOOL.

KNOW THAT THERE IS ALWAYS MORE TO LEARN.

REALIZE YOU CAN'T LEARN EVERYTHING ABOUT ANYTHING.

DON'T NEGLECT YOUR FAMILY TO STUDY.

INCLUDE SOME SPIRITUAL KNOWLEDGE IN YOUR STUDIES.

CONTINUE TO LEARN ABOUT SOME INTEREST OF YOURS THROUGHOUT LIFE.

PURT' NEAR PERFECT

It's been over forty years since that historic breaking of the four-minute mile barrier and the subsequent lowering of the record by about ten seconds, but I figure the *real* record, established two years before Roger Bannister was even born, may never be broken. Here's the story:

"Coach Haygood, my Daddy says I should run track."

Jimmy Haygood turned around and saw the typical Arkansas farm-boy—tall, lanky, a shock of hair that had been combed down but with a rooster tail sticking up. He was dressed in a short-sleeved plaid shirt, faded blue jeans, and had on black high-top Converse sneakers.

"And why is that, son?"

"Well, on my Daddy's farm, we have a herd of cows that I have to bring in from the pasture ever' day, so me and my dog run around the field and get 'em. Sometimes, if the bull gets after me, I have to run real fast. Anyway, I've got some Indian blood in me, and though I cain't run all day like they used to, I can purt'near it. So he thought I should run track while I'm here at college."

Anyone could tell that was probably the longest he had ever talked at one time, but there was something in his eyes that struck Haygood. He had coached sports at Henderson-Brown in Arkadelphia, Arkansas, for twenty-six years, and he saw the look of something special in this obviously untrained boy. He noticed the huge chest capacity and the hard, yet long "runner"'s muscles.

"What's your name?"

"Robert, sir. Robert Harrison. But everybody calls me Harry."

"Well, Harry, let's see what you can do. Here." He reached into a box and tossed him an old faded Reddie track uniform and some track shoes. "Put these on and I'll see you on the track after you warm up."

It was a beautiful Spring day. Track season had been going for two months already, and actually would be over in another two weeks, but in

1927 things weren't as organized or regulated as they are now, so if a new player appeared on an athletic team, it was all right.

Harry walked up. "I'm ready, sir." He still had his black Converses on. "If it's okay, I'd like to run in these—I'm used to 'em."

"Have you ever run track before, Harry?"

"No, sir. Wabbaseka's too small to have a track team. So I just run track in my mind."

"And what do you run in your mind?"

"Well, I'm not too fast, unless that bull is after me, so I'm partial to the mile. I've seen people run a couple before. I've wondered why they don't just run as fast as they can the whole way."

And there the idea was born in Jimmy Haygood's mind. Here was someone so untrained he didn't even think about pacing himself over a long distance, didn't know that it was impossible . . . .

"Harry, do you think you could run as fast as you can the entire mile?"

"Purt' near it, I think. I don't see why not. It's only four times around that track, ain't it?"

Coach Haygood blew his whistle and gathered the team together for an experiment. He got his best in the 100, 220, 440, 880-yard events, and his milers, and told them to run their best race in their event against Harry, all at one time, dropping out as they finished their particular distance. He started them off, and sure enough, Harry was ten yards behind after 100 yards, still about 10 yards behind at the end of 220 yards, and at 440 yards he was about twenty yards behind. But Harry was now gliding along as effortlessly as he had the first lap, a built-in full speed ahead pace, and he continued it through the second lap, then the third, and finally the fourth, now eighty yards ahead of the other milers. He didn't have a "kick", because he ran the entire race that way.

Needless to say, his now-teammates were overwhelmed and overjoyed, as they saw this performance repeated two more times in practice that week. The last regular track meet of the season was against Southern State College, and, as Coach Haygood instructed Harry to follow his teammate for three laps, Harry won easily but no one even noticed. So it was that Robert (Harry) Harrison qualified to run in the AIC (Arkansas Intercollegiate Conference) tournament the following week, May 21, 1927.

This was where the top two qualifiers from each of the eight AIC colleges came together to determine the champions of the small colleges for the state of Arkansas for the year. It was quite a mixture of talent and uniforms—but Harry brought more than a new snickers as he limbered up in his faded red-dyed uniform and black sneakers.

The strategy for the mile hasn't changed much over the years. A "rabbit" would set a fast pace, then drop out. But when he dropped out after the first lap, there was Harry right behind—a :55 first quarter. That was the plan—to run steadily all the way. Jimmy Haygood not only had his stopwatch, he had requested three extra timers for this event, in addition to the two regular official ones. As the second lap ended, and a time of 1:50 was announced, the crowd was abuzz, but anticipating this long-legged boy to fade or drop out as the rabbit had. But Harry kept churning away as hard as he could, his arms pumping and his feet gulping up the yards, his legs not tightening as he lengthened his lead in the third quarter and started the final lap. All other activity stopped as everyone watched Harry, his face now straining but still showing a smile at the sheer joy of it all. The other runners were fifty yards behind now, as they began their kicks, hoping this "who is this hayseed?" from Henderson would soon collapse. But as Harry roared around the last turn and headed for the finish line 100 yards away, the crowd sensed that something special was happening—something no one had ever seen before and never would again—and they were on their feet, cheering their lungs out for this lad from nowhere to be able to continue, to help sweep him to victory, to . . . . And Harry never faltered a step as he crossed the finish line and was besieged by his teammates!

". . . and the time, ladies and gentlemen," the announcer was fairly shouting now, "checked by five official watches—a new world's record of 3 minutes, 40 seconds!" He had done it! The crowd sat in stunned silence for about five seconds for it to sink in, then exploded!

It was a big day for news the next day, as every minute detail of Charles Lindbergh's historic flight was covered, so the AIC track results, including the mile, appeared in the ARKANSAS GAZETTE in a one-column summary. No one else paid any attention, so it was overlooked and soon forgotten, except for the few people like me who had witnessed it. Jimmy Haygood knew what an historic event he had just seen, but being a modest man, said no more about it. As for Harry, he was pleased he had gotten to run on a real track, had won, and had made his Daddy proud. "I just ran as fast as I could" was his only quote. Track season was over, and his father died that summer, so Harry never made it back to college or ran again competitively, as far as I know. So I guess this is the only account of the "purt' near perfect" mile.

DO U C WHAT I C?

We Americans love initials! When I first heard "USA! USA!" at the 1980 Olympics hockey match, it sent chills up my spine. What other country can so powerfully, yet so succinctly, broadcast its name?

The sports world loves initials. One can score a KO, TKO, TD, PAT, K (or SO). A DH can hit a HR, RBI, or into a DP to the SS, affecting the BA (and MVP status). We follow the NFL, NBA, WNBA, NHL, MLS, NASCAR, NCAA, USTA, PGA, LPGA, WWF (& WBA, WBC, IBF champion).

We love personalities with initials. When BB hit his 73rd ball over the fence (like a bb?), he replaced MM (not the sex symbol). We want to be like MJ (not the pop star). And don't forget AJ, OJ, TO, and DR. J.

Politicians have prospered with initials—from FDR to JFK (and RFK) to LBJ (& MLK, JR.) to simply W now. The government abounds with initials—like UN, CIA, FBI, DOT, EPA, USDA, and the USMC gives their ETA for an SOS call (hopefully no MIA, POW, or DOA).

We watch ET and AI (not from MGM) on DVD or a VCR, HBO, CNN or JAG, ET, ER, and CSI on ABC, NBC, or CBS TV. We listen to EP on an old LP or CD, put a CD-ROM in our IBM PC or surf the WWW.

We take an MRI or EKG to see ASAP that we don't have ALS, MS, or HIV. We fly from JFK in NYC, NY to LAX in LA, CA or DFW in Big D, TX on AA (not TWA now). We make an A or B to take the SAT or ACT to get a BA, BS, MA, MS, PhD, or MD from VMI, MIT, or NYU.

We drive a DOHC VW, BMW, or GMC SUV (LXi) with ABS and AWD. We trade GE, AT&T, and WMT on the NYSE or NASDAQ.

We drink OJ and RC and eat at KFC, BK, or McD (not a BLT). We measure in OZ, LB, K, G, KM, M, CM, MM, YD, FT, L, or QTs. Our time is AM or PM, BC or AD. We even ID ourselves as DR, MR., MRS, or MS.

See? You actually understood everything! So, with all of these initials, I C U R OK! (I M 2.)

A FABLE

"Tremendous!" "Outstanding!" "The best I've ever seen!" So went the comments that came from anyone who had seen Tony Johnson in action. What a prospect; all were licking their chops trying to get him—the Lions, the Bears, and the Vikings. Everyone wanted Tony!

And why not? He was 6 feet 2 inches tall, 210 pounds, quick on his feet, could survey the situation in an instant and react to it, seemed to remember anything he was told or read, was cooperative, hard working, creative, handsome, and articulate! And he had just graduated from college with the highest honors possible.

The draft was loose and of little actual value in that a prospect was not required to sign with the organization that drafted him but with any group he chose, depending on location or other factors important to him and, of course, salary.

Johnson was no fool, although he didn't have an agent. He talked with everyone who had an offer, listened intently, and politely asked questions but did not commit to any one organization. He knew that his career lay ahead; he hoped that he would have many productive years before the daily requirement, the stress, the constant pounding, or an injury took their toll on his body and mind. But now he was twenty-two years old, in tip-top condition, on top of the world, loved what he was doing, and was obviously very good at it.

The day of the draft came, and so did the media. Cleveland picked Johnson as its first choice, but New York, Miami, and other organizations quickly upped the ante. Then the haggling began, and the scene resembled an old-fashioned horse trading or a Middle Eastern bazaar. Johnson simply sat quietly in the background as the principals went back and forth, upping each other's offer.

Finally the organizations had reached the limit they could offer, and the final proposals were presented to Johnson. He and his family went into another room to consider the offers and emerged some time later. Reporters rushed forward as Johnson went to a podium to announce his choice.

"I appreciate all of the wonderful offers I've received from the various cities," Johnson graciously began. "After considering them all, and other personal factors, I've made my choice. I plan to make my home nearby in the rolling countryside, which I love; there are many nearby cultural, historical, and entertainment events that I enjoy; and it will be a good place to work with an established, yet forward-looking organization. It has a great history, and I hope I can help make it have an even greater future." He seemed to be enjoying the suspense, as people mentally eliminated cities from the clues he was giving. You could have heard a pin drop.

"Of course, the money in Baltimore isn't bad either," he suddenly concluded, holding up a giant replica of a check indicating an annual salary of $6.2 million dollars, guaranteed for twenty years, for a total of $124 million!

An audible gasp was heard from the onlookers. Then the room erupted in a tumult of sound and the flash of cameras taking pictures of the check Johnson was holding while smiling broadly.

At this point, the head of the Baltimore contingent took the podium. The crowd became quiet.

"We're very happy to have some of Tony Johnson's ability as part of our team, and feel he's worth every cent that we've invested in him. Frankly, our future depends on him and others like him. He obviously brings a great deal to our organization, but what one person contributes can be much more than just what may be seen. How can you count the value of someone who does what he does so well? Who knows what influence he may have on child and adult alike as a role model, what his fellow comrades may gain from his work ethic and his professionalism, and how the country or even the world may be changed by what he both represents and imparts to others? It is with great pride and pleasure we welcome Tony as the highest-paid teacher in the world!"

A SCHOOLBOY'S PROOF OF FERMAT'S LAST THEOREM

Every person who has studied Geometry hopefully knows the Pythagorean Theorem—in a right triangle, "$a^2 + b^2 = c^2$".

Probably the most famous "unsolved" problem of the past three centuries is Fermat's Last Theorem, which says there are no positive integers "a", "b", "c", "n" such that "$a^n + b^n = c^n$," if n > 2. A brilliant mathematician, but not his chief occupation, he wrote in a book, "I have discovered a truly remarkable proof which this margin is too small to contain."

Although it was finally proved in 1994, the proof is so long and complicated that it is probably not what Fermat had in mind. What was the proof Fermat discovered? Possibly, the following:

In trying to prove something true for all natural numbers, the classic method is by "Mathematical Induction". In trying to prove something is not true, the classic method is by an "indirect proof". Combining these two methods produces this proof:

Let n = 3.

Do there exist positive integers a, b, c such that $a^3 + b^3 = c^3$, (with c>a and c> b therefore)?

Assume $a^3 + b^3 = c^3$ for some integers a, b, c.

Then $a * a^2 + b * b^2 = c * c^2$.

Thus $(a/c) * a^2 + (b/c) * b^2 = c^2$ (dividing by c).

But $(<1) * a^2 + (<1) * b^2 = c^2$. **CONTRADICTION** (to integers existing such that $a^2 + b^2 = c^2$ by the Pythagorean Theorem).

Therefore, what we assumed is incorrect—and the case for n = 3 is true (which has also been proved elsewhere).

Let n = k.

Assume there are positive integers a, b, c (with c > a and c > b) so that

$a^k + b^k = c^k$. We need to show true for n = k+1—that is, $a^{k+1} + b^{k+1} = c^{k+1}$.

But $a * a^k + b * b^k = c * c^k$, and, dividing by c,

$(a/c) * a^k + (b/c) * b^k = c^k$ and

$(<1) * a^k + (<1) * b^k = c^k$. **CONTRADICTION** to the given assumption.

Therefore what we assumed is incorrect, and thus the case for n = k+1 is true, and, by the principle of Mathematical Induction, therefore true for all natural numbers.

Therefore, for n > 2, there are no positive integers a, b, c such that

$a^n + b^n = c^n$, proving Fermat's Last Theorem.

(If a more rigorous proof for the integers is desired—if both "a" and "b" are even, both odd or one even and one odd, then working with "2n" and "2m-1", etc. by the same method, it can similarly be show to be true in all three cases.)

Thus we have a "truly remarkable" and simple proof, but a little too long to write in the margin!

GUESS WHO'S COMIN' TO TOWN?

It was Christmas Eve, there was no doubt of that. All the Christmas shows were on the 3-D TV, Christmas music flowed through all the halls, shops, and even the individual compartments of the space station, unless you turned it off yourself.

But Johnny wasn't about to do that. He had loved everything about Christmas all his life, and he was already seven! He fondly remembered the wonderful times he had had at Christmas back on Earth—Santa Claus coming, all the presents—and, of course, the true meaning of Christmas, the coming of the Christ child. His face lit up as he thought of the way he had felt that year when they had been snow-bound, and for three days he had just played games with his Mom and Dad, watched movies on the DTV, baked cookies, sung Christmas songs, and fallen asleep lying by the fireplace wrapped in his mother's arms.

But that was then, and times had changed! The awful mono-glide accident, Dad saying Mom had to stay in the hospital for a while, that he was being transferred to New Earth II to work on his experiment, and here they were! Of course, Johnny got to talk to his Mom every day over the view-phone, so he could even see she was getting better, but, still, she wasn't here. And Dad was so busy on his scientific project that Johnny was alone much of the time.

And Johnny was feeling alone. Christmas was certainly going to be lonely this year—Mom in the hospital, no shuttle either way for another two weeks, and today was Christmas Eve!

He was jolted out of his thoughts by his favorite Christmas song on the radio—"Santa Claus is Comin' to Town". He especially liked this version, by some singer a long time ago with a funny name, Bing. He went over and punched a button on the entertainment system. Immediately a piece of paper came out of a slot—the words to the song. He glanced over it. He'd tried not to cry or pout, and he'd been good, so he'd be on Santa's list. But there'd be no way Santa could reach him up here! There'd be no toys or anything else this Christmas!

The song was ending—"You mean the big fat man with the long white beard—he's comin' to town!" Johnny smiled in spite of himself.

That was still his connection between Santa and the baby Jesus who had come—the picture he had formed of God when he was younger. Old, but jolly, friendly, wanting you to be good, and always ready to give you all the presents you really wanted!

Johnny didn't want lots of presents this year—in fact, no presents would be all right if he could just have his parents with him, all snug and laughing again.

The phone rang, indicating an intercom communication. It was his Dad. "Johnny, we're right in the middle of an important experiment, so I'll be late. Go ahead and eat. I'll be there before you get to bed."

"Okay, Dad," sighed Johnny, as he hung up, knowing he would be alone for the rest of the evening. A wave of loneliness hit him and engulfed him as a wave at the ocean would. Mechanically he went to the refrigerator, got a carton out of the freezer, and put it in the microwave. After a few seconds it was ready. As he ate, he thought about what his Mom had said earlier that day as he had talked with her by view-phone back in the hospital on Earth. "Remember, I love you—and that Santa Claus is comin' to town!"

"I wonder why she said that?" he mused half aloud. Then, muttering bitterly to himself, "but no one, especially Santa Claus, is coming to this town this year!" He slumped on the couch, punched a button to turn on the DTV, and fell asleep to the late movie.

"Johnny!" He awoke with a start, then, seeing his Dad, he slowly stretched, yawned, and tried to rouse himself. "Johnny," his Dad repeated, "wake up! It's Christmas!"

"Why is he so excited about that this year?" Johnny wondered. Then, his eyes finally open, he looked around. There was a Christmas tree, all decorated—a real tree, even! He could smell its freshness! The lights were all shining brightly, the star on the top almost brilliant! And there were presents under the tree, all wrapped and looking inviting!

"How . . . . where . . . .?" Johnny started to ask, astonishment in his voice.

"Are any of those presents for me?" a voice interrupted. His Mom's voice! He whirled around—and there she really was—in person! He jumped up and ran to hug her and his beaming father.

"Mom! How did you get here?"

"Well, your father calls it 'tele-kineti-portation'. I call it a miracle, but let's just say, Santa Claus came to town!"

A CHARACTER

I grew up in a small town in Arkansas, and my doorsteps were about a hundred yards from his. As long as I knew him, Cecil Stephenson looked the same: lean, almost frail, a wrinkled face with glasses and a pug nose, and thin gray hair covered by a hat unless he was in bed (or perhaps taking a bath).

As a child, he kept me in balls as I would play and lose them. "A boy has to have a ball" he would say. I told him I would buy him one someday, and a few years ago I did, on his 70th birthday.

He was a farmer, from cotton to hay wagons, through the first machinery to harvesting rice with combines; for thirty-nine years he made a crop on 1000 acres he leased. When offered a chance to buy it, he felt he couldn't afford it and didn't. "The worse mistake I ever made," he told me. One summer while on a break from college I stayed in his home and farmed for him. He woke me up at 4 a.m. by pulling on my toe. When we got to the field at five, I wondered at all the time spent oiling and checking the tractors. "Before you do something, you've gotta get ready" was his reply.

He knew everyone in the county, and they knew him. If some boy had grown up so that he didn't recognize him now, no put-on nor embarrassment for him. A straight out "Who are you?" started them off talking about the old days, the things he'd done for them, and what they'd learned from him.

He has always been a wit and teller of yarns, and he remembered every name and date that anything happened to anyone. I would sit for hours and listen to stories, he'd look over his glasses and smile, and I'd fall laughing at his feet. I always thought he'd be terrific on those late-night shows. One example: "In our town of 300, there are three people whose mentality and speech are about that of a 4-year-old. A stranger drove into town one day. Since the river was up and he couldn't cross the ferry, he stopped someone on the street—there weren't too many—to ask how to go around. Not quite understanding the directions and gestures given by the incoherent person, he stopped another. Getting alarmed now, he made one more try—of course choosing the third "4-year-old". You could almost hear him say, "My God, what kind of town is this?" as he immediately sped away!"

A constant battle of wits with his wife brought these comments: after driving 150 miles to visit us, we asked who had driven. "She did," he replied, "I just held the wheel." Upon proven correct in one of her statements, he retorted, "Why, Bertha, you talk so much, you're bound to be right once in a while!"

He was always a unique individual. While driving in a nearby town, a police car followed him for several blocks with a flashing red light. Finally he turned in and stopped. When the policeman, who knew who it was going 10 mph, asked why he hadn't stopped earlier, he simply answered, "I hadn't got to where I was going!" No ticket—only a smile and shake of the head.

When a doctor once told him he would die from appendicitis in hours if he didn't have an operation, he stated that he didn't know what was wrong but he knew it wasn't appendicitis and went home to dig potatoes. An ulcer was later found to be the problem.

In a restaurant one time he ordered a steak—and it came cooked very rare. He looked at it and handed it back with the comment, "Why, Hell, I've seen cows sicker than this get well!" It was returned to him in a few minutes nicely done.

When I was considering marriage, he told me to be thrifty, but never try to scrimp on three things—good food, a good doctor, and lingerie for my wife. After being married now for forty-three years, I call that wise.

We had given him some stylish (then) tight pants with which to make his first trip to Washington, D. C, at the age of 79. "I had to grease my legs to get these on," he said, but he went with us. Not missing a thing, he reasoned, "I'm afraid you'll see something and won't tell me." And, commenting on the lit-up city, "They sure don't care about their electric bills here, do they?" On the way home, a freak storm allowed him to have a snowball fight with people he'd never met at a restaurant.

He could get away with things like these because he was completely free and honest. He told me you could make friends with a lion if you tried, and he could. Many times we've gone somewhere and he would simply find a place to sit and talk with someone. It didn't matter if they were 15 or 80—openings like "You look smart enough to be governor", "you look rich—how about a hundred?" or "you know, I've never seen anyone as ugly as you" would always break the ice.

He also had a special way with criticism. I remember thinking he could probably tell a man anything and the man would thank him. He simply told it exactly as it was, with no hard feelings, and when he had finished, he was still the man's friend, willing to do anything for him. I never knew anyone who was ever mad at him.

Oh, he had faults, from which I gained a lot. One of the biggest was alcohol. After ten years he decided that was enough and quit. He later told me that drinking was probably what he regretted the most having done in his life, but if seeing him the way he was when drunk had helped me to stay away from it, then it was worth it. It has been.

He never seemed a religious man, although I knew that years before he had been a mainstay in the church. But he thought about it a lot. One day when he asked me if Jesus was really all He had said He was, and I answered that I believed so, that seemed to settle it. Church still wasn't for him too much, but he knew what it meant to live justly, love mercy, and walk humbly with God.

Any old people he saw barely creeping along would draw comments like: "He's not going to be with us long," "You can hear the buzzards following him," "They're going to be carrying him off down the hill some time soon." He joked with the local undertaker, "Get your hands off me—I don't want you touching me." But recently he passed away as he had wanted—caring for himself, coming from town to check the mail, with his hat on, my picture in his billfold. Everyone loved "Mr. Cecil". But I called him "Granddaddy"!

A TALE ABOUT TAILS

I'D LIKE TO TELL YOU A TALE ABOUT TAILS—ALL KINDS OF TAILS AND TALES.

THERE ARE TALES TO HEAR—"CANTERBURY TALES" AND WAR TALES AND TALES OF ADVENTURE AND CRIME TALES AND ROMANTIC TALES AND TALES OF THE OLD WEST AND TALL TALES AND FISH TALES AND TALES OF THE SEA AND LONG TALES AND SHORT TALES AND TALES OF LONG AGO AND FUNNY TALES AND SCARY TALES AND TALES OF RICHES AND GHOST TALES AND RELIGIOUS TALES AND TALES OF SPACE AND SILLY TALES AND "THE TALE OF PETER RABBIT" AND PETER COTTONTAIL AND "A TALE OF TWO CITIES".

THERE ARE CATTAILS AND TAIL FEATHERS AND TAIL FANS AND FANTAILS AND LONG TAILS AND SHORT TAILS AND ANIMAL TAILS LIKE MONKEY TAILS AND CAT TAILS AND WAGGING PUPPY DOG TAILS AND BOBTAILS AND BIRD TAILS AND SHARK TAILS AND WHALE TAILS AND WIGGLY PIG TAILS AND ALLIGATOR TAILS AND KANGAROO TAILS AND SNAKE TAILS AND SWISHING HORSE TAILS AND COW TAILS.

THERE ARE TAILS TO WEAR—PIGTAILS AND PONYTAILS AND RATTAILS AND DUCK TAILS AND SHIRT TAILS AND TUXEDO TAILS AND DRESS TAILS, AS WELL AS TAILBONES.

THERE ARE TAILWINDS AND WINDMILL TAILS AND FLYING FOX TAILS AND TAIL FINS AND TAILSPINS AND AIRPLANE TAILS AND TAILPLANES AND TAIL ROTORS AND TAIL SKIDS AND TAIL BEAMS AND TAILORED TAILPIECES AND TAILSTOCKS AND LONG COMET TAILS AND TAILRACES AND TAILBACKS.

YOU CAN CATCH A TIGER BY THE TAIL AND FISHTAIL AND TAIL SOMEONE BY THEIR TAILLIGHTS AND TAILPIPE UNTIL YOU TAILGATE THEIR TRUCK'S TAILGATE FOR A TAILGATE PARTY. YOU CAN CALL "TAILS" AND HIGHTAIL IT OUT OF TOWN AND HAUL TAIL AND TURN TAIL AND RIDE COATTAILS AND FIND DETAILS ON RETAIL SALES AND, IN THE DEEP SOUTH, EVEN STAY AT A BUDGET "MO-TALE"—AND I'LL LET THAT BE THE TAIL END OF MY TALE!

WITH APOLOGIES TO E. B. B.

HOW DO I LOVE THEE? LET ME COUNT THE WAYS.
I LOVE THEE TO THE DEPTH AND BREADTH AND HEIGHT
MY SOUL CAN REACH, WHEN FEELING OUT OF SIGHT
FOR THE ENDS OF BEING AND IDEAL GRACE.

(I MORE THAN EXIST WHEN WITH YOU—I AM FILLED
    WITH
THE PERFECT KNOWLEDGE OF GOD'S LOVE, MERCY, AND
    HELP,
AND MY SOUL IS COMPLETELY FILLED WITH YOU.)

I LOVE THEE TO THE LEVEL OF EVERY DAY'S
MOST QUIET NEED, BY SUN AND CANDLE-LIGHT.

(YOU HAVE THE LITTLE THINGS THAT MAKE LIFE RICH
AND MEANINGFUL, EXUBERANT AND GLOWING AS THE
    SUN—
SOFT AND GENTLE AS CANDLE-LIGHT.)

I LOVE THEE FREELY, AS MEN STRIVE FOR RIGHT.

(AT ALL TIMES, IN ALL PLACES, OPENLY AND NEVER
    CEASING,
KNOWING GOD'S GREATEST PERFECTION WAITS, I LOVE
    YOU.)

I LOVE THEE PURELY, AS THEY TURN FROM PRAISE.

(HUMBLY, TRULY, WITH A QUIET, SIMPLE SINCERITY,
    FOREVER

TRUSTING AND KNOWING IT FULFILLED, I LOVE YOU.)

I LOVE THEE WITH THE PASSION PUT TO USE
IN MY OLD GRIEFS, AND WITH MY CHILDHOOD'S FAITH.

(ALL THE FEELINGS EVER FELT FOR ANYONE, OR IN MY
DREAMS,
ARE POURED FORTH TO YOU, KNOWING THAT THEY WILL
BE
UNDERSTOOD AND CARED FOR.)

I LOVE THEE WITH A LOVE I SEEMED TO LOSE WITH MY
LOST SAINTS—

(A NEW, SPECIAL ANGEL HAS BEEN GIVEN ME TO
CHERISH, ADORE,
AND RECEIVE HER WATCHFUL LOVE.)

I LOVE THEE WITH THE BREATH, SMILES, TEARS, OF ALL
MY LIFE!

(IN ALL I DO OR SAY OR THINK, JOYFUL MOODS AND SAD,
ANGER AND
REPENTANCE, INSPIRATION AND LAZINESS, THIS WILL
NEVER LEAVE ME.)

AND, IF GOD CHOOSE, I SHALL BUT LOVE THEE BETTER
AFTER DEATH.

NINE MONTHS—AND COUNTING

THE FIRST MONTH begins and ends with the stunning words of the nurse, "We'll wait to find out for sure if your wife is pregnant before we bill you." Although somewhat forewarned by her a few minutes earlier, after five years of marriage you're never quite prepared, and you try to hide the giddy, frightened shock with a straight face and calm, "Fine. Thank you."

THE SECOND MONTH makes sure. You've now asked and read and envisioned enough so that you can almost, but not quite, see yourself holding a baby. You may even see yourself changing him (you've insisted on calling it "him") some time.

You have seen her trying valiantly to remain as usual, but that's hard to do when she's either nauseous or sleeping (that's one way to diet!). You feel sorry for her and you, as you note your first extra duties as a father-to-be. You see yourself as a destitute, forgotten, slave-to-be.

THE THIRD MONTH corrects that somewhat. She's bounced back now and is giving you that special treatment as always. In fact, nothing seems different at all, and you almost forget about this change-in-your-life-to-be. And then you hear that rapid heartbeat of YOUR CHILD for the first time, and you really realize that she wasn't putting you on all this time.

THE FOURTH MONTH she starts putting it on, and loosely-fitting clothing isn't too loose. She even wears some of those maternity smocks, but, other than that, everything is normal—except she thinks she's getting uglier. A little funnier looking, perhaps, but her special glow seems to make you overlook that.

She keeps saying it's so, and finally one day you sneak up on him and, amazingly, actually feel him kicking! Build up those muscles, boy!

THE FIFTH MONTH finds those muscles building as you actually feel him kicking you in the back as you sleep. She suddenly blossoms and balloons, and you know she must be uncomfortable. You give her special treatment, not so as to spoil her, but you do find yourself lifting things for her and buying cantaloupes even though they're 'way too high. But she's still pretty much normal.

THE SIXTH MONTH finds her tiring. She can't last as long at anything without having to rest or nap, and it's much harder for her to get up out of a chair. You could play basketball with her by now, and the skin is so tight you wonder how it can possibly stretch more. It's hard for her now to relate to anything not connected in some way to the baby, home, or fixing up the room.

THE SEVENTH MONTH finds her very pleased that the room is fixed up and cute—her nest is ready. She can still work surprisingly hard at times and gets around well even though she looks burdensome. And her skin can stretch more. Swimming is her favorite past-time—I guess she floats easily. Spirit-wise she floats along on a cloud of bliss.

THE EIGHTH MONTH finds that cloud both fluffy-white and gray. She is still excitedly anticipating but is also easily irritated and just a little frightened about what the future holds for her precious-one-to-be. He shows he's pretty tough by belting her with everything he's got from the inside. I guess he's getting crowded—and ready.

THE NINTH MONTH finds her ready too. She has finally grown a little weary of being large and waiting. I still marvel at how non-incapacitated she is. She works faithfully on her exercises and breathing techniques (she's to have it by the Lamaze method—without anesthetic, with me coaching) as the countdown continues closer and closer to the estimated day of arrival.

We get to bed at 11 p.m. the night before the EDA. At 1 a.m. I'm awakened by her breathing. As she writhes in pain, she tells me the breathing exercises aren't working! We wait for the false labor pains to leave. I time the contractions and read the summary sheet to see things to look for and do. There is a definite time sequence between contractions and so I tell her when to get ready for them. Now her breathing is beginning to help, as she knows what to expect. We still wait for the contractions to end, and she changes position often. About two hours later, as they not only haven't ended but have continued at 5-minute intervals for over an hour, we decide to call the doctor to check on it.

He says to come on in to the hospital and he'll check her out. So we begin to pack her things and slowly get ready. Whose baby comes the morning of the due date (and a Saturday, when I'm off from teaching school, to boot)? Forty-five minutes later, the doctor calls back to see if we understood. I tell him we're leaving right then. She stops to have another contraction, then goes to the car, hospital, meets the doctor, has a contraction sitting in the elevator, and finally to the examination room.

The doctor tells me the baby is on the way! I dress up like a doctor (my mother should see me now!) and go to help her however I can. It's now 4 a.m.—really a good time. You've got everything in the hospital all to yourself, it seems.

She has a picture of a pretty mother and baby that I tape on the wall to help her concentrate. The nurses keep interrupting that, but she stays with it—on and on, doing beautifully. She is hurting some (maybe not even a little) and working a lot, but progress is being made. The doctor has gone to sleep down the hall as we draw nearer to the final countdown.

About 9 a.m. the nurses finally say it's coming (I'm up at Jeanie's head—I'm not that brave), and I'm wondering when they're going to take her to the delivery room and get the doctor. Finally, they do. He barely gets his equipment on in time to reach down and catch a new life being launched! I am a squeamish person, but I have never seen anything more beautiful—not at all what I expected! I only hear the doctor say, "It's a beautiful boy," as my eyes have misted over. She lies there, suddenly no longer exhausted, a big smile on her face and a l o v e l y glow about it.

The countdown has gone along and ended perfectly. Only this time the missile was sent from Heaven to Earth!

A DOUBTER'S PRAYER

I HAVE SUCH LITTLE FAITH AND TRUST, O LORD. I AM FILLED WITH DOUBT, ANXIETY, FEAR, AND HARSHNESS OVER SOMETHING I KNOW LITTLE ABOUT THAT SOUNDS HARD OR UNPLEASANT. HAVE YOU NOT ALWAYS GUIDED ME AND KEPT ME, GENTLY SHOWING ME THE PATH OF YOUR PURPOSE? AND I HESITATE AT YOUR CALLING! HELP ME TO KNOW WHAT THAT IS, SO I MAY GO FORTH GLADLY.

YOUR GRACE IS SUFFICIENT FOR ME. YOUR STRENGTH IS MADE PERFECT IN WEAKNESS. WHY DO I FEAR WHAT MAN CAN DO TO ME? IF YOU ARE FOR ME, WHO CAN BE AGAINST ME? AND, IF SO, HOW LITTLE IT MATTERS.

STRENGTHEN ME AND GRANT ME THE COURAGE TO SEIZE THIS OPPORTUNITY TO SHOW YOUR MERCY, POWER, AND LOVE. MAY YOU GROW WITHIN ME SO THAT I AM ALWAYS WITH YOU, AS YOU ARE WITH ME UNTIL THE END OF TIME.

THY ROD AND THY STAFF COMFORT AND PROTECT ME; MY CUP RUNNETH OVER WITH YOUR GRACE, LOVE, AND POWER; SURELY GOODNESS AND MERCY SHALL FOLLOW ME ALL THE DAYS OF MY LIFE, AND I SHALL KNOW THAT YOU ARE DWELLING IN ME, AND I WITH YOU, FOREVER.

AMEN.

REMEMBRANCE

It was late Fall, and the sycamore trees in front of my grandparents house had lost their large, fan-like leaves. St. Charles, Arkansas was a good place for a boy of twelve to be growing up. Located on the White River (the best catfish you ever ate comes from there), it was a small town, only 256 population, but the rice and cotton farmers didn't need much more than a grocery store, a general store, a post office, three churches, and a barber shop. (The local joke was, for a big Saturday night, go there and watch him cut hair.)

We were proud of our historic town, for it was in both RIPLEY'S BELIEVE IT OR NOT and the encyclopedias—in the center of the street was a monument erected in memory of the Union soldiers killed in the battle of St. Charles, where "the single most destructive shot of the Civil War" was fired. (A cannonball hit the boiler of a gunboat and blew up, killing 105 and wounding 44.) The old Belknap mansion still gave evidence of the war with holes and blood and names with dates scratched into its mud walls.

But that was in the past. Now, I threw a rubber ball against the front steps, grabbed the hot grounder and threw the imaginary runner out at first. It's amazing how, even though I was playing as fair as I could, the Yankees, my favorite team, were almost always able to pull it out in the last inning and win.

But baseball season was over, and it was now basketball season. The only court in town was only about thirty seconds away, and I spent hours on it. I must have gotten a foot of dirt on my hands through the years, 'cause it was a dirt court! If I kept my basketball by the back fence while doing jobs around the house, I could run over and get in five minutes of practice maybe before my mother missed me and called me home with another chore to do.

My father was Superintendent of the school there, all twelve grades in two buildings. It even closed for two days when harvest time came and deer season started, knowing that no boys would be there. But it was an important part of the community in several ways. It was the only education some of the poor farmers' or river people's children ever got. My dog

Prince probably went to school more than some—he would go with me, and if the door was closed, he'd jump from flower basket to flower basket outside the windows until he found a window open so he could come in. Daddy was also the Authority for the community. If some students needed glasses or were sick and couldn't afford a doctor, he saw that they were taken care of. If they needed discipline, he provided that. "I been there three days and I ain't said nothin' yet!" came from the wildest first grader imaginable, and it continued on through high school.

The school offered the social events for the community, as the nearest town was sixteen miles away. Wednesday night movies, a Halloween carnival, box suppers with square dancing filled the auditorium with excitement and opportunity for all. After a sixth grade school bus trip to Little Rock and the State Fair, a boy who'd never been out of town was asked, "Harry, your eyes are so red. Are you all right?" He answered, "I seed so much today I just can't see any more."

School also offered the opportunity for sports. But the only athletic team we could afford was basketball, and it was now basketball season! As I said, there was only one court in town, so the different teams had to take turn on it, and if it rained, we couldn't practice at all. Naturally, that also meant we had to play all of our games AWAY. Almyra's gym was hardly better than no gym, as the backboards were nailed to the walls and the ceiling was only as high as the top of the backboard, so if you arched your shot, it hit the ceiling and was the other team's ball. Still, we could usually beat them pretty easily.

Then one day Daddy announced (he was also the coach of the teams) that we had a game with Cotton Plant! Now that was exciting for three reasons—it was across the river, they had won the Championship for their region, and they had a large gym with an actual marble floor, I heard.

Crossing the river doesn't sound like much, but the problem was, there was no bridge or ferry at that time. St. Charles was the end of the line. It took five hours to drive around to get twenty miles on the other side of the river. Rather than do that, Daddy decided we'd cross. He had someone drive a bus around earlier in the day, then, when time came for us to go, we all simply drove down to the river, and there, waiting for us, were three boats the fishermen used each day. Four or five of us would get in a boat, they'd take us across, and then come back for another load. I still remember how cold and scary it was, especially in the dark.

But we all made it and were on our way to The Game. We arrived, and the stories about the gym were true. The Junior team (I was on) and Girls played, and then it was time for the Senior Boys to play. You could sense their concentration to play a perfect game, with no mistakes—hustling, rebounding, waiting for a good shot—the only possible chance they had to actually win. And that's how they played. I still can see Jimmy Harrison stealing the ball and going in for a lay up, how they scrapped and stayed in it until, with a minute to go, St. Charles had the ball and were only one point behind.

Determination was written on their faces as they passed the ball around again and again, looking for an opening, until Johnny Mack Price, a burly, grizzly-bear hunk of a man who'd lost a finger in a hunting accident, got the ball in the corner, went up and hung there, and then let go that four-fingered jump shot that hit the bottom of the net just as the buzzer sounded, and we had won!

I felt the warm glow of that victory all the way home, even crossing that cold river, and I knew that if preparation, determination, hard work, and faith could bring someone from the dirt to victory on the marble—anything was possible!

RANDY

I first met him when was about ten—a true Huck Finn Southern country boy with his blonde, tousled hair, freckles across his nose, barefooted, one pant leg rolled up higher than the other, a fishing pole over his shoulder as he ran to the pond to fish and back home again as his mom called him to supper, and always with a large toothy grin on his face, completely full of joy. He was the youngest of three brothers who were checking me out carefully as a suitable beau for one of their two sisters—and I believe he approved of me when I later became her husband.

When you live far away and don't see or communicate much through the years, you don't really know another person. But I do know he had a motorcycle, guns, and loved to hunt and fish like his father and brothers, he did his plumbing job to the highest standard and quality possible, he was always nice to me, and he was a friend to all, helping and laughing with them whenever possible.

He grew up to be a strong, handsome man, and I feel he did the best he could to provide for his wife and family during tough times and that he was a wonderful, loving father to a handsome son and a beautiful daughter.

Things were not easy for him through the years and they finally got even worse. Mental illness struck his wonderful son; his beloved daughter, with three children of her own, got a divorce; and then his wife left him also. Then he found out he had a rare disease. He bravely smiled as he bore the pain and watched his weight and strength waste away.

Finally, as a dear sister held his hand, his big blue eyes widened even more and he smiled his largest smile ever as he saw Jesus coming for him—and as she urged him to "run, Randy, run," he ran as fast as he could, full of joy and peace and strength once more, all the way Home.

RELIGIOUS REFLECTIONS

THE KING

A king began as a defender and protector of the people, and the people trusted and obeyed him.

Then he owned the land, and they received a portion, and they became stewards—everything they had belonged to their lord. He considered how much of what he had they would be able to keep.

Jesus is a different sort of king—no castle, no army, no land. His power comes from love—and he doesn't demand, but invites us for him to be our king and us his people. We owe everything we have to God. How much will we give to Him as an expression of our gratitude and love?

OUR CHOICE

We, like the disciples and the rich young ruler, have a choice of whether to follow Jesus or not.

We wouldn't be free to develop our character and talents if we couldn't choose our own path, so God lets us, giving His resources to help or change a pattern to complete His plan for us.

But we can choose: God, as Jesus, is either like the man hanging there on the cross or like the men who hung him there.

FEAR

"Why are ye fearful, o ye of little faith?"

The opposite of fear is not courage, but faith. It may not save us from calamity or even death, but it does save us from the fear of it. We are afraid to follow Christ because it costs too much, although we may know in our hearts it's the only way to peace and joy and life.

SALT

Salt is never used for its own benefit, but to help others:

to enhance another's flavor;
to preserve and prevent decay;
to irritate open, painful sores that continue to fester in us;
to reduce the swelling of pain and despair to allow quicker healing;
as a catalyst to help make things happen.

We, like salt, are valuable but may be invisible, as salt is naturally in foods. So we may be in our everyday actions. Who we are and what we do speak louder than what we say. There is much need for salt in our world today—has our salt lost its flavor?

THE WAY

The way to live is not just written in the text of scriptures, but in the very texture of our lives.

If we don't know where we're going, waiting to get there is even harder. Faith is the willingness to act in the midst of fear and doubt and anxiety. Faith is related to doing something—not just a feeling or thought. We are not called to do everything—but something specific and personal to us. God calls us and we respond—not to be perfect—just faithful.

We're always telling God what we can't do, instead of seeing what He can do through us. He promises to be with us, blessing us to be a blessing to others.

THE SOLID ROCK

When Christ died for us, it relieved us of our obligation to pay for our sins. We can trust and have faith in Him. We have a responsibility to a higher calling and action. We have a vision of what's going to happen, so we don't have to worry. Upon this solid rock we can stand and build our lives.

BLESSED

He is truly blessed who enthusiastically prepares to live each day—the present—to the fullest as the gift from God that it is . . . and confidently and joyfully also prepares to die so that he may truly live forever in a Heavenly paradise with Jesus.

THE HOLY SPIRIT

The Holy Spirit is present with us when we couldn't or wouldn't do things more than we can afford, deserve, try, or even hope for. Our enthusiasm for Him is God in us, the Holy Spirit at work.

The Spirit is present as:

Our Advocate—asking God to forgive our sin;
Our Comforter—giving us peace when there is none;
Our Helper—giving us what we need to do any task God asks of us;
Our Protector—guarding and saving us from countless dangerous situations;
Our Teacher—guiding us to know and live in God's way;
Our God—sent to us, covering the entire world every moment, as the wind blows, when Jesus as a man couldn't be with all of us physically.

C-H-R-I-S-T-I-A-N

C is for Christ, and the
Hope He brings to those who
Really seek Him and try
In all they do to follow and
Serve Him and others,
To always be a witness
In the best way possible to
All they meet and fill their
Needs—so they too may know God.

THE "C"s

The "C"s of Christianity do not include Control—that is in God's hands; do not include Competition—we are all brothers and not against one another; do not include Coincidences—they are God-incidences;

The "C"s of Christianity do include Cooperation—always working together with one another to do God's will; do include Concern and Compassion—actually doing works, not just saying words; do include Consecration—sealed by God as His and held in the palm of His hand; and do include the most fulfilling "C"s of all—Christ-filled and a true Child of God.

THE KINGDOM OF HEAVEN

While we can't put ourselves in God's Kingdom, He invites us there, perhaps even to the head table. It is something given to us as a gift, not what we earned—a free garbage service, all of our iniquities gathered up, bagged, and hurled into the depths of the sea. It gives us a different perspective—all of life looks different from the Kingdom of Heaven: joys are deeper, hope is always present, peace is prevalent, love is the driving force behind all we do, and death is a gate into which we walk into glory.

May we never forget the people that are not seeking the Kingdom of Heaven, so we can tell them what it is like.

COMMITMENT

Our commitment to God is not Multiple Choice—prayer, gifts, service, and presence; it is All of the Above.

Prayer: pray in the morning, at night, all through the day, continually, listing those you pray for, asking for His will in you, and thanking God for all of His blessings;

Gifts: respond to God's grace and resources for those things that require support to do His will;

Service: look for ways in which you can serve in your church and community and world;

Presence: God promises to be present with us, and our presence with Him pleases Him as He touches us in some way and offers encouragement to others—the presence of God through us is very powerful.

POWER COMPANY

It is almost impossible to imagine life today without electricity to make our lives more comfortable.

Seeking to do God's will, God will supply the power through the Holy Spirit in us, making it available to all persons and in all situations—doing works even greater than Jesus did.

We are like the power company, converting the power of the Holy Spirit into useful work and distributing it to people in need—to resist temptation, stand up for what is right, endure pain and suffering, feed the hungry, comfort the sorrowing, teach about God, and face death confidently.

Without electric power, people suffer for a while; without God's power, people suffer forever.

TRINITY

Thinking about God helps us understand Him better. God relates to us in different ways, in whatever way we need most to bring us closer to Him.

As the Father: creator, friend, husband, pastor, caretaker, the role above all.

As the Holy Spirit: comforter, strengthener, sustainer, protector—always there in time of need—whenever, wherever, however, God will be with us.

As the Son: teacher, healer, and Savior, assuring us we are forgiven, as he laid down his life to pay the price of death for our sin.

COCOON

We are into "cocooning"—retreating into our safe, comfortable homes and ways. But Jesus told us that following Him would involve risk and danger. He promises that he will protect us and strengthen us and guide us.

We promise that we will serve him—as we do unto the least, we do unto Him. If people need to be fed, hugged, healed, forgiven, our hands, God through us, will do it.

To be happy, learn how to serve—in order to find true J O Y: Jesus first, Others second, Yourself last.

●

PRAYERLESSNESS

Perhaps the only prayer Jesus prayed for himself was "If it be possible, let this cup pass from me," sweating blood at the time.

What is the reason for his agony? The fear of pain and suffering, of the temptation to save himself, of denial by all of his followers, of betrayal by those he had come to save, of death, being in a grave, losing his life with nothing remaining?

He knew the path that awaited him and why he was here, so he finished his prayer with "Nevertheless, not my will, but Thine be done." He took the guilt and sin of the entire world upon Himself, asking that they be forgiven for killing God's son.

May we pray we are open to the Spirit and do not enter into the temptation of prayerlessness. Or worse, go to God in prayer and don't rely on God after prayer, not believing what He promises us.

GOOD-BYE

It is hard to say good-bye, whether things are good or bad.

Abraham said good-bye and left his good life, land, reputation, and job to go out in faith to where he knew not, to what he knew not—to end up being a blessing to all.

The woman at the well had to say good-bye to her sad way of life, broken relationships, isolation, hatred, and failure—to receive living water that would refresh and satisfy her thirst for God forever.

May we be willing to do no less.

THE LESSON

We try to differentiate among ourselves, competing for the affection and love we see as in limited supply.

The Pharisee was a good man, and he was proud of and thanked God that he was. Seeing a sinner, he said, "There, but for the grace of God, go I." We use our goodness to feel superior, better off, and think "why me—I don't deserve it" when bad things happen.

The tax collector simply admitted his dependence upon God's grace and that he needed saving. We need to focus more on the vertical than the horizontal—that God loves and sees all men the same, all are His children, all are of sacred worth.

We don't have to compete with one another for God's attention, grace, love, forgiveness, gifts, blessings—they are there for all, for the asking.

WINNERS

Those who want to run the race before us and win must learn the fundamentals of the faith in the midst of the toughness of life—the teachings, ideals, love of life, goodness of life, joy, peace, hope, that God conquers and rules all, guides us on how to live, gives purpose to our lives, forgives us and loves us so much that He gives us salvation in spite of our actions—if we just have faith.

PERSISTENT PRAYER

More important than the words we say in prayer is the attitude—how we are to pray. Our prayers should be persistent, tenacious, unyielding—not to get what we want, but to get to know Him and His will for us better.

If nothing seems to happen—keep with it! It may transform what we ask into what is more important. God gives to us what we need to serve others—how much more will He give the Holy Spirit to enable us to do things we couldn't by ourselves.

Jesus didn't get what he wanted when he asked for the cup to pass him by, but he got what he needed—the strength and will to follow through with the purpose God had for him—to save us all.

A FOOLISH MAN

A man is foolish if he places his confidence and security in his possessions instead of God. He will never have enough money, and the pursuit of money gets in the way of other, much more important, things.

We act as if everything is ours instead of a gift—it won't belong to us when we die. If, instead, we focus on God and his love as our measure of being happy, we'll have security and happiness overflowing on the bottom line.

May we not build bigger barns, but bigger hearts to receive his love, eyes to see the needs of others, and the will to do His will for us.

THE LAW

What are our responsibilities under the law? The priest and the Levite knew the law and stuck to it; both fell short of doing what they could and should have done for someone in need.

The Samaritan followed the law of love and did what he himself could. If we look for the least we can do under the law, we lose the point of Jesus' love.

There are times when we are helpless and bleeding beside life's road. Then Jesus, like the good Samaritan, comes to pick us up, carries us, and even pays the price for us to be made whole—both now and for all eternity.

WHO ARE YOU?

"Who do you say that I am?" We have to answer the question that Jesus asks based on what we experience of God in our life. It doesn't call for a belief in God or religion in general, but for a personal, individual belief and decision—an intimate encounter with God. We have to look at ourselves and decide who we are.

You may be a businessman or wife or teacher or father or minister or politician, but are you truly a disciple of Christ? When God calls us into His service, nothing changes until we say "I'm your servant. Send me." He will, and we will be able to do things we've never thought we could do before—to actually be what He wants us to be.

THE WAY TO HEAVEN

"The way to Heaven is through the good life" is a misleading sign along the road of life. There are many wrong signs that we may read, but there are signals that we are going in the wrong direction—stress, unhappiness, discontentment, lack of joy, peace, hope, love.

Only one sign in the world says "This is enough." God's grace, freely given, is enough. We don't need more. God's grace is sufficient. God, our helper, is enough.

COMMITMENT

A lack of commitment is a big problem in our time. The church itself is not involved or concerned as it should be, and as the early church was.

Certain things hold us back from following Jesus: regret from what might have been, a sense of longing for the past and feeling that the future won't be better, and fear—a lack of trust that God can deliver what He promises.

But nothing should be more important than following Him—nothing should take His place as our God. It is time to stop "going with" Christ and time to marry—be totally committed for life, follow Jesus, with no turning back to the old ways.

WELLNESS

"If anyone suffers, it must be a punishment for their sin" was a common thought—and it still is today. God may test us to help make us strong and believe in Him more, but He does not cause us to suffer—He helps and heals us in suffering.

If God treated us as we treat Him, we would be in big trouble. We don't get what we deserve. When we are faithless, He remains faithful. God's goodness does not depend upon our goodness.

Gratitude and faith follow what God has done for us. Healed, we recognize it was because of God's blessings—an awareness of God's presence and source of strength. If we can but believe God is always with us, it will make us truly well.

FAITH

When we say "give us faith" we may really mean to "have God do things for us"—but it should be the other way around. We may feel if we do enough good things, then God owes us something. But we should realize we will always be in His debt—God gives because He loves us, not owes us.

If we believe that God has already done everything needed to save us, then we can serve Him in faith. We are not earning a reward, but expressing our gratitude for what He's already done for us. We can never do enough—no coffee break, no vacation, no retirement. We will always be able to do what God would have us to do.

Why do it? It's the most rewarding experience life has to offer, knowing He will supply whatever is needed when we are doing His will.

STEWARD

We need to realize that all things really belong to God, that we are only stewards of what He has given us—and we should be the best stewards of it that we can be. And that includes not only physical things, but our talents as well. When we think of ourselves and our talents as worthless, we reflect on Him. As the saying goes, "God don't make no junk." As the Bible say, as he created each thing, "He saw that it was good."

PINK SLIP

Many people have received a "pink slip" in their lives during perilous economic times. At that time, things can either be disastrous or opportunities, as it forces us to make a choice in life, to see what we're consumed by and what gets put aside.

It gives us a chance to reinvest our life with what is the highest priority. If we are only chasing money—although necessary for living—we can't expect more than that. We are ignoring spiritual values and the chance to receive help from God when we need it—to naturally trust and depend on Him. A pink slip may give us the time to discover why God created us and what is truly important in life.

THE LOST SHEEP

It is not easy, in a large flock, to feel warm, loved, and wanted. When we are lost, there is nothing more comforting than the knowledge that Jesus seeks us and we alone are on the receiving end of such caring.

Afterward, back with the other 99, it's easy to feel that God doesn't care for us anymore, even though we are together with others who have also been found and saved, resting in green pastures beside still waters. We have to know the lost one will receive caring from the rest of the flock, and thus we care for one another, as He cares for us.

LAW OR LOVE

The law was given to us for our protection, even though we may think of it as bad, negative, tough, harsh, punishment, whereas love may be thought of as good, positive, easy, tender, special treatment. Jesus thought the law was good, but love was better, so he extended and deepened the law. We should not kill but also should not even be angry or it is the same thing.

It may be easy to keep the letter of the law, but it's far more difficult to act in love—in fact, we can't. We can only try. God's love for us takes care of our penalty under the law—we don't have to do anything more than love God in return.

IN CHARGE

We have so much of God in us—and Satan acting on us—we sometimes act like we are God, exactly what the devil would like us to think until he can take control of our lives. We need to be reminded of who created us and everything else in the universe, who rules all the forces of nature, who is the author of love and everything good in the world, and who will ultimately actually live with us forever if we will let Him.

WAITING

As a child, it seemed forever before Christmas came. It comes much more quickly now. But, waiting, preparing for Christmas makes it more meaningful and enjoyable. Just like Christmas, we await some word from the Lord. It's easy to give up hoping for something better; there is a fear that we may not survive. In the wilderness, we need to prepare the way for the Lord to come.

Then God comes and that is the joy of Christmas—darkness becomes light, death becomes life, the wilderness becomes joy to all those who wait, believe, and endure.

THE PURPOSE OF PRAYER

We tend to feel that the purpose of prayer is to get what we want, to dial up God when we need something. In reality, the purpose of prayer is to restore our communion with God, which He wants much more than we do.

Jesus tells us that those who ask will receive, those who seek will find, and those who knock will find the door opened—if it is God we are asking, seeking, and knocking for. We will always find Him there, giving us the Holy Spirit that enables us to be closer to God, even praying for us when we don't know how. The purpose of prayer is to grow in our relationship with God, and that is the one request that will never be denied.

THE COST

Everything costs—either now or later. Belief in Jesus, instead of ourselves, is the first thing being a disciple costs. The second is doing something—go and serve, make disciples, help others, greet in hospitality, feed, clothe, heal—whatever He has for us to do. The third is a battle for Christ—situations that are painful or unpopular. Then we will be a true disciple, building for eternity.

RE-CREATION

Great moments in Biblical history are a re-creation of a Christian's life:

Creation and the Garden are our beginning as a Christian—and we too fall away.

Noah's flood shows God washing all our sins away.

Abraham's journey is our walking in faith to distant lands, willing to give all to God, and then—He sacrificing His son in our place.

Exodus represents our freedom, not by anything we did—even as we may grumble.

In the Promised Land, after being in limbo in the wilderness, God is our leader and we triumph.

The Fall of Jerusalem and Exile leave us with no hope of His promise.

The Prophets show us to wait on God to act again.

Jesus is a re-creation of the past, as he is Adam, Abraham, Moses, David, and the fulfillment of God's promises from the Prophets wrapped up in one person.

God's consummation of history will be again as it was in Eden—a perfect world, walking with God himself.

A SERMON

We may be many things:
    Merchants, bankers, and carpenters, butchers, bakers, also fishermen
    Shepherds, soldiers, and servants, draftsmen, craftsmen, noblemen
    Farmers, teachers, and holy men, mothers, fathers, and children
    Though we are from different ways of life, surely Jesus came to
        relieve our strife.

He says to love your neighbors:
    He says that we should care for those who taunt and hate us
    To forgive them we must
    He says that God will love us no matter what we do
    He says that God our Father forgives us and loves us and
    We, like the Father, should also love and forgive.

Crown Him with many crowns:
    Worker of miracles, healer of pain
    He made the blind to see, he healed the lame
    He could make soldiers quiver with fright
    He could slay armies with his great might
    He came as a lamb to the slaughter
    He came to save every son and daughter.

As we pray together:
    Father, thank You for Your love, which lets us grow from day to day
    Thank You for forgiving our sin
    Thank You for promising to be with us always
    Keep us steadfast in your will
    In all we do, in all we think, in all we say.

Go now in peace:
    Go now to share the word
    Take all the love that you've heard
    Spread it around each city and town
    That the glory of God may abound.

OUR MODEL

(A ONE ACT PLAY IN THREE SCENES)

CAST: JESUS
         JAMES, his brother
         MARY, his mother
         ANNA'S FATHER
         SERVANT GIRL
         GUESTS (scene one, scene two)
         ZACCHAEUS
         MARK
         PETER
         JAMES
         JOHN
         NARRATOR

SCENERY: Each of the scenes takes place inside a large room. Three tables are needed—one stage right, one stage left, one downstage center in the first scene, one stage right and the other two together downstage center in the second scene, and all three downstage center in the third scene.

A Narrator will introduce the play, each scene, and offer comments at the close of the play. The rest of the set will be blacked out, while a single spotlight will be on the Narrator, at these times.

NARRATOR: Today we're going to present three scenes about well-known events in the life of Jesus, put in modern-day language and filling in details as they might have occurred. Remembering that Jesus was as fully human as we are, we'd like you to especially notice his normal, everyday actions in the different situations.

The first scene takes place at a celebration—a wedding in Cana.

(SCENE 1 : A LARGE ROOM IN A HOUSE OF JESUS' DAY, WHERE
GUESTS ARE MINGLING AT A RECEPTION, EATING TIDBITS AND
DRINKING WINE.)

JAMES: Jesus! (Coming up to him) This is terrific! I appreciate
                you putting in a word with Mom for me to let me
                come too—I knew she'd listen to you.

JESUS: That's all right, James. (Joyfully greeting him) I
                figured you were old enough to come join in the
                celebration, and I haven't seen you since I've been
                on the road. And, besides, you used to play with her
                brother as much as I did Anna.

JAMES: Yes, it's good to see him again. And Anna looks so
                pretty—she's just beaming! Are you a little jealous?
                After all, she used to like you when you both were
                young and she lived in Nazareth.

JESUS: Oh, that was just a childhood crush she had on me.
                I've got other things to do, she looks very happy, and
                I'm pleased for her.

JAMES: She really was pleased to see us, I think, although
                it seems like they have more people here than they
                anticipated coming.

JESUS: I had noticed that the food trays and punch bowl
                have had to be replenished several times already.

JAMES: Especially the punch bowl! I got to try my first wine
                today. It didn't taste too good at first, but after a few
                cups it's getting better and better.

JESUS: now don't drink too much too fast—you're not
                used to it, and you don't want to get drunk the first
                time out! Remember the proverb: Wine is a mocker,

strong drink a brawler; and whoever is led astray by it is not wise.

JAMES: You're always quoting scripture to me! I'll be careful!

JESUS: please do! Anyway, you know how Mom is—she'll skin <u>both</u> of us alive if you drink too much!

JAMES: Oh, I don't know. I've seen her have several cups herself. Uh oh, maybe I spoke too soon—here she comes.

MARY: (Coming over to where they are talking) James, take it easy! Just because we're celebrating and it's free is no reason for you to try to empty the punch bowl! Remember, this is your first time, so you're not used to it like your brother. (Sidling up to Jesus) By the way, have you noticed that they're running out? I don't want them to be embarrassed.

JESUS: What's that got to do with me?

MARY: You know very well what you can do to help! (To a servant girl) Whatever he tells you to do, do it! (Looks at Jesus as a mother expecting her son to do as she wishes, then hurries away to join the other guests.)

JESUS: (to the servant girl, after pondering a moment, then coming to a decision) Fill those jars over there with water, then, when the punch bowl is empty, fill it up from them from now on.

SERVANT GIRL: (Puzzled, doubtfully, but used to obeying orders whether she understands them or not) Yes, sir.

JAMES: What are you going to do? I've heard of thinning
                          the wine with water before, but pure water? People
                          aren't that drunk yet!

JESUS: Shh! Don't say anything to anybody. Just be first in
                          line to get up both a cup when she fills it up from the
                          jars.

                          (James makes his way over toward the table, Jesus
                          to the jars that the servant girl has now filled with
                          water. He stretches his hand over the jars a moment,
                          then walks away to chat with other guests, leaving
                          the servant girl looking puzzled as she goes back to
                          serve at the punch bowl.)

                          (People have continually gone to the table for re-fills,
                          and the punch bowl is now empty. Anna's father
                          comes over to it, looks at it in despair, then hurries
                          off. The servant girl sees it's empty, so obediently
                          goes to the jars, gets one, and pours it in the punch
                          bowl. She looks at it in amazement, as does James,
                          when they recognize it is wine that has come out of
                          the jar. She then replaces the jar, looking in awe back
                          and forth at it and Jesus. She then goes and serves
                          James, first in line, at the punch bowl. James gets
                          two cups full and brings them to Jesus.)

JAMES: (Handing a cup to Jesus) How'd you do that? (as
                          they both take a sup) Wow, this is good!

                          (In the background, others, having taken a cup and
                          samples it, are also nodding their heads in approval
                          and remarking among each other.)

JESUS: Yes, it is, isn't it? (Looks pleased)

                          (Anna's father hurries in, is interrupted by a guest.)

GUEST: Most people serve their good wine first, then their other later when it doesn't matter as much what it tastes like. Why did you wait to serve the best last?

FATHER: (Rushing toward Jesus) How can I thank you enough? I don't understand how you did it, but you've saved me—and Anna—great embarrassment! Can I repay you in some way? (As Jesus shakes his head, indicating "no") I certainly owe you one!

JESUS: (laughing, reaching for the father's cup and handing him his empty one) How about this one, and we'll call it even!

              (They all laugh, as a quick blackout ends the first scene.)

(SCENE 2: A LARGE ROOM WHERE A PARTY IS GOING
ON, ONE TABLE FOR DRINKS AND A LARGER TABLE
PREPARED FOR DINNER IN THE BACKGROUND.)

NARRATOR: Our second scene take place at the home of a man Jesus found up a tree—literally—Zacchaeus! He has been invited to a party that Zacchaeus is throwing for his friends.

ZACCHAEUS: (as Jesus, Peter, and Mark enter the room, already full of other guests) Jesus! I'm so glad you actually came! Welcome, all of you!

JESUS: Thank you—it was good of you to have us on such short notice.

PETER: (looks around.) (To Jesus) If you don't mind, I think I'll wait outside for you. (Quickly leaves without a response)

ZACCHAEUS: (To Mark) Just mingle around all you like—drinks are there on the table; help yourself; we'll eat in a little while. (To Jesus) I'd like to introduce you to some people—it's such an honor having you. If you'll just come with me . . . . (to servant girl, as he starts leading Jesus by the arm) Quick! A drink for Jesus! (She gets it and hands it to him as they walk toward a group in the background.)

GUEST: (Having observed Jesus arrive, to Mark, as they get a drink at a table in the foreground) I'm surprised that Jesus came—dining with tax collectors and sinners, you know. He's got his reputation to think of!

MARK: He's not worried about that. He'd rather have a good time.

GUEST: Well, I certainly would, but, then, partying is part of my reputation. But everyone seems to think he's somebody special.

MARK: Well, he's certainly special in many ways, but he also likes to just be one of the boys from time to time.

GUEST: But what will the priests say?

MARK: Probably a lot, but they do no matter what he does, so it doesn't matter. Maybe that's another reason he came tonight.

GUEST: And what's the main reason?

MARK: Well, as I said, he like to socialize as much as you would. It helps him unwind from a hard day's work. He's got a tough schedule.

GUEST: I've heard he does—people coming to him all the time with their problems.

MARK: They do flock to him.

GUEST: It seems like he wouldn't have time to come to a party.

MARK: Something like this helps people identify with him even more, so he can work with them better—though this is fancier than most places he goes.

GUEST: I guess you're right. (Looking over at Jesus, drink in his hand, telling a joke to a group, who laugh heartily) He seems to fit right in and even be the life of the party.

MARK: Just wait awhile, when he really gets going. No one can tell a story like he can!

GUEST: I also notice that women like to be around him as much as possible. That girl's filled his cup every chance she's gotten.

MARK: Yes, they're actually his biggest supporters. They'll probably follow him all the way to his grave.

                 (Two men start a small scuffle off to the side. Jesus quickly steps between them and immediately breaks it up; the situation calms and returns to normal in seconds.)

MARK: See that? He always seems in control of himself, and the situation, no matter how much he's had to drink.

GUEST: I guess you're right. I've never heard of him being unruly. (Pauses) I guess it still just surprises me some, him being a minister and all. The priests I know . . . .

MARK:	I told you he was different—he's a <u>modern</u> minister. See? He's got you interested in him, and you haven't even heard him say a word.
GUEST:	I must say, he does look like my kind of man! I think I <u>will</u> go over and hear what he's got to say. Coming?
MARK:	Sure. (Both get another drink.) Everyone's drawn to him in the end.
	(They walk toward Jesus as a blackout ends the second scene.)

(SCENE 3: A LARGE ROOM WITH ONE LARGE TABLE IN THE BACKGROUND, SET WITH BREAD AND WINE.)

NARRATOR:	Our third scene takes place the last night Jesus was with the disciples before his crucifixion—in the upper room.
	(Jesus and some disciples are talking seriously in the background at the table, filling their cups from time to time. Two disciples are upstage right, talking and drinking.)
JAMES:	(Sarcastically) Boy, this is some cheery atmosphere!
JOHN:	Well, we <u>are</u> celebrating the Passover. It <u>should</u> be serious.
JAMES:	I know, but it's more than that. All his talk about suffering, dying, ...
JOHN:	Yeah, "This is my blood, shed for you"—and then the red wine! Why, I almost couldn't drink it!

JAMES: I know what you mean! And then he said one of us would betray him. What a downer! (Takes a big gulp from his cup.)

JOHN: Did you notice Judas couldn't take it anymore and left?

JAMES: Well, I don't blame him. It was either that or drown himself in his misery, like we're doing. (takes another big gulp from his cup.)

JOHN: But even Jesus is different tonight. He keeps filling his cup like he almost <u>wants</u> to get drunk.

JAMES: As I said before, all he's thinking about tonight is suffering, so he's just trying to ease the pain.

JOHN: "give strong drink to him who is ready to perish, and wine to him in bitter distress", the proverb goes. He does seem in bitter distress!

JAMES: Yeah, he's definitely tense tonight. Did you hear him flat out <u>tell</u> Peter that he'd deny him three times tonight? He's off sulking a bit.

JOHN: He was also pretty abrupt with <u>us</u> earlier—remember? When we asked if we could sit on his right and left when he came into his kingdom.

JAMES: When we entered Jerusalem the other day, I thought it was about to happen!

JOHN: But now . . . . he seems so depressed.

JAMES: All this traveling, crowds all the time, and criticism more and more may be getting to him. (pauses) Maybe it's good he's drinking so much tonight—it'll make him forget his worries!

JOHN:	I know, but it's already so late. If he'd just go to sleep, everything would probably be all right in the morning.
JAMES:	Yes, I'm feeling "mellow" right now myself, so I am getting a little sleepy.
JOHN:	(As Jesus gets up and comes toward them) Oh, here he comes. Maybe he's finally going to tell us all we'd better get to bed.
JESUS:	I want you two to get Peter, and come with me.
JAMES:	Where are we going?
JESUS:	Gethsemane. (Walks out resolutely)
JOHN:	Gethsemane?
JAMES:	He still looked pretty serious to me.
JOHN:	(As they prepare to go) Goodness, he's going to have us up all night, I bet! I hope I can stay awake! . . . . I still think it'd be better if he just went to bed.
JAMES:	It looks like there's no stopping him now—he's got his mind set on . . . something.
JOHN:	I'll get Peter. (Yawns, stretches.) Boy, I'd better get some sleep tomorrow night or I'll never be the same!
	(He goes, motions for Peter to come, and all three are leaving as blackout ends the third scene.)
NARRATOR:	Three well-known events in the life of Jesus, as they might have occurred. We've seen Jesus as He celebrated a special occasion, mixed socially with

people at a party, and faced suffering He didn't want to face.

This play is not necessarily meant to be enjoyed—it's offered as a challenge, and needs to be pondered. Let me help you get started.

First, it may simply have made very little sense to you. There are several small, mixed messages possible, and you may have gotten confused by it, or not seen a point at all. Think about some of the things you heard, and perhaps what I will be saying next will also help.

Second, it may have opened your eyes to a different way of looking and thinking about Jesus—and yourself. Jesus was a hearty man who loved people, being with them, and making them happy. He mixed with all sorts of common people, where they were, and this was one of the things He was criticized for by those who were too religiously wrapped up in rules and proper behavior. We need to recognize this Jesus, think about it, and see if we are too much like the Pharisees.

And third, it may have bothered, offended, or even angered you. You may know someone like this, but certainly not Jesus! We simply can't think of Jesus in this way, because he was not this way! Everyday attitudes about using alcohol are evident in the play, but more than just moderation or self-control in all things should be thought about here. Setting the best possible example, doing nothing that may cause a weaker person to fall, always wanting the best for others was Jesus' way of life. He was more than just a "good old Joe". He went wherever people were, but He didn't just become one them—He tried to raise them to become one of Him! As depicted in this play, was Jesus "our model of behavior"? If <u>not</u>, then this is not the way <u>we</u> should live either.

From Ephesians: "Be imitators of Christ, as beloved children." "Put off your old nature which belongs to your former manner of life, be renewed, and put on the new nature, created after the likeness of God." "I therefore beg you to lead a life worthy of the calling to which you have been called."

(Blackout, Curtain)

QUIZ ON THE BIBLE

(ANSWERS AT THE END)

1. HOW MANY BOOKS ARE IN THE OLD TESTAMENT?
   _____

2. HOW MANY BOOKS ARE IN THE NEW TESTAMENT?
   _____

3. WHY WAS THE FIRST ANIMAL KILLED? _____

4. THE OLDEST MAN WHO EVER LIVED WAS NAMED
   _____ . HE DIED AT THE AGE
   OF _____ .

5. ABRAHAM WAS _____ YEARS OLD WHEN HIS SON,
   _____, WAS BORN.

6. WHO SURVIVED THE GREAT FLOOD? _____WHAT
   SIGN DID GOD GIVE THAT HE WOULD NEVER DO THAT
   AGAIN? _____

7. JACOB HAD HOW MANY CHILDREN? _____

8. THE LORD PROMISED SODOM WOULD NOT BE
   DESTROYED IF _____ RIGHTEOUS PEOPLE LIVED
   THERE. WHO LOOKED BACK AND WAS TURNED INTO
   A_____? _____

9. MOSES SPENT _____ DAYS ON MT. _____
   RECEIVING THE TEN COMMANDMENTS. IN WHAT BOOK
   IS THIS RECORDED? _____

10.   _____ WAS SOLD INTO SLAVERY BY HIS BROTHERS
        FOR _____ PIECES OF SILVER. JESUS WAS BETRAYED
        FOR ____ PIECES OF SILVER.

11.   THROUGH MOSES, GOD BROUGHT ____ PLAGUES
        UPON EGYPT BEFORE THE EXODUS. NAME THEM.
        _____

12.   WHO WRESTLED WITH AN ANGEL? _____ HIS NAME WAS
        CHANGED TO ____.

13.   _____ WAS PUT IN THE DEN OF LIONS. WHY?
        _____ WHO WAS PUT IN THE FIERY FURNACE,
        UNHARMED? _____

14.   WHAT CAUSED PEOPLE TO SPEAK IN DIFFERENT
        LANGUAGES? _____

15.   SAMSON'S STRENGTH FROM _____ WAS DISCOVERED
        BY _____.

16.   DAVID   KILLED   THE   GIANT   _____. HOW?
        _____

17.   _____ WENT TO HEAVEN IN A CHARIOT; HIS
        SUCCESSOR AS A PROPHET WAS NAMED _____.

18.   NAME THE FOUR GOSPELS. _____

19.   IN WHAT BOOK IS THE LORD'S PRAYER? _____
        CHAPTER? _____ IN WHAT BOOK IS THE STORY OF
        THE PRODIGAL SON? ___ CHAP? _____ IN WHAT BOOK
        ARE THE BEATITUDES? _____ CHAPTER? _____

20.   WHO WAS THE FIRST PERSON TO KNOW JESUS HAD
        RISEN? _____

21.	WHO DENIED JESUS 3 TIMES? _____ WHO BETRAYED HIM? _____

22.	WHO WROTE "REVELATION"? _____ WHO WERE JAMES AND JUDE, THE AUTHORS OF THE BOOKS WITH THE SAME NAMES? _____

23.	PAUL'S REAL NAME WAS _____; PETER'S REAL NAME WAS _____.

24.	WHAT BOOK LISTS THE 12 APOSTLES? _____ CHAPTER? _____ NAME THEM. _____ _____ WHO TOOK JUDAS' PLACE? _____

25.	THE FIRST MARTYR WAS _____; THE FIRST GENTILE CONVERT WAS _____; FOLLOWERS OF JESUS WERE FIRST CALLED CHRISTIANS AT _____; THE APOSTLES FIRST RECEIVED THE HOLY SPIRIT _____.

ANSWERS:

1.	39, 27
2.	CAIN (GEN 4:1)
3.	TO CLOTHE ADAM & EVE (GEN 3:21)
4.	METHULELAH, 969 (GEN 5:27)
5.	100, ISAAC (GEN 21:5)
6.	NOAH, HIS WIFE, 3 SONS & WIVES; RAINBOW (GEN 7:13; 9:13)
7.	13 (GEN. 30:20,21; 35: 22-26)
8.	10, PILLAR OF SALT, LOT'S WIFE (GEN 18:32, 19:26)
9.	40, SINAI, EXODUS (EXODUS 20:2-17)
10.	JOSEPH, 20, 30 (GEN 37:28; MATT 26:15)
11.	10, RIVER TO BLOOD, FROGS, GNATS, FLIES, LIVESTOCK DIE, BOILS, HAIL, LOCUSTS, DARKNESS 3 DAYS, FIRSTBORN DIE (EX 7:17; 8:2, 16, 21; 9:3, 9, 18; 10:4, 22; 11:5)

12.   JACOB, ISRAEL (GEN. 32:24, 28)
13.   DANIEL, PRAYED TO GOD INSTEAD OF KING DARIUS; SHADRACH, MESHAK, ABEDNEGO (DAN 6:16, 3:20)
14.   BUILDING THE TOWER OF BABEL (GEN 11:9)
15.   HIS HAIR, DELILAH (J'UDGES 16:17)
16.   GOLIATH, STONE FROM HIS SLING AND CUT OFF HIS HEAD, THE PSALMS (1 SAMUEL 17:50, 51)
17.   ELIJAH, ELISHA (II KINGS 2:11, 12)
18.   MATTHEW, MARK, LUKE, JOHN
19.   MATT 6:9-13 & LUKE 11:2-4; LUKE 15:11-32; MATT 5:3-12
20.   MARY MAGDELENE (MARK 16:9)
21.   PETER (MATT 25:15), JUDAS (MATT 26:47, 48)
22.   JOHN, BROTHERS OF JESUS
23.   SAUL (ACTS 13:9), SIMON (LUKE 6:14) OR CEPHAS
24.   MATT 10:2-4, MARK 3:16-19, LUKE 6:14-16; PETER, ANDREW, JAMES, JOHN, PHILIP, BARTHOLOMEW, MATTHEW, THOMAS, JAMES, SIMON, THADDEUS, JUDAS; MATTHIAS (ACTS 1:26)
25.   STEPHEN (ACTS 7:59); CORNELIUS (ACTS 10:31 . . .); ANTIOCH (ACTS 11:26), AT PENTECOST IN JERUSALEM (ACTS 2:4)

CHRISTIAN SEMESTER EXAM

(2 CORINTHINANS 13: 5-7)

GRADE YOURSELF A, B, C, D, F ON THESE:

1.   I JOHN 4:15. DO YOU CONFESS JESUS IS THE SON OF GOD?

2.   1 JOHN 4:20, 21. HOW MUCH DO YOU LOVE GOD?

3.   1 JOHN 4:20, 21. HOW MUCH DO YOU LOVE YOUR BROTHER?

4.   I PETER 3:15. HOW PREPARED ARE YOU TO ACCOUNT FOR THE HOPE IN YOU?

5.   1 PETER 4:9. HOW HOSPITABLE ARE YOU TO OTHERS?

6.   1 PETER 5:6. HOW HUMBLE ARE YOU BEFORE GOD?

7.   1 PETER 5:7. HOW WELL DO YOU CAST YOUR ANXIETIES ON HIM?

8.   1 PETER 5:8. HOW WELL DO YOU WATCH AND RESIST TEMPTATION?

9.   1 PETER 2:1. HOW WELL DO YOU PUT ASIDE DECEIT, ENVY, AND SLANDER?

10.   1 PETER 2:20, 21. HOW WELL DO YOU SUFFER FOR WHAT'S RIGHT?

11.   JAMES 1:19, 20. HOW QUICK ARE YOU TO LISTEN, SLOW TO ANGER?

12. JAMES 1:22. HOW WELL ARE YOU A DOER OF THE WORD?

13. JAMES 4:18. HOW WELL DO YOU DRAW NEAR TO GOD?

14. JAMES 4:11, 12. HOW MUCH DO YOU RESIST JUDGING?

15. HEBREWS 13:3. HOW MUCH DO YOU REMEMBER THOSE ILL TREATED?

16. HEBREWS 13:4. HOW MUCH DO YOU HONOR MARRIAGE?

17. HEBREWS 13:5. HOW FREE ARE YOU FROM THE LOVE OF MONEY?

18. TITUS 2:4-8. HOW WELL DO YOU FULFILL THE MODEL OF CHRIST?

19. TITUS 3:1, 2. HOW WELL DO YOU SHOW COURTESY, ETC.?

20. 2 TIMOTHY 2:22. HOW WELL DO YOU AIM AT RIGHTEOUSNESS?

21. 2 TIMOTHY 3:1-5. HOW WELL DO YOU AVOID THESE TRAITS?

22. 1 TIMOTHY 2:1 HOW WELL DO YOU PRAY FOR OTHERS?

23. 1 TIMOTHY 2:8-10. HOW WELL DO YOU CONDUCT, ATTIRE YOURSELF?

24. COLOSSIANS 3:1, 2. HOW WELL DO YOU SET YOUR MIND ON ABOVE?

25. COL. 3:5. HOW WELL DO YOU PUT TO DEATH EARTHLY THINGS?

26. COL. 3:8-10. HOW WELL DO YOU NOT LIE OR SAY FOUL THINGS?

27. COL. 3:12, 13. HOW WELL DO YOU FORGIVE?

28. PHILIPPIANS 4:4. HOW WELL DO YOU REJOICE IN GOD?

29. PHIL. 4:8. HOW MUCH DO YOU THINK ON THESE THINGS?

30. EPHESIANS 6:13-17. HOW MUCH ARMOR DO YOU HAVE?

31. EPH. 6:1, 2. HOW MUCH DO YOU OBEY AND HONOR YOUR PARENTS?

32. 2 CORINTHIANS 9:6, 7. HOW CHEERFUL A GIVER ARE YOU?

33. 1 COR. 3:16. HOW MUCH ARE YOU GOD'S TEMPLE?

34. ROMANS 12:6-8. HOW WELL DO YOU USE YOUR GIFTS?

35. ROM. 12:9-21. HOW WELL, OF ALL THIS, DO YOU OVERCOME EVIL?

36. PSALM 15. HOW WELL DO YOU QUALIFY TO DWELL WITH GOD?

37. THE LORD'S PRAYER IS FOUND IN THE ____ CHAPTER OF _____, VERSES _____, IN THE _____ TESTAMENT.

38. THE TEN COMMANDMENTS ARE FOUND IN THE ____ CHAPTER OF _____, VERSES _____, IN THE _____ TESTAMENT.

39. YOU CAN NAME 10 ___, 8 ____, 6 ____, 4 ____, 2 ___ COMMANDMENTS.

41.   YOU CAN NAME 12 ___, 10 ___, 8 ___, 6 ___, 4 ___
       DISCIPLES.

XC: YOU CAN NAME ALL 66 ___, 50 ___, 40 ___, 30 ___, 20 ___
       BOOKS OF THE BIBLE.

HOW DO YOU RATE?

_____ X 4 = _____
(NO. OF As)

_____ X 3 = _____
(NO. OF Bs)

_____ X 2 = _____
(NO. OF Cs)

_____ X 1 = _____
(NO. OF Ds)

             = _____
                (TOTAL)

A TOTAL OF 144 (90%) OR HIGHER AWARDS YOU AN **A**.

A TOTAL OF 128 (80%) TO 143 GIVES YOU A VERY FINE **B**.

A TOTAL OF 112 (70%) TO 127 GIVES YOU A NICE **C**.

A TOTAL OF 96 (60%) TO 111 GIVES YOU A PASSING **D**.

A TOTAL BELOW 96 FAILS TO GIVE YOU A PASSING GRADE.

DID YOU PASS YOUR SEMESTER EXAM?

YOU HAVE ANOTHER CHANCE—GOD GIVES THE FINAL EXAM.
                          (JESUS IS THE ANSWER.)

A PRAISE OF WIFE FOR HUSBAND

Jay Downs is so very special to me for all the things he is and does. I thank God and sing God's praises for matching me to Jay. I admire and love Jay for being:

A man of God
Honest
Loving to his children
Loving to others
Faithful to God
Faithful to me
Faithful to his children
Faithful to his students
There when we all need him and expect him
Loyal to his beliefs
Loyal to God
Loyal to his family
Loyal to his employer
Slow to anger
Slow to find fault
Slow to criticize
Slow to judge
Slow to make important decisions
Slow to do his work well
Fast to get to work
Fast to see a need
Fast to direct a child
Fast to direct me
Fast to tend his little flock
Fast to attend to chores
Fast to make a living
Fast to hear our voices
Fast to sense deception
Fast to see a phony

Fast to reject a lie
Fast to stop gossip
Wise to seek God
Wise to keep His will
Wise in his counsel with his family and others
Wise in his decisions
Wise in his use of time
Wise in his consumption of food
Wise in self-control
Wise to pray
Wise to avoid straying
Wise in his desire for things
Wise in his desire for sex
Wise not to lie
Wise not to steal
Wise not to lust
Wise to read
Wise to keep learning
Wise to exercise moderation in all things
Wise in his choices
Wise in his example

Lord, you know the areas of his weaknesses—strengthen him that he may resist temptation. Expose evil lurking in the shadows ready to exaggerate his faults. Please keep sharp his awareness of self-deception that he may continue to be your servant. Please continue to bless his years that he may grow old and prosperous, giving you the song of his praises.

Thank you for the twenty years I have known this man. My love and respect for him have only increased. Forgive me for unnecessary burdens I have placed on him and the lack of sensitivity to the load he has shouldered like a noble man. Forgive me for over-indulgence in my weaknesses. Please forgive me for falling short of the supreme queen I would have like to have been. Help me, Lord, to make sufficient sacrifices that I might serve him with grace all the long days of his life. Mold me and shape me that I might be a wonderful help-mate. Please give me sensitivity to him that I can anticipate his needs and share his joy and pleasures.

Thank you for your forgiveness. Thank you for the hope, faith, and love you promise. Thank you for eternity and the taste of paradise that you provide here—a mere appetizer of what awaits us. Thank you for sharing the Essence of love with me—Jay.

Amen.

Jeanie, 18th anniversary (1986)

GROWIN' UP DOWN HOME

Everyone has a "home town"—where he or she was raised. The feelings one has are probably the same no matter where that place is, but the experience of growing up in a small town may be special—though shared by millions. I hope some of the situations and feeling I share here will be familiar to you—and bring back some fond memories of "growin' up down home."

"Down home" may automatically remind you of a small Southern town, like Andy Griffith's "Mayberry". But DeWitt, in my case, was a large town of 3000—I'm talking about St. Charles, Arkansas, population 256. The nearest doctor, drug store, or movie was eighteen miles away on a narrow road. My small town had 2 general-type stores, an ice and fish house, a barber shop, and a post office—as well as a school. St. Charles is right on the White River, and, until a ferry and finally a bridge came many years later, it was a dead end. You had to travel almost one hundred miles around to get to towns on the other side of the river. The river was the livelihood of fisherman, White River catfish the best in the world to me—but rice and cotton (and later soybean) farming on the prairie was the major activity of the area, as it had been for a hundred years.

St. Charles did have a claim to fame—a couple in fact. DeSoto passed through as he was exploring that area (some artifacts found confirmed this), and it was the site of "the single most destructive shot" of the Civil War, as the encyclopedia called it. A Union gunboat was hit by a cannonball, exploding the boiler and killing 193 sailors. Ripley's "Believe It Or Not" noted the fact that a monument to Union dead had been erected right in the middle of the street of a Southern town. Cannons were still around to crawl on, and the old Belknap mansion (a crumbling two-story dirt house) had bloodstains, bullet holes, and names and dates carved in its wall to show it had served as a hospital during the Civil War.

So, though unique in several ways, as all towns are, my home town was like thousands of other small towns—where everybody knew everybody (and would tell your parents if you did something wrong)—a wonderful place in which to grow up!

FAMILY

Although born in St. Charles (in my grandparent' house with no doctor present), we moved away for a few years during World War II, then came back when my father was appointed Superintendent of the school there and my mother second grade teacher. I was five, so my first real memories are of St. Charles. Where you grow up stays with you for a lifetime, I guess, as the setting of many of my dreams even today (with no connection whatever) are surroundings of my home town.

My father's name is Charles, so St. Charles seemed to me to be named for him. He was the epitome of what one should be to me—hard working, respected in the community, and what he said at school went. But he also loved sports and games, and I shared that love. Cards, dominoes, and Monopoly are not only fun, but ferocious battles to win. I learned to catch and throw a baseball with him, and to shoot a basketball, and many summer days we went fly fishing on Stinkin'Bay or swimming in the canal at Crockett's Bluff. Some bone-chilling days we went over to the cold school building to play ping pong as I was learning. So I guess Daddy was my role model, in many good and bad ways. (Being thrifty is wonderful, for example, but always thinking you can't do something because you can't afford it probably isn't good for you.)

Mimi, as we called my mother, was the overseer. She saw that things went right at home, were neat and clean, and taught us how to keep things that way—with lots of practice! But it must have rubbed off, because I do like a neat and orderly house today. She was the best second grade teacher in the world to me, and her energy revolved around making it so. Before I was old enough to go to school (we had no kindergarten there), I would go with her sometimes to her classroom, do things with the other students, and marvel at all the wonders that were everywhere you looked in her room. She taught me to want to learn, and to enjoy it. I remember wanting to learn to count higher, so I could do those wonderful dot-to-dot books. She was the center of our lives, everything revolved around her, and we were close—close enough for just us two, years later, to make a trip together to the World's Fair in New York.

I had one older brother, Steve. I didn't think about it then, but it may have been good for me to have had a sister too for a learning experience, and, seeing my sons with their sister, I would have enjoyed it. But I enjoyed my brother plenty. When small, he would push me around in a little car. I didn't seem to last long pushing him, so he just pushed me some more. We would spend hours in a huge sand pile making houses with our hands before pulling them out to dig tunnels through them, until finally they got smashed by a monster or washed away by a flood (hose).

We were quite different at that time (it's funny how you get more alike as you get older), me loving games and such and him only tolerating them. He was fair in sports and a good runner, but mainly creative in art and music. I think we got along pretty well, actually, because we liked and cared for each other. He must have picked on me some, because Granddaddy told him, "Just wait until he gets big enough to pick on you," and I did. He got mad once and whopped me one, and I think that stopped it from both sides. I always knew, even though I usually didn't need it, that I had a big brother to watch out for me—and he did. That's a comforting thought to a little brother anytime, but especially when just you two take a train trip to Baltimore at age ten. A small-town boy in a city needs some looking-out-after, even visiting relatives. He was probably scared and unsure too, but I never knew it and it was a comfort to me. So all my life growing up, I was very proud to have Steve as my brother.

Mama and Granddaddy, my grandparents, are central figures in my life. Besides being born in their house, which I don't remember of course, I spent many hours of every day there or around there while growing up. If I ran fast, it was twelve seconds from my back door to their front door, which had glass prisms on either side so that sunlight sprinkled rainbows on the floor of their living room.

The house itself was large—full of big rooms with tall ceilings, some special hiding places, porches where we sat in the evening, drinking milk shakes. Mama ran a grocery store located to the rear of the house, and a huge garden, chicken house, pig pen, and field lay behind this. (After seeing all of this after being grown, I'm amazed at how small things really are, that looked so large to me then. If a child only comes up to your waist, things are big to them, I guess.)

Since Mimi was late getting home most days, and food was Mama's specialty in life, she cooked and I carried our supper home many school evenings. And Sunday lunch was always there—with fried chicken and ham, at least five vegetables and three desserts. She had so much I could pick what I liked, so I didn't learn to eat a big variety, but I sure grew up healthy on those wonderful home-cooked meals.

Mama was always ready for a picnic, and she might just stop beside the road with Steve and me, get out her goodies, and we'd have a grand time there. Going to DeWitt always included a stop at the drug store for a milk shake (she liked a lime), and I couldn't mow the yard for too long before she'd appear with something cold and "good for you" to drink.

Granddaddy was a rice farmer, overseeing a thousand acres it seemed like. (His biggest mistake, he said later, was not buying that land when it was almost shoved on him to do so.) I would ride with him in the late afternoon to pick up the "hands" from the field, or to DeWitt, or up to the post office to get the mail. I did that from the time I was five; he was proud and glad to have me ride with him, and I learned to drive in that truck.

He was a man who knew how to tell a story, and commonplace happenings, as he told them, left you rolling in the aisle. He was a good and gentle and kind as anyone you could ever meet. "You can make friends with a lion, if you try," he'd say, and he never met a stranger—they were just people he didn't know yet. But I also learned two important lessons from him in a negative way. His smoking stifled me, so I never started smoking, and he became a different person when he drank alcohol. As a child, seeing someone you love become different, staggering to his bed where he would sleep for the rest of the day, is devastating. I didn't understand it; I only know I hated the alcohol that made him like that, and that has remained with me to this day, as I see or hear of it repeated countless times every day.

Auntie, Mimi's sister, still lived at home there a couple of years when I was very young. We had a special liking for each other, and I was her dog "Jip" when we played and "Jaybird" all of my life to her. A wonderful time we shared on occasion was when I would spend the night at Mama and Granddaddy's and get to sleep with Auntie. We would read in bed a while and have a snack (crackers were a favorite, but not very nice to sleep on later) before going to sleep. She also made me milkshakes a good bit, and could open the refrigerator and pick up things with her toes, which I thought was neat, but one night she was very sleepy when she went to make me a milkshake and accidentally used buttermilk instead! (I don't recommend it.) She still laughs at the face I made!

I was the ring bearer when she got married, and she has never forgotten me or my family in the years since. Silver Auntie (because of her hair and a gift of silver each year after I got married) was just another special part of the love and nurturing I received while growing up.

FRIENDS

My first recollection, when we had just moved back to St. Charles, is sitting in the sand pile, hearing "Hi," looking up, and there was Sammy. His yard was three giant steps from mine, and little did I know that he would be my best friend and almost constant companion for the next nine years. He was a year younger than I, and his sister a year older, so the four of us (with Steve) had many good times together. We'd always see what they got for Christmas as soon as we could, they'd join us at the movies in DeWitt (at 14 cents each)—for meanness, we got to where we would wait until Sammy invariably said, "I wish I could go" before inviting them—and all four of us could ride Old Pet (the true old gray mare) at one time.

In a small town, we knew everyone, of course, and I'd go to their house to play some, but usually everyone would end up at our place. Large groups would come to play "War", usually in the gullies near our house, all day or all week even with ongoing battles, or we would play "Cowboys"—complete with saloon in the chicken house. We sold little glasses of water and crackers, (Steve always the boss, Nancy the saloon girl, and I always had to be the good guy with my Peacemaker, like my heroes, Roy Rogers and the Lone Ranger.) Stick horses made from mop handles with cord tied around them for reins lined up at the saw-horse hitching rails, and when we had play fights, people loved to tumble over them backwards as if knocked over them. The movies had nothing on us, as we imitated everything we'd seen last Saturday.

The only time anyone got hurt was playing Indians with real bows and reeds as arrows. We got the bows so strong the reeds would shatter against the chicken house, and Glenn got hit in the eye. (He could see, but wore glasses from then on. How stupid we were!)

I don't even know where most of these old friends are now, but that's not something you think about when you are young. You just enjoy them—and I did.

GIRLS

Add a "late bloomer" to someone shy with little knowledge of girls, and, as you can imagine, you come up with very little, girl-wise. For a long time, I simply had no interest in girls, as I was consumed by sports, play, school, etc. When I finally did become curious, I was so shy there was simply no hope. I would go early with Daddy to the movies he showed on Wednesday nights at school, find a good seat, then wish Jeanne would come sit by me when she came. Naturally, she never did. Classic Charlie Brown! (Boys, don't be that way. She really did want to sit with me, but I made it too hard for her. Think of the other person instead of yourself, and that may help.)

Another time, all the children got to play outside the school one night while a meeting was going on. I'm not sure how it started (some girls for sure), but the game was for the girls to chase the boys, and if caught, she got to kiss him. Well, most of the time Jimmy and I hid in a ditch where we could see all the running around, but nobody could see us. We were finally discovered, and off we took. Lou Ann raced after me, but I was determined no girl could catch me. We must have gone two hundred yards, and I was getting tired and ready to stop, when she did, and then she turned around and walked back. I guess that did it, because she never was interested in me again, although we were always friends. (She never know that she was the only one I would have liked to have caught me, and how much I'd wished she had.)

Of course, those were the days of "Spin the Bottle" (of course, I was still too fast to catch.) and "Post Office". The parties I went to were few, and what did I do? I was the "Postmaster", or "You just walk around the house with Jay." Sandra, though, either hadn't gotten the word or was determined to change things. She called for a "Special Delivery" from me, and, as we went into the night, I could tell this was it. But fate stepped in, or at least I did, right in a big mud puddle, ruining our shoes, pants, and her big chance. (It really was an accident!) I've wondered since how things might have been different (possible better or possibly worse) in later years if I had kissed someone during this time (instead of finally three years later), and how a small, insignificant event could really possibly change the course of your life, whatever it may be.

I also think it's good to be particular, and I was—but possibly too much—for some good, fun times were lost because I chose not to go somewhere, rather than go with someone who was only a friend or who chiefly only liked me. It may have been unfair to them to have gone, or it may have been wonderful for them, but it led to some lonely times for me.

SPORTS

I loved games and sports of all kinds! My parents would have a big Canasta night weekly, and I would watch until I had to go to bed (too early). I learned Old Maid, Fish, Slapjack, Hearts, and on up until I could also play a nice Canasta game. Dominoes was THE game that was always going at Granddaddy Downs' when we visited there, and I remember how big I felt when I could actually join the men in a game and hold my own.

Monopoly would take up all Sunday afternoon sometimes, as the bargaining got cut-throat, and Joe would swear we'd all ganged up on him. And reading a Hardy Boys book, rocking away and eating Puffed Wheat at the rate of the action was an enjoyable activity. But, when it came down to it, what I loved most was something to do with a ball!

I had several versions of baseball I could play. With friends by the side of our house, we designated that tree for first base, the big one for second, put something down for third, and where the paths crossed was home. It was about an acre in size, but if you hit it hard enough over short, it would go down the road and was a sure home run. This, and watching the grown-ups play on Sunday (where the farmers transformed into winning ballplayers over neighboring towns), actually led us to have a PONY

League baseball team one year. I played second base, being a good fielder but not possessing a strong arm, and hit lead-off. I was small, watched well for strikes, and timid enough not to swing wildly, so I got walked a lot. But we had a good team and went through our schedule undefeated, and finally we were to meet the only other undefeated team for the championship. They were tough and had a good, fast pitcher.

As I came up to bat at the start of the game, the first pitch was a bullet down the middle. I reacted, blasted it over the center fielder's head for a triple, and we were on our way. Hey, if he can hit it like that, we certainly can! We blew them away (they must have been rattled also) and actually got to go to Little Rock for the State Tournament. There a case of big-field-with-lights jitters and a curve ball we had never seen before quickly sent us home, but it had been a great season.

There were also simpler baseball games I played alone. The front steps on Mama's house were concrete, three feet high and six feet wide, and made a marvelous batter for a rubber ball. Inning by inning, I would pitch against the steps, play the grounder and make the imaginary pitch to first, judging if safe or out. It also gave easy pop-ups, a line drive, or even sometimes all the way over me, which could be a home run if I didn't get to it in time. Game after game, with me playing fielders for both teams, were played on those steps, and I usually got finished before a foul ball would fly back against the screen door and Mama would call for me to stop. A rug placed right in the middle of the steps became strikes if I only wanted a "pitcher" game with only walks and strikeouts. I spent many an hour entertaining myself at those steps.

In front of their house was a dirt road, which would be freshly graveled from time to time. A cut off mop handle made a perfect bat, and the rocks were balls. I would now bat for both teams, doing the sportscast in my head as Mickey Mantle would come to bat, this time batting left-handed. I sprayed rocks all over that field, tossing them up and slamming them with that mop handle, again judging if a hit or an out. The Yankees were my favorite team, and it's remarkable how they would come from behind in the last inning and win, even I told myself I was trying to be fair—maybe I was just working harder since I wanted them to win.

If it was raining, not to fear. A dishcloth makes a wonderful, safe ball, and if I folded it right, I could almost make it curve or drop or be a fast ball. I loved that, since I couldn't do it with a real baseball and liked to win by out-thinking rather than overpowering an opponent. Daddy would play this game with me, with certain places the dishcloth would land being designated singles, doubles, and so forth. The bat? A dish towel, of course! It could send the dishcloth soaring twenty feet or so. A wonderful moment: Daddy up, one run behind, last of the ninth, two outs, bases loaded, two strikes. I'd wind up and throw it—and watch it unfold, catch the wind, stop, flutter, and drop as he swung away for strike three, and we would die laughing!

The side of our house was perfect for softball, and the front was for football. The football games were touch or "gentle" tackle usually (with no protection of any kind, it's a wonder someone didn't get hurt, but no one ever did), and plays usually had to be passes. With Lynn cutting across and Dickie going deep, we could beat most teams three on three, even though we were smaller. Whoever got 100 points first won, then we'd rest awhile and start all over again. (If alone, I'd pass the ball, run down and try to catch it, then pretend being tackled or not, but I couldn't keep that up for long like baseball.)

Basketball was my other great love. We only had one dirt court at school, and it was about one hundred yards from our house. I started playing when I was so small I couldn't get the ball up to the rim "pump-handle" style. But finally I did, and over the years developed a set shot from anywhere on the court and worked on a jump shot for when I was older. My hands stayed black from the dirt off the court that got on the ball. After school and on week-ends, I would hide my basketball out in the yard, so that when I got through doing a chore for Mimi I could run out, get my ball, run over to the court and shoot a few before she discovered I had finished that job and called me to do another.

A great joy was when I was actually old enough to play on the St. Charles Wildcats junior basketball team in the sixth grade. I was small, but fast, and passed well, played defense well, and shot pretty well. (Daddy was the coach of all the teams also, and he always had me play against one of the biggest players, it seemed.) Having only a dirt court, we couldn't play any games at home, of course, and there were no schools our size anywhere close to play, so we played very few. It was always nice to play Almyra though, as they were only about an hour away, and they always had a weak team, so you knew everyone would get to play. Their gym was so small the free throw circles touched the center circle, there was one foot of out-of-bounds space on three sides and only about four on the side where the teams sat. If you went in for a lay-up, the wall was only one foot away, and the ceiling was about fifteen feet high, so you couldn't arch your shot much at all. But it was a gym, and it was nice to win a few games.

There were some teams across the river that we could play, but, again, transportation was a problem. So Daddy got someone to drive a school bus around to the other side of the river, and we boated across, two or three at a time, in some of the fishermen's boats. It was so dark and cold usually that I'm sure someone would have drowned if he had fallen in, but nobody did, and we were again able to play teams only thirty minutes away. (We moved away when I started the ninth grade, but I'm sure this laid the groundwork for my basketball playing there, finally culminating in our team winning the District tournament my Senior year, but that's another story.)

If it happened to be raining or too cold to get out and play real basketball, a small rubber ball came to the rescue. We had cornices over our windows in our house, and they were about eight inches from the ceiling and stuck out from the wall about three inches—just enough room for a 2 ½ inch ball to fall through, if shot just right, of course. I couldn't dunk the ball, but lay-ups and shots from all over my 6 x 8 foot court were possible. I spent many a chilling hour (we didn't heat the back bedroom) playing one-on-none, most games being won in the last few seconds, as I again played for both teams in my imagination.

I have continued to love and follow sports all my life (tennis being my game later, and even coaching it for twenty-seven years at the high school where I taught—but, again, that's another story), but never so much as when I was growing up.

SCHOOL

As I indicated earlier, the social life of St. Charles revolved around school and its activities. With my father as the Superintendent and mother a teacher, I was naturally around there a good bit. The large, long red brick building housed first through twelfth grades—probably about 250 students in all, many coming from outlying towns with no school there. We ate lunch by grades, lining up when it was our class's turn to go. Older students would sometimes help in younger classrooms, and the Seniors were in charge of hiding the eggs for the big Easter egg hunt by the smaller children.

Everyone seemed to work together well, but it was a big thing to be able to get back into the main building after completing sixth grade.

Before I was old enough to go to school, I went many times, and, when Steve was in the second grade in Mimi's class, I would go with him some. I would do everything they did (as much as possible) and learned a lot, as well as getting me a head start on the first grade. My love of math today probably came from playing "Champion" in that class (two people would go to the blackboard, work an arithmetic problem given orally by the teacher, and the first to get it correctly was the winner. Defeat others selected by the one having to sit down and you were Champion!)

It's said your personality is shaped by the time you're five. That could be true. Two examples in the first grade caused some concern for the teacher, who told Mimi the problems: I never would let her see my work until finished, which was a little funny but understandable, but the second completely baffled her. Why did I color everything in purple? Coming to no deep psychological answer, Mimi decided to ask me. It was simple—that was the only crayon I had left!

Fourth, fifth, and sixth grades were situated in an older wooden building where the lunch room was also housed. It was not as nice, but easy to get to lunch on rainy days and close to the ball field at recess.

Prince went with me every day to the sixth grade. A Manchester rat terrier, he was as smart as any student there. When the teacher shut the door on him, he'd scratch on it for a while. If that didn't work, he'd jump on the flower boxes outside the windows until he found one open, then he'd come in the classroom and go and lie down by the stove. He seemed to sense when Daddy would be coming around to check attendance, for he'd get up, saunter over to a table that had a skirt on it, and disappear under it until the coast was clear. He was never a problem, and the teacher almost always let him stay. Why, he even answered a science question on how one could tell what kind of tree it is besides its leaf . . . . Bark! Bark! (Sorry about that—I couldn't resist!)

Being the social center for the community, activities at the school abounded (that may not exactly be the proper word). Some (of the not-quite-the-latest) movies were shown regularly on Wednesday evenings, nobody minding as the movie stopped to change reels on the one projector, and about once a month a pie or box supper would be held. Here ladies would fix a complete meal, put it in a wrapped-fancy box, and bring it to the school. They were all put on a table in front, then, one by one, be auctioned off to the men. Whoever bid the most on a particular box, with no hint of whose it was or what was inside (supposedly), got to eat the meal afterward with the lady who brought it. (Sometimes it might get out that someone's girl friend had brought a certain box, and that poor chap paid twice as much as normal as they would run up the bid.) I can't remember if the children would eat before we came or the mother would simply fix enough, but it was no problem as we were running around anyway. (A pie supper was similar, except only pies were brought, not complete meals.) The evening was then topped off with a square dance. Probably 200 or 300 people would come to this event from all the surrounding communities.

Another big event at the school was the Halloween carnival. Every class had a project or booth it sponsored, with prizes given for a cost of a dime at the fish pone, ball throw, etc.; the Bingo tables were always full and the cake walk had ample customers all night (a giant doughnut shape was drawn on the floor with chalk, numbers put in slots equally around it, then everyone walks around the circle as music plays; when the music stops, the people do, one to a number. Whoever standing on a drawn winning number wins a cake!) There was always a haunted house in the basement room, and you could even get married with a certificate and all (with kissing the bride, of course)! A big fund-raiser, it was always great fun for all and a huge success.

School was also, of course, <u>school</u>. I did enjoy it, did well, and feel that the basic education I got in that small school with almost no facilities compared to today's still prepared me well for the future. I believe when someone wants to learn and the opportunity is there, he can learn at any size school. But I also think I had some excellent teachers in that small school in Arkansas, and, on behalf of all thankful students everywhere, I'd like to tell them how much I appreciate them.

PRINCE

It may be true that a dog is man's best friend, but it was certainly true for me that a dog is a boy's best friend. I remember when I was very young we had a dog named QT, and another called Rags, and that they died, but the dog that was truly a part of me was Prince, mentioned earlier.

He lived up to his name. His pointed ears only lowered if he was scolded, his tail stopped wagging only when it was broken when a car ran over it (how happy he looked when he could wag it again), and his face and eyes gave an impression of intelligence, understanding, and joy.

And that's what I found with him. Where I went, he went. Not an "inside" dog, he roamed around all he wanted (what a blessing to live where a dog can run free without bothering anyone), but was always at the bottom of the steps waiting for me when I came out of the house. Every once in a while I would sneak out another door very quietly to try to get to Mama's without him sensing me, but almost always he would catch me, run as fast as he could towards me, then jump up as high as my chest as I dodged his assault. Then I'd run off, with him right at my heels. Sometimes he would lie in wait for me, and pounce on me as I walked along the path. Whenever we camped out, Prince would be the one who would snuggle up and keep me warm. If I just lay there thinking, looking up at the stars, or in the grass looking up at the clouds change their shapes, he would just lie quietly and enjoy the peace.

He did have two faults: his territory was off limits to other dogs, and he would defend it at all costs, no matter how much larger the other dog was, which scared me; and he liked to chase cars. A man told me what he'd seen one day: as Prince came alongside the car, it swerved to hit him. Prince jumped over the hood of the car and ran off the other side of the road. The man swore it was true. I guess that cured him, because Prince never chased another car again.

I enjoyed all the other animals that were around, and even had a wonderful horse that was a little too high-spirited for me, but there is a special bond between a boy and his dog—at least, that's how it was with Prince and me.

SNOW

Snow either may be no big deal to you or you may think that it never snows in Arkansas. Not true! Granted, it isn't Buffalo—a three-inch snow is a big deal, and since there is very little snow equipment available, people are snowed in almost anytime it snows.

To a child, it's about the most wonderful thing that can happen. You're definitely off from school, the trees and shrubs are covered with a magical white cover that makes everything beautiful, and friends are over to make a snowman or have snowball fights.

A special treat for me was snow ice cream. Just put some Pet milk, sugar, and vanilla in a bowl, add snow until it's the consistency of ice cream, and you've got a wonderful treat in about a minute. It will, of course, freeze your insides until it hurts if you eat too much too rapidly. If you've just come in from romping (there's no other word for it) in the snow, all fingers and toes frozen, then some hot chocolate is just what the doctor ordered.

There is a little entertainment you can do outside in the snow while inside. We'd get a cardboard box, turn it upside down and put some bread crumbs or whatever under it, then prop up one end with a stick that had a long string tied to it—so long that we could stick it through the window. Then, we would watch as birds came to get the scraps. When one was far enough under the box, we'd pull the string, and, if lucky, the box would fall quickly enough to trap the bird under it! We, of course, would simply go out, pick up the box, and let the bird fly free—the fun was in the trapping. Most were too quick or shy to be caught easily.

The biggest thrill in the snow was to go down the big hill by the graveyard on a sled. It was probably a hundred yards long, at a 60 degree slope, and to make it more exciting, there were several trees scattered around near the bottom you had to dodge—and then you had to watch out or you'd end up in a gully at the bottom. Hours and bruises later, we would wearily but happily trudge home.

If the snow lasted too long, or had ice with it, the electricity would usually go out. Besides going to bed early, candlelight made playing cards even more fun. So overall, when it snowed, there was great joy over the special gift we'd received from the sky.

THE 4TH OF JULY

There's something about the 4th of July. It not only makes you feel patriotic, but, in a small town, gives you a chance to get out, do something, and see everybody, instead of just sitting around panting in the heat.

St. Charles was no different. One in particular I remember: Steve and Kay were in charge of the parade. (You've got to have a parade.) You may wonder what kind of a parade a town of 256 can have—well, we thought, a good one! Bicycles were decorated with streamers through their spokes and all, clowns appeared along the way and someone dressed up as Uncle Sam on stilts, girls with batons marched before veterans carrying the flag, the mayor and sheriff rode in decorated cars, and a kazoo band (of which I was a member) rode on a flatbed wagon playing patriotic songs and even playing and singing one we'd made up for the event. For you music lovers, here are the words, sung to a lively tune I guess we'd concocted also:

> Oh, when the 4th of July rolls around
> We eat until we have to lie down,
> And in the morning we'll have lots of fun
> Because the big parade has just begun;
> And in the evening there'll be fireworks—
> So many it gives us the jerks—
> We'll have fun in every way
> Upon this great, big day!

After the parade, people would get together for a fish fry. Huge black kettles of frying catfish were provided by the men, and everyone brought covered dishes to go with that—and desserts of all kinds. Miss Bertha's (Mama) strawberry shortcakes were always gone as soon as she set them on the table. The children kept going back for more helpings of anything as we played chase among all the parked cars. Again, there must have been two hundred to three hundred people that came to these fish fries.

By then we were full, worn out, and hot, so usually we had to lie down for a rest at least (you could read if you were old enough not to have to take a nap).

By early nightfall it was time for fireworks. They were nothing to even speak of compared to all the displays today, but, there and then, to see some rockets burst high up in the air (and to be big enough to <u>light</u> them), to hold some Roman candles, write your name with sparklers, then run with them, making loops and throwing them, watching them blaze across the night sky, seeing a few fountains or showers of sparks, and, of course, setting off firecrackers under cans or, if brave enough, holding them as you lit them, then throwing them. As the mosquitoes took over the evening, it was time to come in, clean up, and get in bed at the end of another terrific 4th of July.

HUNTING AND FISHING

Living in a small Southern town certainly lent itself to learning how to hunt and fish. And I did, but was no great enthusiast for a couple of reasons.

Not being a real rugged type I guess, I got to where I could put a worm on a hook correctly and not mind too much, and take a fish off the hook without getting finned, but I didn't care for it too much. (I notice I don't mind now, but my children did, so maybe it has to do with age or simply if you do it enough to get used to it.) But I loved to fish. Whether it was a two-inch-long sun perch in Davidson branch, or big ones up at the farm, there really is something peaceful, yet exciting, as you wait for the cork to bob, then try to be quick enough to get the fish hooked. It was a real joy when I graduated up to where I could <u>fly</u> fish (no more worms) and even go out in a boat and cast toward the shore. (I got to where I was really pretty good, I thought, being able to put the fly right in there where I wanted it between branches of a fallen tree.) And it was great watching that fly disappear and feel that weight on your line as you brought it in.

I still didn't care for the messy part of cleaning them, but, luckily, almost always either Mama did them for us or we'd give them away to someone who would clean them and eat them for supper.

Hunting was also a big thing there. So big, in fact, that school would actually let out the first day of deer season. People from all over would come for "deer camps", and Mr. Malcolm and others would hire out as guides. I never went; at first, because I was too young, and, then, because it was considered too dangerous by Mimi. I didn't mind, since standing out in the cold all day waiting for a deer to come by didn't sound too fun to me. Besides, every time I had ever camped out with the Boy Scouts or anything it had always rained, making it generally miserable.

Daddy took me duck hunting several times (nearby Stuttgart being the "duck hunting capital of the world"), after I had graduated from a BB gun to my own 20-gauge shotgun. It was a tremendous sight to see the entire sky literally covered with ducks (which kept decreasing each year until finally there were only a few flocks). We would get to the rice field before sun-up, wade in the icy water to the duck blind (Daddy carried me at first if I didn't have high enough boots), and be there waiting when it was time to start. It was exciting to seem them circle to a duck call, then flare and start to come in. That's when we'd throw up the top of the blind and start shooting. There was a nice basic manly feeling if you knew you'd gotten one and got to wear the little tail feather in your cap. But as the ducks grew scarcer, the limit lower, getting up at 4:00 a.m. in the freezing cold grew less appealing to me.

A few times I would just walk in the woods up at the farm, playing like Daniel Boone I guess, to see what I could find. But I never wanted to shoot anything—I liked to see if I could hit it, but I didn't want to hurt it. When I got a .22, it was fun shooting blackbirds (to keep them from the rice) and rats (that infested one of the building on the farm), because I felt I was helping.

It did pay off, as I was familiar with arms and could shoot decently when I was in the Army. But it was also a rite of passage, a trial I had to undertake when seriously dating Jeanie years later. Her father and brothers were great hunters, so on one of my first visits to her home they gave me a .22 and said, "Let's go hunting" (even after I had expressed a disinterest in it). As we walked in the woods, we saw a squirrel 'way up in a tree. "He's yours," Jeanie's Dad said. I drew a bead on him, fired, and down he fell. They never asked me to go again. (After I also played basketball and football with them and more than held my own, I guess they decided I may be all right after all—and Jeanie became my wife.)

MISS STELLE

Her real name was Estelle Deane, but it came out "Miss Stelle" when I was small, and it stayed that way. She was special to me in several ways: rather large and grandmotherly-looking for as long as I can remember, there was a look and graciousness about her that made you think this was the last of the true genteel Southern ladies. She always had a kind, gentle look about her that made her seem to glow. And she was in her realm when sitting behind a coffee-pot serving people.

She was also my eighth grade English teacher, and I attribute the ease with which I later did vocabulary, spelling, and an appreciation of literature to her. One teacher along the way can make a difference for the rest of a student's life. She made a difference in a lot of people's lives.

She also ran a "general" store in town, where everything from material to nails was sold. The first Christmas present I ever bought by myself was a "Junior Commando" helmet for Steve at Miss Stelle's.

And even though I never had her as a Sunday school teacher, she was always at church, and that example was not lost on me. If a strong faith did her some good, and she thought it important, then it must be. (She finally passed away in her bed after attending church that day.)

She had a temper, I understand, and was extremely thrifty with her money, but a gracious, grand lady full of the quest for knowledge and a love for life.

THE POST OFFICE

Going to the Post Office each day was a treat, something you looked forward to. Actually twice a day, as Miss Jim Crabtree would drive her mail truck, back end also filled with passengers, to DeWitt to get the mail, bring it back, then, later in the afternoon, take mail back to DeWitt, pick up more mail (and any prescription or the like anyone may need) and people returning to St. Charles, and bring them back. Walter Duty would have the mail sorted and in mailboxes within thirty minutes, so everyone converged on the Post Office. It must have been more social than anything else, as rarely was there anything too exciting in the mail as far as I can remember. But I know how much we looked forward to going to get the mail, and how big I felt when I was able to go to town by myself, open the combination by memory, and bring the mail home.

What a basic need there must be to communicate, to anticipate surprises, to be part of a community—and that need was met by a small-town Post Office.

THE FARM

Possibly the best, if not only, wise business deal Mama made in the store was buying a small farm from someone who owed her a large debt. And did she love and have dreams for the farm—not as a farm, necessarily, but as a refuge possibly—an escape from the everyday pressures into a childhood fantasy herself perhaps. The "Club House" and a couple of other small building were painted white, furnished with an old wood stove and the like, white chickens and guineas dotted the place, and a large dam was made so a lake was created, and it was stocked with fish.

Mama would faithfully go up to the farm every day to feed the animals, gather eggs, and linger awhile just to dream. Steve or I would usually go with her. One of my joys was to fish in the lake, watching in the clear water at the edge as the fish were tempted by the bait, then snatched at it as I jerked the pole and caught them (throwing them back). I still remember what a thrill it was when Mama caught a fish that almost pulled her in and was about two feet long. It was like a physical reality to her dream. I think she had that fish in her freezer for the rest of her life.

It was not too long before she was unable to keep the farm up; we had moved, and it went downhill. But when Mama and Granddaddy died, they left the farm to Steve and me to help in the future with our families, so the cherished memories live on.

CHRISTMAS

Of all the good times and holidays we had in St. Charles, Christmas remains the highlight. Growing up, the anticipation and excitement of Santa Claus coming, seeing the multitude of presents under the tree, and wonderful food, and the pageant at the church were all blended to make this the most marvelous time of the year. And if it just happened to be ripe for snow, well, that just added immensely to the warm feeling.

With both parents and grandparents there, our Christmas stockings overflowed, and, for a few days after, when Steve and I would sing "Away In a Manger" for Mama before going to bed, our stockings magically had something new in them the next morning. A twelve—foot ceiling in their house lent itself to large Christmas trees, and they liked a lot of small gifts rather than one or two larger ones (as well as going overboard, I'm sure), so there were presents all around. I got to set up the tiny plastic reindeer on the coffee table, then the manger scene, and, as I grew older, the lighted houses on the TV, the tree, lights, decorations, and garlands themselves. Granddaddy would know just where to go to chop down a tree, and I remember how crazy it seemed the first time I had to buy a tree (years later when I lived in a city.)

Mama's role was cook, which she relished. She would be up at 4:00, baking and cooking. For breakfast there would be quail and tenderloin with scrambled eggs and biscuits. Dinner found two or three meats, six or so vegetables, with all the trimmings, and at least three or four different desserts, my favorite being "Karo-nut" pie. (It was literally years before I knew it was officially called pecan pie in restaurants.)

The Christmas program at the church consisted of candlelight, cedar decorations, singing favorite Christmas hymns, and a portrayal of the manger scene as the appropriate scripture was read. Being "Joseph" one year was a great honor to me.

The blend of Christ and decoration and gifts and family and love kept me coming to St. Charles every year for twenty-three years—until it was no longer possible. This remains one of my favorite times of the year, and I am able to remember it and incorporate parts of the tradition in my family now each Christmas season.

CHURCH

For such a small town to have four churches may be unique, but that's how it was in St. Charles. We belonged to the Methodist church, your basic "looking-like-a-picture" white building with a steeple, bell (that lifted you off the floor) that rang on Sunday morning, and traditional pictures of Jesus hanging about.

I went to Sunday school, church, and the Methodist Youth Fellowship regularly. It was pretty simple and basic as I remember, but I grew up learning about God, believing in Christ, and I joined the church when I was twelve. I always enjoyed Sunday school, MYF was fun (especially "Piggy wants a motion" after the lesson), and church was usually inspiring. Once when the preacher was giving a "money sermon" (which I didn't realize) about giving and you would receive double what you gave, it impressed me so that I gladly dug in my pocket at the offering time and surprisingly found a quarter rather than the nickel I usually had. I probably hesitated, then decided to put in the entire thing. I felt good about it, and my childish faith was given a personal boost immediately as I left church. There, in the dusty road walking home, I found a half dollar! God did what He said!

The simple faith I gained during those years growing up in that church, surrounded by that small group of faithful people, has stayed with me through the years. It has reminded me of what is good and right, how God expects us to live, and what strength, peace, and joy can come from knowing God. Like everyone else, I've not always remembered that and certainly have not done it, but it has basically sustained me all of my life.

I gained much from all of these places, events, and people in my life. I'm so pleased I was able to grow up as I did—"down home".